Sanctum Sanctorum

Sanctum Sanctorum

On the One Whose Name Is Holy

JUSTIN MANDELA ROBERTS

☙PICKWICK *Publications* · Eugene, Oregon

SANCTUM SANCTORUM
On the One Whose Name Is Holy

Copyright © 2019 Justin Mandela Roberts. All rights reserved. Except for brief quotations in critical publications or reviews, no part of this book may be reproduced in any manner without prior written permission from the publisher. Write: Permissions, Wipf and Stock Publishers, 199 W. 8th Ave., Suite 3, Eugene, OR 97401.

Pickwick Publications
An Imprint of Wipf and Stock Publishers
199 W. 8th Ave., Suite 3
Eugene, OR 97401

www.wipfandstock.com

PAPERBACK ISBN: 978-1-5326-5690-3
HARDCOVER ISBN: 978-1-5326-5691-0
EBOOK ISBN: 978-1-5326-5692-7

Cataloguing-in-Publication data:

Names: Roberts, Justin Mandela, author.

Title: Sanctum sanctorum : on the one whose name is holy / Justin Mandela Roberts.

Description: Eugene, OR : Pickwick Publications, 2019 | Includes bibliographical references and index.

Identifiers: ISBN 978-1-5326-5690-3 (paperback) | ISBN 978-1-5326-5691-0 (hardcover) | ISBN 978-1-5326-5692-7 (ebook)

Subjects: LCSH: God (Christianity)—Holiness. | Holy Spirit. | Theology. | Theology, Doctrinal.

Classification: BT147 .R63 2019 (paperback) | BT147 .R63 (ebook)

Manufactured in the U.S.A.   11/07/19

To my long-suffering and dear wife Abbie

"What good does it do to speak learnedly about the Trinity if, lacking humility, you displease the Trinity? Indeed it is not learning that makes a man holy and just, but a virtuous life makes him pleasing to God. I would rather feel contrition than know how to define it."

—Thomas à Kempis, *The Imitation of Christ*

Contents

Preface | ix
Acknowledgments | xi

    Introduction | 1
    Creating Space in Transcendental Thought | 7
    Transcendental Criteria | 10
    Views of the Holy | 13
    Outline of Chapters | 19

1 **The White Light of Holiness** | 21
    Introduction | 21
    The Preeminence of the Holy | 22
    Transcendental Liturgy | 33
    The Eclipse of the Holy | 41
    Conclusion | 56

2 **The Invisible Father** | 57
    Introduction | 57
    Being in Repose | 58
    The Revelation of Life | 65
    Divine Reverence | 74
    Presence/Absence | 81
    Conclusion | 89

3 **The Holy's Spirit** | 91
    Introduction | 91
    The Consecrator | 92
    On the One Whose Name Is Distance | 100
    Holiness and Touch | 106
    Conclusion | 112

4 **Nosferatu, A Symphony of Horror** | 115
   Introduction | 115
   The Play of the Absurd | 116
   Horror without Remainder | 126
   The Grotesque Will Save the World | 130
   Conclusion | 142

5 **The Secret** | 144
   Introduction | 144
   Secrecy and the Gift | 145
   Faith as Secret Keeping | 151
   The Mask and Its Rituals | 154
   Conclusion | 159

Bibliography | 161
Index of Names and Subjects | 173

Preface

THIS BOOK CAPTURES A moment of transition in my life. I have been moving steadily over the past several years from the world of Protestant thought to the greater catholic Christian legacy, which I tend to call "participatory" for short. From the earliest days, this participatory tradition has helped re-enchant the world for me. It enables me to see all things living and moving and having their being *in* God. It also helps me see that beauty is not a trite matter but is of immense spiritual weight. Among the many aspects that were opening up to me, I was most lured by the Holy, which drew all things to itself in deepest reverence.

Because of my Protestant background, it was quite natural to think that holiness somehow stood at the very depths of God, or represented a pinnacle or summit in his nature. Even at the harshest points of Protestant theology, all God's loving aspirations are bound by the brooding demands of his more elemental quality, namely holiness. But I have come to see that this instinct of seeing holiness at the root of God's nature was less natural for the participatory tradition. I was introduced to the wealth of reflection on things like Truth, Goodness, Beauty, and Being, for instance, but that initial lure of the Holy felt somewhat unfulfilled. To this day, we can find lots of biblical scholarship on the theme of holiness. We can find phenomenological accounts of the Holy, along with other studies in the areas of anthropology, sociology, and world religions. We can find ecclesial and moral treatments of holiness and sanctity. However, the tradition seems to lack a certain metaphysics or ontology of holiness itself.

As my affections for the theology of the tradition grew, so did my longing towards the Holy. That biblical instinct remained of seeing holiness as the deepest part of God, and "Holy" as our greatest praise of him. As Ambrose says, "We too find nothing of more worth, whereby we are able to proclaim God, than the calling Him holy." What I soon realized

Preface

was that this seemingly innocent truth, namely that "Holy" is our greatest praise of God, makes a radical impact on our understanding of God. For with Dionysius the Areopagite, all names, such as Truth and Goodness, *are* praises of God, and their essence and character are perceived according to *how* they praise God in union with all the other names. Thus, to follow this original instinct through the Dionysian door leads to a substantial amendation to the tradition's metaphysics of God. If, going back to Plato, the Good is the conductor of all things, then the Holy is the music. This book then is my initial effort to sketch a metaphysics of the Holy.

Acknowledgments

First, I would like to thank Steve Studebaker and Gord Heath. They supervised the dissertation out of which this book came. You showed me immense generosity and understanding, and encouraged me to pursue the things that were most pressing in my heart and mind. For your support and guidance, I have the deepest gratitude.

I also think of a few friends in particular who helped me explore and test the contents of this book, and perhaps most importantly, fuel the fire of discovery with shared affections: Joel Knapp, Corey Stephenson, Jesse Newton, and notably David Fuller, without whom I am helpless.

Thank you to Wipf and Stock Publishers for the opportunity to contribute to their great collection.

As this work grew out of my doctoral studies, I want to thank my mom and aunt Karen, who have been a great support to me throughout the journey that this book represents. Above all, I thank my wife Abbie, my perfect companion, support, and part-time editor. For your selflessness and steadfast love, thank you!

Introduction

HOLINESS IS AMONG THE least controversial theological confessions and infused in every strand of heretical thought and practice as surely as in its orthodox counterparts. Its rather uncontroversial career does not ease but hinders a proper inquiry of its nature. The church, after all, has so often discovered the depths of its own discourse by writing *contra* heresy. Holiness permeates every conceivable level of existence, as a descriptor of God, heaven and its beings, time, space, creation, humanity, food, liturgy, behaviour, experience, and the church. The near-at-hand definitions of holiness—including otherness, purity, and transcendence—fall short of expressing what makes such a wide range of references to the holy possible. Can "purity" substitute for the titanic range of experience conjured by the thought of what is holy? Purity may well be a quality of the holy, but such things cannot define the holy as such. Efforts to explicate the holy so easily veer away from the determinative question that must be addressed directly if one is to approach the topic: what *is* the holy? What do we talk about when we talk about holiness? This line of questioning has prompted the present thesis.

I will argue that holiness is included in a special category of divine names that Christian metaphysics calls "transcendentals" (which are five: being, one, truth, goodness, and beauty). Moreover, holiness stands in a hierarchical relationship to the other five transcendentals, as the culmination or concentration of the rest. Only by understanding holiness as the "head" of the transcendentals, as "the" transcendental, can one account for all the complexity the idea of the holy conjures. Therefore my thesis is: holiness is the transcendental *of* the transcendentals. Each transcendental is said to add an "aspect" to existence (e.g., the good, desire and truth, relation). Holiness adds the aspect of reverence to existence, and as such it is constituted by the formula *sanctum sanctorum* (Holy-*of*-holies) which extends from the divine nature through the triune life to all creation.

One sees the need for such an investigation in John Webster's treatment of the topic in *Holiness*, which offers a *"trinitarian dogmatics of holiness."*[1] The "context and content" of that dogmatic enterprise "derive from revelation (the gift of God's presence as the Holy One)," and therefore do not constitute a "transcendent critical inquiry but an attempt at rational speech about the Holy One."[2] Webster continues, "and so such a theology is not poetic but positive, not an activity of naming but one of confessing. It finds its content, its norm and its limit in Holy Scripture."[3] On the nature of human experience he says, "Accordingly, its primary task is exegetical rather than comparative or phenomenological . . . and is unpersuaded that much is to be gained from reading the canon as an expression of the experience of the holy-in-general."[4] For Webster, this is not about "some ontological participation in the divine holiness."[5]

Webster's virtue is his combination of truly pious articulations with a dogmatic vision of Christian Scripture. However, he seems to exemplify why the nature of holiness remains as confused as it is. As we saw, he begins by making questionable dichotomies: is there an antithesis between the poetic and the positive, naming and confessing, contemplation of transcendence and dogma? Consequently, it becomes difficult to know what he means by "holy." Webster sees holiness as "a conceptual attempt to point to the concreteness of God's identity," which is "'enacted' in the sense that it is accomplished in God's free action towards his creatures as creator, reconciler and perfecter."[6] Therefore, he says, "Holiness is thus God's personal moral relation to his creatures."[7]

Webster seems to take it for granted that the word "holy" has content in itself. As a "conceptual attempt to point to the concreteness of God's

---

1. Webster, *Holiness*, 1.

2. Webster adds, "A Christian theology of holiness is an exercise of holy reason, and holy reason is reason segregated by God so that God's communicative presence as Father, Son, and Spirit can be known and loved" (Webster, *Holiness*, 99).

3. Webster, *Holiness*, 99.

4. Webster, *Holiness*, 99.

5. Webster, *Holiness*, 57.

6. Webster, *Holiness*, 100.

7. Webster, *Holiness*, 100. Webster further explains the word "holiness": "As Father, Son and Spirit, God's holiness is a way of indicating the 'name' and 'works' of God, that is, the identity which God enacts" (Webster, *Holiness*, 100).

identity," which is "enacted" by God and defined by "God's personal moral relation to his creatures," holiness remains devoid of meaning. What does "holy" *say* conceptually about God? What is "enacted"? What does "holy" tell us *about* God's personal moral relation to his creatures?

How is holiness—which is confessed properly of God—said of the church? The holy people of God have holiness as an "alien sanctity: gift, not possession; grace, not achievement."[8] The church's holiness is "visible in the primary act of the Church, which is confession," which he explains is "acknowledgement or recognition of the sheer majesty, transcendent worth and goodness of God."[9] The primary act that makes the holiness of the church visible is "confession," and this confession is a human mode of perceiving the transcendence and goodness of God. After denying that confession is "transcendent critical inquiry," or "phenomenological," he insists that the primary activity of holiness is a response to the *experience* of God in a transcendent fashion. Moreover, we might ask, what is it about this "recognition" of God's transcendence that makes it holy?

Webster further explains that holiness "is not self-achieved perfection but a pointing to the perfect reality of the holy God."[10] Again we are left asking, what of this "pointing?" Webster continues to speak as if holiness has some meaning (some essence or "is") but cannot bring himself to face the question due to methodological convictions. His understanding of dogmatics severs what have been decisive modes of theological inquiry throughout Christianity history, namely philosophy, mystical reflection, and literature. Not only does this severing limit his theological resources, but it sets him decidedly against the prospect of ever answering the "is" question.[11]

Such a question—namely what is the holy—occupies Socrates in Plato's *Euthyphro*. Hearing that Euthyphro is prosecuting his own father for murder, Socrates is shocked as much by the philosophical confidence of this man (to know what the holy action is in this circumstance) as by the fortitude of his moral conviction. In characteristic flattery, Socrates wishes to be taken as Euthyphro's pupil and begs that he teach on "what you just

---

8. Webster, *Holiness*, 101.
9. Webster, *Holiness*, 101.
10. Webster, *Holiness*, 101.
11. Webster says "the Church is holy; but it is holy, not by virtue of some ontological participation in the divine holiness, but by virtue of its calling by God, its reception of the divine benefits, and its obedience of faith . . . the Church's holiness is that which it is by virtue of its sheer contingency upon the mercy of God" (Webster, *Holiness*, 57).

now asserted that you knew so well."[12] "Tell me then," he says, "what do you say holiness [ὅσιον] is, and what unholiness?"[13] Here at the beginning of the dialogue, Socrates clearly sets out the question Euthyphro must answer, but one he inevitably evades and never satisfies: "Is not holiness always the same with itself in every action and, on the other hand, is not unholiness the opposite of all holiness, always the same with itself and whatever is to be unholy possessing some one characteristic quality?"[14] By inquiring after that "one characteristic," he sets out to establish the essence or nature of holiness itself, the kind of essence one would require to do something as extraordinary as prosecute his own father.[15] Euthyphro does not grasp the nature of his question and offers an unintelligible proposal: the holy, he insists, is that which I am doing, prosecuting a man guilty of murder, just as Zeus put his own father in bonds.[16] Socrates is willing to put aside his general skepticism about Greek mythology for the moment, because the question has not been addressed; he is not interested in knowing what acts are holy, but "the essential aspect, by which all holy acts are holy."[17]

Euthyphro tries another: "what is dear to the gods is holy."[18] But this voluntarist suggestion finds no favour with Socrates. Even among the gods one finds disputes over such matters, which begs the question, what is that over which they fight? In other words, if two people were to solve a dispute of the length of a thing, they would measure it; if they were fighting over a mathematical issue, they could apply arithmetic.[19] What is the definition

12. Plato, *Euthyphro*, 5c.
13. Plato, *Euthyphro*, 5d.
14. Plato, *Euthyphro*, 5d.
15. On Euthyphro, R. E. Allen says, "As essences, Forms play a regulative role in dialectic. They rule out of court certain kinds of answers which merely offer a distinguishing mark characterizing things which have the Form, as distinct from a definition of the Form itself. You cannot say what a characteristic is as such by merely offering a mark for distinguishing its instances" (Allen, *Plato's Euthyphro*, 76). See also Judson, "Carried Away in the Euthyphro," 33; Vlastos, *Platonic Studies*, 410–17.
16. Plato, *Euthyphro*, 5d–6a.
17. Plato, *Euthyphro*, 6d. Socrates says, "For, my friend, you did not give me sufficient information before, when I asked what holiness was, but you told me that this was holy which you are now doing, prosecuting your father for murder.... Now call to mind that this is not what I asked you, to tell me one or two of the many holy acts."
18. Plato, *Euthyphro*, 6e.
19. Plato, *Euthyphro*, 7b–7c. Timothy Chappell says "Socrates is not arguing that 'what is holy' is *not* 'what the gods love.'... The point of his argument is that the mere description 'what the gods love' cannot serve as a *definition* of 'what is holy.'" (Chappell, "Euthyphro's 'Dilemma,'" 64).

INTRODUCTION

that could put the question of holiness to rest?[20] Frustrated after many exchanges on the issue of whether divine will can determine the nature of holiness, Euthyphro says the most truthful thing yet, "Socrates, I do not know how to say what I mean. For whatever statement we advance, somehow or other it moves about and won't stay where we put it."[21] Later, he tries this: "the part of the right which has to do with attention to the gods constitutes piety and holiness."[22] But what is this "attention"? What *characterizes*, *defines*, and thus *delimits* the attention that "is" holiness itself? Through more exchanges, Socrates finds that Euthyphro's suggestion of praise and sacrifice is called holy *because* it delights the gods, which brings the discussion back to the beginning (namely defining what *is* holy by what the gods will).[23] Finally, Socrates woefully begs for resolution but resigns his hopes in a bitting indictment: "tell me the truth.... For if you had not clear knowledge of holiness and unholiness, you would surely not have undertaken to prosecute your aged father for murder for the sake of a servant."[24]

Rudolf Otto's *The Idea of the Holy* (first published as *Das Heilige* in 1917) may be the most significant attempt to look "at" the holy itself, a task that for one reason or another has proven difficult or undesirable. He does not treat holiness among other concerns, thus obscuring the presuppositions that guide one's thinking on the matter, but abides in the question, what *is* the holy? Otto is a product of the German intellectual heritage, navigating critically or otherwise a Kantian paradigm. Though he shares the German distaste for hellenic influence—as he says, "the tendency to take refuge in a Greek terminology being here, as so often, nothing but an avowal of one's own insufficiency"—one sees that he formulates the "idea" of the holy in something of a Greek (and Medieval) way.[25]

---

20. Socrates says, "Is that which is holy loved by the gods because it is holy, or is it holy because it is loved by the gods?" (Plato, *Euthyphro*, 10a).

21. Plato, *Euthyphro*, 11b.

22. Plato, *Euthyphro*, 12e. Euthyphro explains later: "I say simply that when one knows how to say and do what is gratifying to the gods, in praying and sacrificing, that is holiness, and such things bring salvation to individual families and to states; and the opposite of what is gratifying to the gods is impious, and that overturns and destroys everything" (Plato, *Euthyphro*, 14b).

23. Plato, *Euthyphro*, 15b.

24. Plato, *Euthyphro*, 15d. Socrates says, "Oh my friend, what are you doing? You go away and leave me cast down from the high hope I had that I should learn from you what is holy, and what is not" (Plato, *Euthyphro*, 15e).

25. Otto, *Idea of the Holy*, 116.

Otto says that primitive religions interpret miraculous "signs" as manifestations of the holy; however, a reality as finite as signs cannot contain the holy, which would be "a confounding of the category of holiness with something only outwardly resembling it . . . it was not a genuine '*anamnesis*,' a genuine recognition of the holy in its own authentic nature, made manifest in appearance."[26] One must go beyond the conditions of appearance to the transcendent thing itself. Otto prompts us to consider how this "transcending" aspect of holiness is *like* the nature of beauty. Even in one of a crude and undeveloped aesthetic taste, a feeling for the beautiful can begin to stir, which "must come from an obscure *a priori* conception of beauty already present."[27] In the misapprehension of beauty and what is deemed beautiful, one's dim conception mistakes the material for the higher reality of beauty itself.[28] The educated have learned to look beyond the "quasi-beautiful but not really beautiful thing" to judge rightly, "i.e., to recognize as beautiful the outward object in which the 'beauty' of which he has an inward notion and standard really 'appears.'"[29] In the words of the Greek tradition, Otto is describing the contemplative ascent from the thing in which beauty (or the holy) appears—a work of art or piece of music for example—to Beauty (or the Holy) in itself.

Otto argues that the holy is an *a priori* category, as "numinous experience, beliefs and feelings [are] qualitatively different from anything that 'natural' sense-perception is capable of giving us."[30] He argues that these numinous experiences are "peculiar interpretations and valuations, at first perceptual data, and then—at a higher level—of posited objects and entities, which themselves no longer belong to the perceptual world, but are thought of as supplementing and transcending it."[31] Otto says he is describing *a priori* categories (that admittedly go deeper than Kant's); however, the best parts of his formulation touch upon a more ancient and compelling way of thinking of such things, namely the notion of the "transcendental" (goodness, truth, beauty for example). In many ways, Otto appears decisively modern, but his idea of the holy is in continuity with transcendental thinking rooted in the Greek philosophical tradition, which was explicated

---

26. Otto, *Idea of the Holy*, 148.
27. Otto, *Idea of the Holy*, 148.
28. Otto, *Idea of the Holy*, 148.
29. Otto, *Idea of the Holy*, 148.
30. Otto, *Idea of the Holy*, 117.
31. Otto, *Idea of the Holy*, 117.

in the Middle Ages. The "deep" and "obscure" categorical *a priori* out of which the idea of the holy comes is most profoundly captured by Augustine's saying that the God who "*is*" goodness and beauty, being and consciousness, is "more inward to me than my most inward part, and higher than my highest."[32] "Beauty" (and Holiness) is an *a priori* category of reason insofar as reason is an extension of infinitely conscious being that is "in-and-beyond" everything through participation. Otto, of course, does not go as far, but his "response" to Socrates implicitly and explicitly brings one's mind to transcendentals, which is the springboard for the present study.

CREATING SPACE IN TRANSCENDENTAL THOUGHT

The number and nature of the transcendentals have varied throughout history. The first explicitly systematic account of the transcendentals originates in the medieval period. No textual evidence for the term *transcendentalis* exists in the Middle Ages, as its appearance is due to the work of modern editors.[33] The more commonly used word is the participle *transcendens*—as an adjective or substantive noun—with its neuter plural form *transcendentia*.[34] Jan Aertsen traces the ambiguities of this word and concludes it has two defining uses: (1) as a reference to that which is transcendent; and (2) to what is universally predicated of all things.[35] The former (1) sense of the word goes back to Plato, who contemplated the Good "beyond being."[36] The verb *transcendere* appears first in Augustine's characterization of the Platonists.[37] One can trace this sense through Neoplatonism, Augustine, and Dionysius, though *transcendens* as a reference to the transcendent (1) is the less common usage in the medieval period. Albert the Great's treatise *Dialectica Monacensis*, dated to the first quarter of the thirteenth century, offers one of the earliest known examples of *transcendentia* in the latter sense (2).[38] Still, there is no systematic analysis of the order and number of the transcendentals themselves.[39] Aertsen points out the irony that the

---

32. Augustine, *Confessions*, 3.6.11.
33. Aertsen, *Medieval Philosophy as Transcendental Thought*, 13.
34. Aertsen, *Medieval Philosophy as Transcendental Thought*, 13.
35. Aertsen, *Medieval Philosophy as Transcendental Thought*, 20.
36. Plato, *Republic*, 509B.
37. Aertsen, *Medieval Philosophy as Transcendental Thought*, 21.
38. Aertsen, *Medieval Philosophy as Transcendental Thought*, 31.
39. Aertsen, *Medieval Philosophy as Transcendental Thought*, 31.

origin of the name *transcendens* is without a doctrine, and the first doctrinal articulation (Philip the Chancellor) is without the name.[40] Philip's *Summa de bono* sets forth the following transcendentals (what he calls *communissima*) in order: *Ens* (Being), *Unum* (One—indivision), *Verum* (Truth—indivision of being and that which is), and *Bonum* (Good—indivision of act from potency).[41] Philip also brings the two senses of *transcendens* together within his understanding of the transcendental; for example, the good belongs to God as such (*per se*) and for the sake of itself, and only subsequently to creatures as they are from him and towards him.[42] By making the same good identical with God (primarily) and indirectly "in" creatures (secondarily), he expresses an "analogical" relationship that would be championed by later thinkers, though curiously this exact word is not present in his discussion.[43]

One can see that at this point in the history of the transcendentals, no unified conception or theory governed the debates. The contemporary emergence of five transcendentals comes from a long dialectical process of discovery, and nowhere is this more clearly seen than in the case of beauty. Medieval writers discussed "the beautiful" primarily because of the influence of Dionysius.[44] Only two writings explicitly defend the transcendentality of beauty. The most significant work is an anonymous treatise from the library of Assisi, which was given the title *Tractatus de transcendentalibus entis conditionibus* (which is an extract from the *Summa Halensis*).[45] The author divides the work into three articles, "the good," "the one," and "the true;" however, at the beginning, he says there are four "conditions" of being: *unum* (one), *verum* (truth), *bonum* (good), and *pluchrum* (beauty).[46]

---

40. Aertsen, *Medieval Philosophy as Transcendental Thought*, 31. Medieval accounts of the transcendentals are typically part of a *Summa*, a commentary on Aristotle, or a collection of questions. Three treatises are entirely devoted to the doctrine: two from the fourteenth century and one from the sixteenth. See Aertsen, *Medieval Philosophy as Transcendental Thought*, 32.

41. Aertsen, *Medieval Philosophy as Transcendental Thought*, 121. See Philip the Chancellor, *Summa de bono*, Q3–7.

42. Aertsen, *Medieval Philosophy as Transcendental Thought*, 123.

43. Aertsen, *Medieval Philosophy as Transcendental Thought*, 123.

44. Aertsen, *Medieval Philosophy as Transcendental Thought*, 105.

45. Aertsen, *Medieval Philosophy as Transcendental Thought*, 169.

46. Aertsen, *Medieval Philosophy as Transcendental Thought*, 170. This treatise gives a synthesizing function to beauty among the transcendentals, but this understanding is not representative of the period.

Introduction

The other explicit treatment of the transcendentality of beauty is found in Ulrich of Strasbourg's *De summo bono*.[47] Most medieval writers restrict their list to the triad "*unum—verum—bonum*" (one—true—good), and remain silent on the nature of beauty.[48] Because the beautiful is often discussed alongside the good, the *Summa Halensis* does not include "the beautiful" among the "first determinations of being."[49] Beauty is not a universal mode of being, and thus could be seen as merely an "epiphenomenon" of the good.[50] Albert the Great's commentary on *De divinis nominibus* establishes the universality of beauty while excluding it from his list of transcendentals, a habit Aertsen says is typical of that time.[51]

The period following Aquinas is equally evasive of the beautiful. Henry of Ghent sometimes refers to "the beautiful" as a "first intension," but he does not include it with the transcendentals.[52] Duns Scotus does not give beauty a place in his order of concepts.[53] The two fourteenth-century works on the transcendentals are silent on beauty (Francis de Prato's *Tractatus de sex transcendentibus* and Francis of Meyronnes's *Tractatus de transcendentibus*).[54] In his *Disputationes Metaphysicae*, Suárez discusses "being" and its properties ("one," "true," and "good") but his theory of the transcendentals omits beauty.[55] Denys the Carthusian remarkably devoted an entire treatise to beauty; in a later work *Elementatio philosophica*, he speaks of the properties of being (*unum, verum, bonum*), but only includes *pluchrum* (the beautiful) as an afterthought because the "divine Denys" says it is convertible with being.[56] Whether or not Aquinas saw beauty as a transcendental is, for Aertsen, more complex. It occupies little attention in Aquinas's work, and does not receive a single question dedicated to it.[57]

47. Aertsen, *Medieval Philosophy as Transcendental Thought*, 171.
48. Aertsen, *Medieval Philosophy as Transcendental Thought*, 172.
49. Aertsen, *Medieval Philosophy as Transcendental Thought*, 172.
50. Aertsen, *Medieval Philosophy as Transcendental Thought*, 172.
51. Aertsen, *Medieval Philosophy as Transcendental Thought*, 173. See Albert Magnus, *Super Dionysium De divinis nominibus*, 4.89.5.
52. Aertsen, *Medieval Philosophy as Transcendental Thought*, 174. See Henry of Ghent, *Summa quaestionum ordinariarum*, 34.3.
53. Aertsen, *Medieval Philosophy as Transcendental Thought*, 174.
54. Aertsen, *Medieval Philosophy as Transcendental Thought*, 174.
55. Aertsen, *Medieval Philosophy as Transcendental Thought*, 174.
56. Aertsen, *Medieval Philosophy as Transcendental Thought*, 175. See Dionysius the Carthusian, *Elementio philosophica seu Compendium philosophiae*, prop. 92.
57. Aertsen, *Medieval Philosophy as Transcendental Thought*, 173.

However, what Gilson calls the "forgotten transcendental" has received more attention in recent Aquinas research than any other transcendental.[58] Moreover, Aquinas's important account of the transcendentals found in *De Veritate* lists six transcendentals, from which beauty is absent: one, thing, being, something, good, and true.[59]

The transcendental "canon" has never been definitively closed. Not until the Middle Ages were the transcendentals categorized as unique, at which time no definite number or order was established. Through the modern period to the present, the canon is openly debated, and as seen with beauty, some of the most influential work in Christian history has been done as recently as the twentieth century. Therefore, the exclusion of holiness from historic accounts of the transcendentals is not necessarily detrimental to its potential inclusion. Continuity with the tradition will have to be determined by deciding whether or not the holy shares the features of a transcendental held by each specific period under investigation, as the role of holiness in Greek, patristic, medieval, and modern thought will all bespeak transcendentality differently.

TRANSCENDENTAL CRITERIA

A transcendental must meet certain criteria. By "transcending" all categories, a transcendental *conceptually* adds a value to being that cannot be reduced to another transcendental.[60] Moreover as Joseph Owens says, "A transcendental predicate runs through all the categories and extends beyond to their first cause."[61] Therefore, the kind of thing under investigation

---

58. Aertsen, *Medieval Philosophy as Transcendental Thought*, 173. See also Aertsen, *Medieval Philosophy and the Transcendentals*, 335–59. For further discussion on the transcendentality of beauty see: Maritain, *Art and Scholasticism*; Pöltner, *Schönheit*; Eco, *Aesthetics of Thomas Aquinas*; Jordan, "Grammar of *Esse*," 1–26; Jordan, "Evidence of the Transcendentals," 393–407; Elders, *Metaphysics of Being*, 136–44; Schindler, *Hans Urs von Balthasar*, 350–421; Bychkov, "'Metaphysics as Aesthetics,'" 147–78. See also Sevier, *Aquinas on Beauty*; Sammon, *God Who Is Beauty*, 236–355.

59. Aquinas, *De Veritates*, 1.1.

60. Aertsen, *Medieval Philosophy as Transcendental Thought*, 174. "Conceptually" here refers to the way transcendentals "are really the same, and differ only in idea" (Aquinas, *ST* Ia.5.1.co).

61. Owens, *Christian Metaphysics*, 111. Aertsen adds: "The term 'transcendental' suggests a kind of surpassing or going beyond. What is transcended is the special modes of being which Aristotle called the 'categories.' Categories are determinations or contractions of that which is: not every being is a substance, or a quantity, or a quality, or a

defies straightforward delimitable definition because technically it does not "fit within" any circumscribable boundary.

On the nature of theological comprehension, Aquinas says that God is called incomprehensible not because he is entirely unseen, but because he is not seen as perfectly as is possible.[62] Citing Augustine, he says: "the whole is comprehended when it is seen in such a way that nothing of it is hidden from the seer, or when its boundaries can be completely viewed or traced; for the boundaries of a thing are said to be completely surveyed when the end of the knowledge of it is attained."[63] The created intellect "knows" the divine in varying degrees and in proportion to its reception of a greater or lesser "light of glory." God's infinite nature exceeds every created intellect. Thus, it is impossible for creatures to "comprehend" God, regardless of how truly one intuits the radiance of his being.[64] Gregory of Nyssa says the divine names (including the transcendentals) are not derived from unmediated apprehension of the infinite, but are "reverent speculations."[65] When we perceive "the Being Who transcends all existences" as the source of creation's continuance, or perceive "the beauty and majesty" of the signs in creation, we get a new range of thoughts about God and interpret them according to a "special name."[66] The good, for example, is the name ascribed to God as life's First Cause.[67] Gregory says our inability to express God's unutterable substance is evidence of God's glory, precisely in and through the poverty of our nature. Thus, the most accurate (non)name we can give to God is "above every name"; the contemplative pursuit is characterized

---

relation, etc. By contrast, the transcendentals are properties that belong to every being. So they transcend the categories, not because they refer to a reality beyond the categories but because they are not limited to one determinate category. Transcendentals are interchangeable or convertible with being that is itself a transcendental" (Aertsen, "Good as Transcendental," 56). Aristotle, *Categories*, 1b25–2a4.

62. Aquinas, *ST* Ia.12.7.co.

63. Aquinas, *ST* Ia.12.7.ad. Moreover: "Everything is knowable according to its actuality. But God, whose being is infinite, as was shown above (Q[7]) is infinitely knowable. Now no created intellect can know God infinitely" (Aquinas, *ST* Ia.12.7.co).

64. Aquinas, *ST* Ia.12.7.co.

65. Gregory of Nyssa, *Answer to Eunomius's Second Book*, 308.

66. Gregory of Nyssa, *Answer to Eunomius's Second Book*, 309. This is the advice of Wisdom: "by the greatness and beauty of the creatures proportionately the Maker of them is seen" (Wis 8:5).

67. Gregory of Nyssa, *Answer to Eunomius's Second Book*, 309.

by adherence to "ineffable majesty" because God transcends every effort of thought and is beyond any circumscribed name.[68]

Holiness will be shown to have a phenomenological profile of transcendence. In other words, while a transcendental is "in" everything—thus we can say that food is "good" for example—it is always qualitatively "beyond" everything. One sees this in Augustine's route to the "thing itself": "This is good and that is good, but take away this and that, and regard good itself," and thus one will see God as "the good of all good."[69] By limiting the scope of one's gaze to the good, one enacts what phenomenologists call a "reduction," as one "brackets" out the objects in view. The reduction reveals a value of existence that does not appear as *an* object but something in and through which "objects" emerge. A beautiful piece of art does not reveal beauty by virtue of any particular form, style, or quality. The humble artistic efforts of a child are not precluded from being beautiful by his or her methodological poverty. This mysterious and sometimes maddening elusiveness contributes to the phenomenological profile of the transcendentals. Augustine can so easily associate the good with God because it would be preposterous to say this elusiveness also eludes God, and it would be equally unthinkable to say God is not good. Therefore, the transcendence proper to God and goodness naturally collide in the unity to which they both belong.

Perhaps most decisively, each transcendental has an intelligible "aspect" that characterizes it and subsequently governs existence. For Aquinas, the good adds the aspect of "desirability" to being.[70] This is interpreted to include a broad ecstatic impulse to "reach," which propels beings towards their perfected forms, guides the body to nourishment, and even "sends" the intellect into the world through the senses. Truth adds the aspect of "relation."[71] Beauty adds "delight" or "pleasure." Because God's simple being is the inexhaustible source of finitude and the Absolute in and through which reality "is," every "act" is simultaneously one of goodness, truth, and beauty. Holiness must contribute such an "aspect" to being that cannot be reducible to another transcendental feature. In addition to adding an aspect to existence, holiness must include the other transcendental aspects for its intelligibility. A *beautiful* painting is made possible by the intelligibility (truth) of the piece that reveals inner beliefs about what is "desirable"

---

68. Gregory of Nyssa, *Answer to Eunomius's Second Book*, 309.
69. Augustine, *Trinity*, 8.3.4.
70. Aquinas, *ST* Ia.5.1.co.
71. Aquinas, *ST* Ia.16.3.co.

INTRODUCTION

(good): the superbly rendered propagandist image of a tyrant is "beautiful" to the grotesque and grotesque to the "beautiful."

Perhaps the most telling and neglected requirement of a transcendental is that by virtue of its convertibility with being—and one, truth, goodness, and beauty—it must be able to further explicate the causal relationships of the divine processions, and demonstrate how the transcendental in question illuminates the Trinitarian life. The Christian tradition has never been hesitant to call the Trinity "holy," but much is left to be done in expositing the Trinity according to the transcendental content of the holy itself. If successful in providing such an exposition, the Trinity will then be the archetype of finite participation in holiness.

VIEWS OF THE HOLY

If holiness has never fully been considered a transcendental, we can still see scattered hints throughout history that holiness ought to be so considered. Plato's dialogue on the holy in *Euthyphro* is significant not only because of its content, but because the holy receives its own treatise just as being, goodness, beauty, and one, and because it is characterized and "ascended to" like its transcendental counterparts. In Plato's *Phaedo*, Socrates discusses why he evinces peace in the face of death. He offers an exposition of "true being" that can be divided into the unchanging invisible and the visible changing being of the material order. The soul he says is most akin to that invisible, the body to the visible. If philosophy is the realization of the mind's lordship over changing corporeality, then it is a kind of death, or the practice of dying; and in this case, death would be the fulfillment of philosophy. Speaking to the transcendentality of being, Socrates asks a rhetorical question: "Is the absolute essence, which we in our dialectic process of question and answer call true being, always the same or is it liable to change? Absolute equality, absolute beauty, any absolute existence, true being—do they ever admit of any change whatsoever?"[72]

In the *Republic*, Plato moves dialectically towards an understanding of the good in a way much like his movement towards the holy in *Euthyphro*. He says the multitude believe the good to be pleasure, while the more refined say knowledge.[73] Both fail to recognize the unique character of the thing in question; the good cannot be synonymous or defined by

---

72. Plato, *Phaedo*, 78d.
73. Plato, *Republic*, 505b.

something like pleasure or knowledge just as the holy cannot be defined by "attention" to the gods, as pleasure and knowledge can accompany the good and the bad. Like his frustration with Euthyphro, Socrates bemoans the inadequate understanding of the good: "'That, then, which every soul pursues and for its sake does all that it does, with an intuition of its reality, but yet baffled and unable to apprehend its nature adequately, or to attain to any stable belief about it as about other things.'"[74] In the *Symposium*, Diotima of Mantinea reasons with Socrates from beautiful things to beauty itself, along the way denying definitions that would fail to regard beauty in its transcendence: "he must remark how the beauty attached to this or that body is cognate to that which is attached to any other, and that if he means to ensue beauty in form, it is gross folly not to regard as one and the same the beauty belonging to all."[75] Socrates also discusses the transcendental nature of the one in Plato's *Philebus*.[76]

The patristic legacy bears witness to the holy in a similar fashion as it does to other transcendentals.[77] Basil speaks in his *On the Holy Spirit* of heavenly beings, those examples of created glory, and says, "The pure, intelligent, and supermundane powers are and are styled holy, because they have their holiness of the grace given by the Holy Spirit."[78] They are not "holy by nature," which would mean they were no different from the Holy Spirit himself. However, their sanctification, "being external to their substance, superinduces their perfection through the communion of the Holy Spirit."[79] Basil says this holy "rank" is maintained by "abiding in the good and true."[80] In *The Fifth Theological Oration*, Gregory Nazianzen makes an argument for the divine hypostasis of the Spirit based on a notion of the holy. He says the Spirit is the medium of one's participation in holiness; if the Spirit was less than a self-existent Trinitarian *hypostasis*, he could not

---

74. Plato, *Republic*, 505e.

75. Plato, *Symposium*, 210b.

76. He says, "We say that one and many are identified by reason, and always, both now and in the past, circulate everywhere in every thought that is uttered. This is no new thing and will never cease; it is, in my opinion, a quality within us which will never die or grow old, and which belongs to reason itself as such" (Plato, *Philebus*, 15d).

77. "Patristic legacy" here does not imagine a homogenous theological identity, but an inherent and received *ratio* or *logos* that can be discerned from within and thereafter traditioned from generation to generation.

78. Basil, *On the Spirit*, 16.38.

79. Basil, *On the Spirit*, 16.38.

80. Basil, *On the Spirit*, 16.38.

INTRODUCTION

communicate holiness to creatures, and if the holy is not understood as a unique quality of the divine, God (the perfect good) could not be God.[81] John of Damascus continues Nazianzen's defense of the "co-essential" and "co-eternal" Spirit of God, who is indivisible of Father and Son, of the same essence with them, sharing the same qualities, filling not filled, participated in not participating; and as such, he is the "fountain of wisdom, and life, and holiness."[82] For the Damascene, holiness qualifies the "Holy Godhead," "Holy Scripture," the three "holy subsistences" (αἱ ἁγίαι τρεῖς ὑποστάσεις), and the "holy and superessential and incomprehensible Trinity" (τῆς ἁγίας ὑπερουσίου, καὶ πάντων ἐπέκεινα, καὶ ἀλήπτου).[83] This holy essence is "identical" also with "authority, power, and goodness."[84]

In *On Virginity*, Gregory of Nyssa exposits the special grace of virginity, which through purity singularly discloses holiness and beauty in an ever complex but refined vision of transcendental intermingling. Speaking of virginity as being phenomenologically "rich" (so to speak), Gregory says, "The holy look of virginity is precious indeed in the judgement of all who make purity the test of beauty."[85] This "holy look" is named by "Uncorrupted," which also is seen in some essential way in the "purity" of beauty.[86] Like beauty, holiness spans the natural-supernatural divide through participation, as the superiority of virginity is shown in the "*deifying*" of those who "share in her pure mysteries, so that they become partakers of His glory Who is in actual truth the only Holy and Blameless One."[87] Of virginity he says its participants are "bathed in the glow of a seeming beauty," a beauty that to the one of "half-grown intelligence" appears to reside in the essence of a thing, but actually transcends every limitation.[88] One must ascend

---

81. He says, "There is something lacking if it hath not the Holy and how would it have this if it were without the Spirit? For either holiness is something different from Him, and if so let some one tell me what it is conceived to be; or if it is the same, how is it not from the beginning?" (Gregory Nazianzen, *Fifth Theological Oration*, 6).

82. John of Damascus, *Exposition of the Orthodox Faith*, 8:9.

83. John of Damascus, *Exposition of the Orthodox Faith*, 8:8–10.

84. John of Damascus, *Exposition of the Orthodox Faith*, 8:10.

85. Gregory of Nyssa, *Virginity*, 1:343.

86. Gregory of Nyssa, *Virginity*, 1:343.

87. Gregory of Nyssa, *Virginity*, 1:344.

88. Gregory of Nyssa, *Virginity*, 11:355. Gregory explains: "The Beauty which is invisible and formless, which is destitute of qualities and far removed from everything which we recognize in bodies by the eye, can never be made known by the traits which require nothing but the perceptions of our senses in order to be grasped" (Gregory of Nyssa, *Virginity*, 11:355).

the "ladder" of analysis and perceive the "Form of Beauty" ("that Intellectual Beauty") in which all other beauties "share" and get their name.[89] In so ascending, one will become "as beautiful as the Beauty which he has touched and entered, and to be made bright and luminous himself in the communion with the real Light."[90] Gregory's understanding of the participatory economy of beauty is given also to holiness. Just as one ascends in beauty, consequently reflecting it, "so the mind . . . under the stress of the spirit becomes pure and luminous in contact with the true and supernal Purity."[91] The virgin places him or herself "like a mirror beneath the purity of God"; one's beauty touches the Archetype, as one's purity "emits light" having itself become "a Light."[92] As one's apprehension of the good and the beautiful is a "science" and "art," Gregory says virginity is like "the practical method in the science of the Divine life."[93] This exposition is a powerful testimony to the inherent Christian "feeling" for the transcendentality of the holy. Seen alongside beauty, both appear phenomenologically in creatures (declared throughout the heavens), require "scientific" or philosophical ascent to be "seen," relate God to creation through participation and deification, intertwine in their appearance (distinguishable though undivided), are archetypically true of God, and reflect in the luminous "mirror" of human beings.[94]

Although holiness may not have been explicitly grouped as a "transcendental" in patristic and medieval thought, contemporary theologians have started to see it as a comprehensive transcendental. Therefore the thesis that holiness is the transcendental *of* the transcendentals (*sanctum sanctorum*) formalizes a general impulse in contemporary reflection on the holy. Orthodox theologian Dumitru Stăniloae offers such an account: "Holiness can be said to reveal to us all the divine qualities in a concentrated

---

89. Gregory of Nyssa, *Virginity*, 11:355. On the ladder, he says "The beauty noticed there will be but as the hand to lead us to the love of the supernal Beauty whose glory the heavens and the firmament declare, and whose secret the whole creation sings. The climbing soul, leaving all that she has grasped already as too narrow for her needs, will thus grasp the idea of that magnificence which is exalted far above the heavens" (Gregory of Nyssa, *Virginity*, 11:356).

90. Gregory of Nyssa, *Virginity*, 11:356.

91. Gregory of Nyssa, *Virginity*, 11:356.

92. Gregory of Nyssa, *Virginity*, 11:356.

93. Gregory of Nyssa, *Virginity*, 5:351.

94. Gregory of Nyssa, *Virginity*, 12:357.

way."⁹⁵ Maxim Vasilijević says "holiness should not be understood as one of the qualities of the nature of God but as the fundamental characteristic of the Triune Persons, unique, unrepeatable and personal Hypostases."⁹⁶ Alexander Schmemann says, "'Holy' is the real name of God, of the God 'not of scholars and philosophers,' but of the living God of faith. The knowledge about God results in definitions and distinctions. The knowledge of God leads to this one, incomprehensible, yet obvious and inescapable word: holy."⁹⁷ Bogoljub Šijaković says "Holiness is *not* just an *attribute* that can be ascribed to beings, phenomena, objects, places so that it would acquire its ontological carrier through them. Holiness means the most real and the most complete Being. Holiness is the *primary 'reality.'* Holiness is not some property of God but the essence of the endless fullness of the Divine Being."⁹⁸

This theme is not limited to the Orthodox. David L. Schindler, a Catholic theologian who has written extensively on the topic of holiness from the *ressourcement* sensibility, says, "In a word, holiness, with its call to share in the perfect love of the Father in the Son by the Spirit, is inclusive of the objective order of intelligence and of the meaning and truth of all created entities. Holiness is intended to comprehend the order of being in its entirety."⁹⁹ P. T. Forsyth also says that holiness "is no attribute of God, but his very essence. . . . It is not a quality in God, but the being of God, in which all else inheres."¹⁰⁰ Melissa Raphael offers a feminist appropriation of Otto's idea of the holy and says "Holiness defines deity: it qualifies all other divine attributes."¹⁰¹ From a theology of the cross, David Willis says "God's holiness is the all-embracing, all-encompassing attribute of God—or, in the language of perfections, the holiness of God is the perfection of all God's

---

95. Stăniloae, *Experience of God*, 1:222–23.

96. Vasilijević, *History, Truth, Holiness*, 1.3.303.

97. Schmemann, *Life of the World*, 32.

98. Šijaković, *Presence of Transcendence*, 1.3.334.

99. Schindler, "Trinity, Creation, and the Order," 412. He adds, "These principles together indicate the historical order of the imago Dei. The point, then, is to integrate all the methods and objects of human intelligence into holiness as articulated in these principles. In a word, and once again, our key presupposition is that holiness, as inclusive of order, is thereby predicable analogously not only of (spiritual) subjectivity but of the objective structure and meaning of all entities in the cosmos" (Schindler, "Trinity, Creation, and the Order," 416).

100. Forsyth, *Revelation*, quoted in Goroncy, *Hallowed Be Thy Name*, 45.

101. Raphael, *Otto*, 40

Sanctum Sanctorum

perfections."[102] Also, the contemplative Thomas Merton says, "His holiness is the culmination of all His other attributes, His being in its infinite transcendency."[103]

The Reformed dogmatitian Louis Berkhof says that though it does not seem proper to speak of one attribute of God as more central or fundamental, "if this were permissible, the Scriptural emphasis on the holiness of God would seem to justify its selection."[104] Berkhof even says that holiness is a "transcendental attribute," but never develops the idea. The puritan John Howe describes holiness almost exactly as our thesis does, if for him this was only an inkling, for holiness "may therefore be styled a transcendental attribute, that as it were runs through the rest, and casts a glory upon every one; it is an attribute of attributes."[105] Finally, John Wesley says that "when God is termed Holy, it denotes that Excellence, which is altogether peculiar to himself; and the Glory flowing from all his Attributes conjoined."[106] If many suggest that holiness is a transcendental name, no one has fully developed this idea in equal measure to that of being, truth, goodness and beauty. Either the transcendentality of holiness is briefly mentioned (Wesley, Howe, Berkhof), or the philosophical framework is unequipped to appropriate the patristic and medieval legacy (Otto). This book seeks to appropriate the participatory ontology of the patristic-medieval tradition and begin developing the holy in equal measure to that of the other transcendentals.

---

102. Willis, *Holiness of God*, 58.

103. Merton, *Island*, 160. He says, "In the holiness of God, all extremes meet—infinite mercy and justice, infinite love and endless hatred of sin, infinite power and limitless condescension to the weakness of His creatures. . . . Yet the supreme manifestation of God's holiness is the death of Christ on the Cross. Here, too, all extremes meet" (Merton, *Island*, 160).

104. Berkhof, *Systematic Theology*, 73.

105. Howe, *Blessedness*, 59. Arthur Pink's book, *The Attributes of God*, popularized this quotation from Howe. Pink, *Attributes*, 42. Pink himself argues that "God Himself singles out this perfection, 'Once have I sworn by My holiness' (Ps 89:35). God swears by His "holiness' because that is the *fuller* expression of Himself than anything else. . . . Thus we read of 'the *beauty* of the Lord' (Ps 27:4), which is none other than 'the beauty of holiness (Ps 110:3)" (Pink, *Attributes*, 41–42).

106. Wesley, *Explanatory Notes*, 667.

OUTLINE OF CHAPTERS

This chapter has introduced issues surrounding the notions of holiness and transcendentality, and offered criteria for evaluating the holy's inclusion into the category of transcendental. It has also shown that while the transcendentals are important aspects of the patristic-medieval legacy, some of the most enduring and enlightened work continues to be done today, and thus the omission of holiness from historic accounts is not detrimental to this thesis.

Chapter 1 will consider the way holiness fits among the other divine names. Particularly, it will elucidate and expand upon the classic Christian analogy of God as light. Holiness is the hierarchical concentration of the transcendentals and "refracts" into rays, as white light refracts into a spectrum of colours. The concept of God as light, which refracts into perceptible "rays," is found throughout the patristics and Greek philosophy. I will argue that holiness is a more fitting apex, as opposed to the good or one, and apply the principle *sanctum sanctorum* to the tradition to show how their thought agrees with my proposed amendment to the order of transcendentals.

Chapter 2 addresses two issues in the discussion of holiness. On the one hand, holiness typically demarcates God's separation from all things, consequent to his awe-inspiring otherness. On the other hand, if something is to be a transcendental, it must be present and contributing to every "moment" of existence, and thus the Trinitarian life itself. It is a part of what makes sense of experience, even an intra-divine one. Thus the issue is: how can God meaningfully experience, know, and be holy in and to himself if holiness is characterized by a division between an all-glorious Other and its spectators, its subordinates? Applying "*sanctum sanctorum*" to the Trinity, I will argue that the divine Son "reveres" the "Holy" Father and is *thus* himself "of holies." Therefore, holiness as transcendental is reconciled with God's immanent life, and the relationship of the Father and Son is shown to further support the theological principle Holy-of-holies.

Chapter 3 will evaluate how the role of the Spirit relates to holiness. Regarding the immanent life of God, I will expand upon the Spirit as gift in unity and distance between Father and Son to show how he contextualizes, makes possible (or "realizes"), *sanctum sanctorum* in the Trinity. This formula requires the distance and unity always ascribed to the Holy Spirit in tradition. More than being merely passive, the Spirit is the principle of consecration (or consecrator), which is the most basic activity of distinguishing what is holy. This chapter will also consider how the Spirit's work applies to the incarnate Christ and extends to the world through the church.

The preceding chapters establish the theoretical basis of the transcendentality of holiness. Because *everything* is now in some measure holy, then *anything* can be further investigated for its measure of holiness. However, recent theological discussion has well understood how holiness permeates the "mundane" and the socio-political sciences, among other things. While this book might give way to further work in such areas, they are not *theoretically* problematic to the very idea of the holy as the transcendental *of* the transcendentals. Thus, chapter 4 considers what might be the greatest problem for this thesis, namely in what sense can one consider obscene atrocities and insidious horrors to be holy? This chapter argues that sanctity is the basis of horror, and thus even the most grotesque realities revere the holy. Moreover, the grotesque has a qualitative and structural affinity to the holy, and thus the latter half of this chapter will offer an *apologia* for a committed retrieval of the grotesque as an aesthetic genre or mood.

The fifth and final chapter argues that the gift is predicated upon the secret, and just as the gift is the dynamic of the good, the secret is the dynamic of the holy. The gift is a symbol of excess that keeps the secret holy and keeps the holy secret. First, it shows how the sociality of the gift discloses secrecy as its precondition. Having amended Dionysius's scheme of divine names, we can connect the gift to the holy and the secret through the *reverential* nature of the good. This theological account supplements the sociality of the secret and the gift. It will also show that because secrecy is the dynamic of the holy, keeping secret is a preeminent Christian virtue and an integral aspect of love. Moreover, it will show that faith itself is an act of secret keeping. And finally, in light of the dynamics of secrecy, it will argue that the mask is an inherent and quintessential aspect of consciousness, insofar as the mask reveals by concealing.

1

The White Light of Holiness

"It was the whiteness of the whale that above all things appalled me."[1]
—Herman Melville, *Moby Dick*

"Let your garments always be white."
—Ecclesiastes 9:8

INTRODUCTION

THIS BOOK ARGUES THAT holiness is the transcendental *of* the transcendentals (as *sanctum sanctorum*). However, the greatest exponents of Christian theology never really reached this understanding of holiness. Therefore, if the holy is to be seen in continuity with the participatory ontology of the patristic and medieval traditions, then we will have to provide a creative re-reading of the thought of key figures. In this chapter, section one argues that the holy is preeminent among the divine names, which amends the preeminence of the good in Dionysius. Section two shows how the

---

1. Melville, *Moby Dick*, 353.

transcendentals are inherently oriented towards the holy in a liturgical fashion; in other words, the transcendentals *hallow* the holy. The third and final section explicates the qualitative distinction between holiness (*sanctum*) and the other transcendentals (*sanctorum*) by introducing "the eclipse of the holy."

THE PREEMINENCE OF THE HOLY

This section will seek to demonstrate how the logic of the divine names in the patristic-medieval tradition anticipates holiness as the preeminent name, even if this order was never explicitly stated. It will look primarily at Dionysius the Areopagite because he summarizes the Christian heritage before him and is definitive for subsequent theology. Particularly, Dionysius argues that the loftiest name good "reveres" the Unnamable essence of God, but because names are "causes" intuited through their effect, the unnamable essence of God warrants the name holy precisely because it *causes* reverence.

In his elegant treatise *The Divine Names*, Dionysius the Areopagite sets forth an explication of the divine names, which are lifted towards what is unnamable.[2] His arrangement and exposition of choice names reveals one exploring the contours of life *towards* the all-blessed, attempting to name and not name in "wise silence."[3] Whatever theological clarity one achieves, names will always be deficient; God's "superessential [ὑπερουσίου] and hidden Diety" beyond every conceivable essence is best rendered by "the name which is above every name."[4] Among the intelligible names, Dionysius exalts a single name above the rest: the Good.[5] At once transcendent of all form and being while also present to everything as cause and end, the good is the desire of all and the condition of motion. Goodness is the

---

2. Dionysius, *Divine Names*, 588A. English translation is John Parker's, which abides more closely to the Greek original than the Paulist Press translation, widely considered a paraphrase. See Knepper, *Negating Negation*, 16.5; Perl, *Theophany*, ix. Dionysius says, "The theologians, having knowledge of this, celebrate It, both without Name and from every Name." This "wonderful Name, that which is above every Name—the Nameless," is "fixed above every name which is named" (Dionysius, *Divine Names*, 596A–B).

3. Dionysius, *Divine Names*, 589B.

4. Dionysius, *Divine Names*, 588A.

5. Dionysuis says this is "the all-perfect Name of Goodness, which is indicative of the whole progressions of Almighty God" (Dionysius, *Divine Names*, 680B).

abundance out of which an infinite glory radiates and to which it inevitably and harmoniously returns.[6] As the agent of cohesion, everything looks to it as its source.[7] Desiring the good, all intellectual beings seek to know it, all sapient beings yearn to perceive it, all lacking perception instinctually long for it, and all lifeless forms turn—in their own fashion—for a share of it.[8]

The inevitable inadequacy of every name likewise befalls the Good. For Dionysius, the true nature and essence of God is a hidden, indescribable, reality without name or expression, "elevated above in the inaccessible."[9] Neither, says Dionysius, "do we apply the very Name of Goodness, as making it adequate to It."[10] Because the good falls short of the ineffable essence of God, the name itself is only possible, is only conceivable, posterior to (*a posteriori*) another mode of divinity. Though from the good erupts an infinite display of differentiated glories, or "beams," which include the remaining panoply of divine names, likened to the sun and its effervescent light, Dionysius still separates the supra-essential identity of God. In *Mystical Theology*, he guides the contemplative into the veiled silence of "superluminous" darkness (ὑπέρφωτον γνόφον).[11]

All divine names are for Dionysius analogical symbols drawn from creatures in praise towards the God who is finally ineffable.[12] Such symbols *never* make the claim of comprehension, but in a sense derive their validity from the liturgical performance they rationally enable; Beauty, for instance, is a name through which creatures "follow" this particular ray of divinity—recognizing the beautiful but never delimiting beauty as an object of observation—which ultimately recedes back into ineffable mystery. Dionysius refuses to give a name to the inexpressible darkness of divinity precisely out of *reverence* to the mystery.[13] One cannot ignore such depth

---

6. Dionysius, *Divine Names*, 697A.

7. Dionysius says, "Goodness turns all things to Itself, and is chief collector of things scattered, as One-springing and One-making Deity, and all things aspire to It, as Source and Bond and End, and it is the Good" (Dionysius, *Divine Names*, 700A–B).

8. Dionysius, *Divine Names*, 700A–B. "Even the nonexistent itself aspires to the Good above all things existing, and struggles somehow to be even itself in the Good—the really Superessential—to the exclusion of all things" (Dionysius, *Divine Names*, 697A).

9. Dionysius, *Divine Names*, 981A.

10. Dionysius, *Divine Names*, 981A.

11. Dionysius, *Mystical Theology*, 997B.

12. Dionysius, *Divine Names*, 981C.

13. We must contemplate "the unrevealed of the Godhead which is beyond mind and matter, with inscrutable and holy reverence of mind" (Dionysius, *Divine Names*, 589A–B).

(which may seem to be a fitting response due to fear or even respect) but must ever steadily enter it. The Dionysian corpus does nothing if not detail the path towards the dazzling darkness of the divine that is without name, but this paradoxical discourse that explicates precisely how God's essence transcends all language is what *every* divine name "*does*" in its own way. "The Good" does not re-present an object, but recognizes the lure of the desirable and pursues it through (and beyond) the name, or more accurately pursues the beyond "in" the name. Therefore, because the sublime mystery of God's supra-essential nature is so utterly transcendent that it elicits *reverence*, it deserves the name which brings the contemplative in and beyond the good towards the inexplicable brilliance of a hidden and invisible darkness, in other words the holy.

As the sun of existence, the good proceeds out of unending immensity into the region of non-being, and after calling everything into existence, choreographs the singular though differentiated voice of the cosmos, which resonates in a doxological tone.[14] This primordial procession of the good, initiated by generosity not necessity, is an act of self-outpouring or *kenosis*. Such self-exteriorizing charity Jean-Luc Marion calls "pure givenness" or *Givenness Par Excellence*.[15] Enthroning goodness over the divine names, Dionysius offers an im-Passioned cosmological vision in which reality is suspended by transcendental *kenosis*. Christ's *descent* into the form of a slave only finalizes the work begun at the first word of creation, both of which instantiate the radical givenness of the good.

To this procession and return, *exitus-reditus*, is added another moment.[16] As Dionysius argues, a hiddenness belongs to God, to which no

---

14. Dionysius, *Divine Names*, 697B–C.

15. For Marion, givenness so characterizes the good that one cannot conceive of a "before" being given, and therefore no "givee" behind the gift. Concerning the phenomenological "bracketing" of the give, Marion says, "It is a question of bracketing the givee. Can we do so without also suspending the entire process of the gift? Certainly. Not only does the bracketing of the givee not invalidate the givenness of the gift, but it characterizes it intrinsically: without this suspension of the givee, the very possibility of *giving* the gift would become problematic" (Marion, *Being Given*, 85; "Metaphysics and Phenomenology," 295).

16. Christian Schäfer brought to light an important aspect of Dionysius's ontology which has been characterized by *exitus-reditus*, procession and return, which is the addition of "repose." This addition overlaps with our argument that Dionysius's thought exhibits a "holy," summative, moment: Schäfer says "rest" (which Genesis connects to holiness) is the "isosthenic completion of all aspects of reality" (Schäfer, *Philosophy of Dionysius*, 39). Moreover, "The final principle of togetherness underlying all differences and opposites is God, the One, Who brings all things together, returning them to Himself

expression can be given; one cannot follow it into its inaccessible dwelling, and even the name "goodness" cannot enter.[17] Precisely by theologizing about God's inaccessible dwelling, Dionysius implies that the good, which enlightens and directs all things, culminates in a reverent posture towards what is beyond itself. The good not only gives from itself but stands towards and gazes at the ineffable, and thus has a transcendent *telos*. The good is not pure givenness, but the *paidagogos* (cf. Gal 3:24) that leads everything up into what is supremely holy, into the inner *sanctum*. The good acts on behalf of the holy.

Though *kenotic*, the good is ultimately *reverential* and thus displays Mariological traits, for historically Mary has been the embodiment of reverence and a paradigm for the church.[18] Humble and unassuming, Mary's virtue is made possible by an infinite, asymmetrical, disproportion between God's gift and her return. Mary is of particularly ignoble beginnings, which primes her to become the Mother of All-Holiness (blessed through meekness). The gift of Jesus Christ to the holy mother is so entirely excessive that it imposes an ultimatum: either, out of pride, she rejects the gift precisely because it has no justifiable warrant in "earthly" terms, or, she accepts the gift, and thus passes through total self-rejection to the serenity of generous receiving, pure gratitude, otherwise known as the fullness of reverence, and thus onto true holiness. Like Mary, the good is given its existence, so to speak (coming from the holy), and exhibits a qualitatively Mariological disproportion towards the ever-transcendent beyond of the holy. The "high

---

in an epistrophic convergence of all opposites towards Himself as their final Cause. The same holds true of the creative procession and its efficient Cause. The ontological 'halt' does not only make us look ahead and remind us of the One as the final aim of the reconciliation of opposites, but it also makes us glance backwards, to remind us of the first and definite unity in which everything has its origin. It is clearly the 'halt' that makes us understand that the regress and the progress of all beings in relation to the One are the same" (Schäfer, *Philosophy of Dionysius*, 39). In the forward, Paul Rorem expands upon this revision of ontological movement: "The 'downward' is the mirror image of the 'upward;' but both are finite and temporal expressions for the infinite and eternal. But what of 'remaining,' the original and/or final eternal? To press the spatial imagery, if the downward procession should be paired with the upward return, should the 'remaining' at the top also be paired with a kind of remaining, or dynamic stability, rest, or 'peace,' at the bottom of the parabola? Hence: procession, remaining, return" (Schäfer, *Philosophy of Dionysius*, xiv). Connecting the two voices together, "rest" or "repose" (which we take as, ultimately, holiness) is in, through, behind, ahead, below, and above reality; in other words, it is transcendental. See also Dillon, "Dionysius the Areopagite," 113.

17. Dionysius, *Divine Names*, 981A.
18. For Mary as the paradigm of holiness, see Gambero, *Mary and the Fathers*, 104.

and lofty one who inhabits eternity, and whose name is Holy" says "I dwell in the high and holy place, and also with those who are contrite and humble in spirit" (Isa 57:15).

Now, by ascribing the name holy to God's supra-essential essence, which is above every name, some might insist that we rupture an inviolable linguistic barrier and subsequently commit idolatry. Returning to Dionysius, names are efficacious symbols that mediate deification less by some fixed content they disclose and more through the spiritual encounter (theurgy) they effect in exceeding intelligibility.[19] Naming God is an act of "onomastic theurgy";[20] or as Alexander Golitzin says, the divine names are "notional icons."[21] Balthasar says that praise, or the "hymnic," is not simply a third moment between apophatic and kataphatic speech for Dionysius. Rather, it functions as the fundamental "methodology of theological thinking and speaking."[22] In all his treatises, Dionysius exposits the mystical way towards God's hidden essence, hoping his readers will be inspired and guided to make that journey themselves. This macro-purpose of his works repeats the micro-reality of *every* divine name.[23]

By insisting, with variety and ingenuity, that God's essence is unnamable, one remains inescapably within the domain of nomination, which

---

19. Theurgy is the "magical" or "sacramental" potency of ritual and material reality to mediate the divine. For Dionysius, the divine names themselves, written and conveyed in scripture and the tradition, are "theurgic" entities.

20. For more on Dionysius's "onomastic theurgy," see Klitenic, *Dionysius the Areopagite*, 85–97. Sarah Klitenic says that because divine names are symbols *par excellence*, "The word itself performs a generative function unleashed at the divine level, but still potent when it functions as human language" (Klitenic, *Dionysius the Areopagite*, 86) and "acting as symbola, names carry a performative capability" (Klitenic, *Dionysius the Areopagite*, 92).

21. Golitzin, *Mystagogy*, 85.

22. Quoted in Jones, "Dionysius," 215.

23. Adrian Pabst says, "If all things immanent intimate their transcendent cause, then it is also analogically the case that all divine names point to something more than themselves—God's excess over all names. . . . Naming the 'Nameless' God ceases to be mere predication and, by liturgical subversion, becomes itself a form of praise of absolute divine transcendence, in the very act of expressing its constitutive indigence" (Pabst, *Metaphysics*, 144). Explicating Dionysius's analogical, and metaphysical, use of "name," Knepper corrects the misconception that divine names are creaturely adornments of an otherwise inexplicable darkness: "Dionysian names are much more than this. They are divine processions that source and sustain the basic properties of the cosmos. . . . Thus it is only because divine names are firstly and primarily *causes of properties* that those properties can be attributed to or denied of those beings that do or do not participate in them" (Knepper, *Negating Negation*, 1). See also Harrington, "Introduction," 6; Rorem, *Biblical and Liturgical Symbols*, 106–16.

The White Light of Holiness

reveals the proper form of apophasis which always paradoxically holds that the "Unnamable," the Ἀνώνυμον, cannot be named.[24] Whether God is called Cause, Incomprehensible, Transcendent One, or Super-Essential Essence, he is *called*, he is indicated. When speaking of God's essence, the Holy is the "it" in "It cannot be named" (which is a variation on the ontological statement that God is the "Is" in both "it *is*" and "it *is* not").[25] Thus, Dionysius's tireless discourse on the unnamable is best rendered in the onomastic performance: "Holy, Holy, Holy." If one asks heaven's beings, says John Chrysostom, they will not speak *about* his "Essence" but sing "the mystic song of His Holiness" (Isa 6:3).[26] This unique name—the divine name *par excellence* one might say—does not risk delimiting God's essence through language, because this name *means* or *effects* noetic excess. While every name may be similarly over-saturated by divine reality, which theological explication of the kind Dionysius partakes would disclose, the Holy is the name which tells *on its surface* of God's excess. Therefore, this name—holy—is behind (in the sense of within and beyond) all names. Consequently, as names are here superseded in the form of a name, "Holy" radically destabilizes linguistic confidence through a resonance of dissimilarity, and thus also stands for "H̶o̶l̶y̶."[27] The playfulness of the paradox is on full display in Bert

---

24. Dionysius, *Divine Names*, 596A.

25. See an explication of this idea see Przywara, *Analogia Entis*, 159–60. David Bentley Hart explains, "Being, simply said, cannot be reduced to beings or negated by them; it plays peacefully in the expressive iridesence of its welcoming light, in the intricate weaving of the transcendentals, even in the transcendental moments of 'this' and 'not this'" (Hart, *Infinite*, 243).

26. Chrysostom, "Homilies on the Gospel," 15.1.

27. This crossed out "Holy" recalls the theological paradox that God is *said* to be beyond *words*; in other words, God is an unspeakable reality we cannot not talk about. For Heidegger, the "Being" which "is" only in Dasein is really nothing, and thus Being crossed out (Heidegger, "Question of Being," 120–51). Jacques Derrida calls the appearance of a word crossed out with an X "under erasure" (*sous rature*): one writes a word, crosses it out, and then prints the word and the deletion, signifying that the word is inaccurate though necessary (Anderson, *Derrida*, 93). See Derrida, *Of Grammatology*, 60. Jean-Luc Marion similarly crosses out "God." He says, "Let us cross out God, with a cross ... which demonstrates the limit of the temptation, conscious or naive, to blaspheme the unthinkable in an idol. The cross does not indicate that God would have to disappear as a concept, or intervene only in the capacity of a hypothesis in the process of validation, but that the unthinkable enters into the field of our thought only by rendering itself unthinkable there by excess, that is, by criticizing our thought. To cross out God, in fact, indicated and recalls that God crosses out our thought because he saturates it; better, he enters into our thought only in obliging it to criticize itself" (Marion, *God Without Being*, 46).

Blans's discussion of negative theology: after discussing Dionysius, he says, "The Holy One cannot be named."[28] Who cannot be named? Blans also says that the Holy One "must therefore be *assumed* to be 'behind' or in the text, or there where the text is silent."[29] Indeed, but the text itself enables one to "see" beyond-text-ness.[30]

Undoubtedly, Greek philosophy influences the elevation of the good, which by itself is unobjectionable. However, given that theological speech is constructed not from plausible words of human wisdom but from the demonstration of the Spirit (1 Cor 2:4), which was granted specially to the authors of scripture, the preeminence of the good should be considered open to emendation (or at least debatable within the realm of orthodoxy, even by Dionysius's own account).[31] For Dionysius himself argues that one cannot speak of "the superessential and hidden Diety beyond those things divinely revealed to us in the sacred Oracles." What makes the authors of scripture especially qualified to speak of God? Whether angels or apostles, shepherds or theologians, adequate theological discourse is predicated upon one's *nearness* to God, the *intensity* of one's exposure to God, and one's creaturely *capacity* to receive God, all of which mutually inform one another.[32]

Based upon this criteria, Dionysius identifies three ideal locations for naming: heaven, the transfiguration, and the eschaton. Led up a high mountain, the disciples see Jesus transfigured in light "a little too bright for their eyes," his face shining like the sun while his clothes become whiter than anyone on earth could have bleached (Matt 17:2–3; Mark 9:3).[33] Bewildered by the theophany, Peter offers to erect altars, his trepidation evinced by his opening "if you wish" (Matt 17:4).[34] Peter's oblation, desperate and yet certain, shares the distinctive characteristics belonging to the Seraphim, of whom Isaiah bears witness. The Seraphim attend to the Lord in an elevated celestial temple, billowing with a cloud of smoke (Isa 6:4), and while hiding

---

28. Blans, "Cloud of Unknowing," 63.

29. Blans, "Cloud of Unknowing," 63.

30. More discussion of how the visible displays the invisible will follow in the subsequent chapter.

31. Dillon, *Dionysius the Areopagite*, 15–50; Perl, *Theophany*, 35–52; Schäfer, *Philosophy of Dionysius the Areopagite*, 55–74. Dionysius, *Divine Names*, 588A.

32. Dionysius, *Divine Names*, 588C–589A.

33. Gregory Nazianzen, *Oration on Holy Baptism*, 361.

34. All Scripture references are NRSV unless otherwise noted.

themselves behind their many wings, they cry, "Holy, holy, holy, is the Lord of hosts" (Isa 6:3). This word, "Holy," is what over-saturated exposure, maximum intensity, and unhindered capacity draws out; it is born from the altar-building impulse of the Spirit of God, by which he gets his name Holy Spirit, τὸ πνεῦμα τὸ ἅγιον: as Basil says, "How could the Seraphim cry 'Holy, Holy, Holy,' were they not taught by the Spirit?"[35] Ambrose also says that "everything which we esteem holy proclaims that Sole Holiness," which is taught by the "Holy Spirit, whose Name is the praise of God."[36]

Isaiah's all-important triadic declaration is repeated nowhere less significant than in John's Revelation, where Dionysius's three ideal contexts for naming coincide, each featuring Dionysius's luminous cloud. Like Isaiah's, John's vision features one seated on a throne in heaven (Rev 4:1–2; Isa 6:1), and with features of Isaiah's vision and the transfiguration mixed together, John sees the throne accompanied by elders and winged beings (Rev 4:4, 6). The elders now wearing Christ's white robe fall before the apocalyptic creatures who cry "Holy, holy, holy, the Lord God the Almighty, who was and is and is to come" (Rev 4:8).[37] In both heavenly visions, the authors use various spatial cues to indicate the special grandeur and clarity of God's appearance: all is seen through an open door to heaven, a place elevated and filled with celestial glory; God sits upon a still higher throne, clothed in mystique or shimmering as light through precious stone; gigantic otherworldly figures cower before the throne; God's presence is evoked by his robe or light, voice and thunder, filling the temple (Isa 6:1–7; Rev 4:1–11). In a sense, John and Isaiah take every opportunity to magnify the spectacle. However, the vibrant imagery can distract from the sparse though precise description of God; while he is described as seated on the throne,

---

35. Basil, *On the Spirit*, 38:24. See also Lossky, *Image and Likeness*, 166.

36. Ambrose, *On the Holy Spirit*, 3.16.110. "Cherubim and Seraphim with unwearied voices praise Him and say: 'Holy, Holy, Holy, is the Lord God of Sabaoth.'"

37. Regarding the thought that holiness is the divine name *par excellence*, Leonard Thompson says of this hymn: "The first expression of heavenly worship heard by the seer of the Book of Revelation is thus the song par excellence of apocalyptic visionaries." Further, "Similar heavenly creatures sing the *Kodosh* elsewhere. According to 1 Enoch 39 those who stand before God without slumbering praise him saying 'Holy, Holy, Holy, Lord of Spirits; the spirits fill the earth' (1 Enoch 39:12). In 2 Enoch the six-winged, many-eyed ones who stand before the throne sing 'with gentle voice,' 'Holy, Holy, Holy, Lord Sabaoth, Heaven and earth are full of his glory' (2 Enoch 21:1). In the later 3 Enoch (3 Enoch 1: 35–40) and perhaps in the Apocalypse of Abraham (Ap. Abraham 16), heavenly creatures also sing the *Kadosh*" (Thompson, *Revelation*, 57). See also Kovacs and Rowland, *Revelation*, 59–60.

one who lives "forever and ever," worthy of all glory and honour and power, none of these descriptions name God directly. All but one word escapes such indirectness; with all cues in place, only heaven's creatures tell *what* God is: "Holy, holy, holy." R. W. L. Moberly says of the *trisagion* that such an emphatic formulation is "tantamount to a definition of the nature of YHWH."[38] Though God appeared to Abraham, Isaac, and Jacob, he did not make himself known to them in his name YHWH (Exod 6:2–3); however, when God revealed his name to Moses, the ground upon which he stood became holy, which was the first appearance of holiness in Israelite history (Exod 3:5, 14). Edward Young also says that the Seraphim set forth "the distinguishing characteristic of God, namely, His holiness. Their hearts burst forth in praise of His very essence."[39]

Among the infinite number of possible words, "holy" is drenched in inevitability, as the only proper name that could possibly here be said. Ambrose says precisely this: "We too find nothing of more worth, whereby we are able to proclaim God, than the calling Him holy."[40] Gregory of Nyssa says likewise. Those who fear God "will even before the naming exalt Him in their thought, it being impossible that words can mount along with thought; still when one shall have reached the highest limit of human faculties, the utmost height and magnificence of idea to which the mind can ever attain, even then one must believe it is far below the glory that belongs to Him," and "the cause of this dignity being so incomprehensible is *nothing else* than that He is holy."[41] If Scripture were to substitute the good for the holy—and the Seraphim cried "Good, good, good"—one would intuitively feel the inadequacy and impropriety of that exchange, which would upset the liturgical effect of this heavenly name for God.[42] The good is implied by holy in a way that holy is not implied by good.

38. Moberly, "Isaiah's Vision of God," 127. Here, he is discussing the *trisagion* in Isa 6:3, and adds that as a definition of YHWH's nature, it "is well captured by the later formulation within the book of Isaiah that 'his name is holy'" (Isa 57:15).

39. Israelite history here excludes God's original act of consecration on the seventh day of creation. Moberly, "Isaiah's Vision of God," 127. On Isaiah's vision: "*Holy, holy, holy*—As here used, *qadosh* signifies the entirety of the divine perfection which separates God from His creation. . . . This is the heart and core of Isaiah's theology" (Young, *Book of Isaiah*, 242–43).

40. Ambrose, *On the Holy Spirit*, 3.16.110.

41. Gregory of Nyssa, *On the Holy Spirit*, 323. Emphasis mine.

42. Rudolf Otto says he invented the term "numinous" to indicate a unique value of the holy, in which absolute goodness is also included though distinct. See Otto, *Idea of the Holy*, 7.

Israel itself liturgically reinforces the preeminence of holiness. Israel demarcates the most lofty and unapproachable dwelling of God as "Holy," הקדשים (of holies), which in the form of tabernacle or temple "ascends" or culminates from the world, through the courts, towards the *sanctum sanctorum* (Exod 26:33).[43] The days of creation also distinguish the uniqueness of the name, as the seventh and crowning day of creation is made holy; six days God considers good, one he considers "holy" (Gen 2:3).[44] Moreover, the good "ascends," or intensifies, towards the holy, as the work of days one through five is called "good" (Gen 1:4; 10; 12; 18; 21; 25), the sixth and final day of work, in which God creates living beings, is called "very good" (Gen 1:31), and the "rest" and completion of day seven God makes holy, ויקדש (Gen 2:3).[45] The Jewish theologian Abraham Heschel makes a similar distinction between the good and the holy. While Heschel is categorically opposed to metaphysical speculation, his distinction comes from the conviction that the biblical witness is formally determinative for theological language, a conviction Dionysius himself defends: Heschel says, "To the philosopher the idea of the good is the most exalted idea. But to the Bible the idea of the good . . . cannot exist without the holy. The holy is the essence, the good is its expression."[46] The supremacy of "Holy" is remembered weekly in the observance of the Sabbath, seen in the landscape of the Israel, and performed in the liturgy of heaven.

---

43. Surveying holiness in the Pentateuch, J. E. Hartley asserts that the tabernacle/temple layout reflects the nature of God: if God's presence is revealed and manifested to Israel in the form of the tabernacle, at the center of which stands the Holy, then in a certain sense one can say that "Holiness is at the center of God's being" (Hartley, "Holy and Holiness," 430).

44. See Hayward, "Sanctification of Time," 141–67.

45. Gordan Wenham says the completion of the heavens and the earth is said to be "'very good,' not merely 'good'" because their full perfection expresses "more adequately the character of their creator than any of the separate components can." The special character of the day is hinted at by the grammatical formula "*the* sixth day" (days 2–5 use "day, Xth" without the article), which it shares with "*the* seventh day" (Wenham, *Genesis 1–15*, 34). Along the same lines as day six, with the specific uniqueness of the day being predicated upon God's nature, the seventh day is made holy, and therefore Wenham says "God is holy: holiness is the essence of his character" (Wenham, *Genesis 1–15*, 36).

46. Heschel, *God in Search of Man*, 17. Rudolf Otto himself agrees that the Bible's magisterial vision of holiness is unequaled: on the numinous aspect of the Holy, Otto says, "There is no religion in which it does not live as the real inner-most core, and without it no religion would be worthy of the name. It is pre-eminently a living force in the Semitic religions, and of these again in none has it such vigour as in that of the Bible" (Otto, *Idea of the Holy*, 6).

Having placed holy atop the divine names, the good retains its classical meaning and function without undergoing radical alteration. Recognizing in Dionysius the ontological convertibility of certain names, Aquinas elects "being" as the primary name of divinity but concedes that the good is prior to being with regard to causality.[47] While the two are the same, being and truth precede the good in idea because nothing can be thought as good apart from the horizon of intelligible actuality. However, the good precedes being with regard to causation because the perfection of beings—in other words their coming-into-being—is caused from the lure of the good "beyond."[48]

Aquinas's appropriation of Dionysius shows that one can exchange which name is centrally positioned without radically altering its meaning and function. If the good is equivocally beyond being, either it will stand over against existence, ever luring but always eluding in a tragic and maddening trick, or it will be an epiphenomenon of transcendence permanently and totally bound to finitude as a mere facade. But if the good "*is*" a wellspring of infinite desire and satisfaction—the endless increase which iteratively gives rapturous experience in every surprising "moment"—then it must be conceived along the lines of being or actuality. However transcendent and invisible the good is, it requires the landscape of infinitely

---

47. Aquinas, *ST* Ia.5.2.ad.1.

48. Fran O'Rourke offers a wonderfully comprehensive book-length treatment of Aquinas and Dionysius. Addressing the importance of Aristotle for Aquinas's understanding of the good as that which is desirable, O'Rourke says, "Desirability, however, is a consequence or result of goodness. To describe the good as that to which all things tend, Aquinas notes, is to indicate by means of a characteristic the presence of goodness rather than disclose its essence or ground. Aristotle's definition indicates what we may term the 'phenomenological' content of goodness—its manifestation to the desiring subject—but does not penetrate to that which fundamentally constitutes it as such. In Plotinus's phrase: 'The good must be desired; but it is not good because it is desirable; it is desirable because it is good.' It is thus necessary to go beyond the *ratio boni* which allows us to recognize goodness, to the *natura boni*, its ontological ground" (O'Rourke, *Pseudo-Dionysius*, 85–86). Moreover O'Rourke further explains the coherence between Dionysius and Aquinas on the good and being: "By definition, the good is what all things desire. But manifestly all things primarily desire actuality, since each thing pursues its own preservation and resists corruption; moreover, what is potential tends towards its realisation. It is thus actuality which constitutes the very nature of goodness. More basically, it is *esse*, the actuality of being, which constitutes the good; the good of each thing is its act and perfection of being. . . . For every thing, it is the same to be and to be good" (O'Rourke, *Pseudo-Dionysius*, 97). As Aquinas did not "sacrifice the causal priority of goodness" when he gave being primacy, we do not alter the causative role of the good by placing holiness "above" it (Hankey, *God In Himself*, 75).

generous actuality. Aquinas thus can be said to inquire after the unique *existence* of the good, which he calls *esse* (being). Divine simplicity ensures that Aquinas's *esse* is as dynamic, inscrutable, and incomprehensible as Dionysius's good, and that Dionysius's good is as actual and substantial as Aquinas's *esse*.

TRANSCENDENTAL LITURGY

As we have seen, divine names have rhythms, tendencies, and "natures" as it were. This section will extend the previous section's discussion of how the good *reveres* the holy to all the transcendental names. We will see that the five transcendental names rhythmically, and by nature, revere the holy, which creates a primordial liturgy from which and to which everything "is."

Dionysius's arguments and presuppositions hint towards the possibility of *prior*itizing holiness. Such hinting may be more than a happy coincidence, but rather unintentionally displays that the inner logic of the divine names is indeed oriented principally towards the holy. The proposed amendment to Dionysius's scheme of divine names does not seek to undermine or surpass him, but to realize theologically what he fortuitously called the "holy hierarchy."[49]

Among his many invaluable insights, Dionysius's analogy of light is exceptionally profound and enduring. By explicating divine substance as analogous to light, which determines what Michael Craig Rhodes calls his "theophanic concept of being," Dionysius anticipates contemporary interest in the appearance or phenomenality of existence.[50] Because substance or being "is" in its appearing, any speculative starting point, by virtue of its

---

49. Dionysius, *Ecclesiastical Hierarchy*, 432C.

50. Rhodes, *Mystery in Philosophy*, 21. Rhodes demonstrates similar notions in two other important Dionysian scholars: Christian Schäfer says "theophany that we call reality" (from *Philosophy of Dionysius the Areopagite*) and Eric Perl, "the whole of reality, all that is, is theophany, the manifestation or appearance of God" (from *Theophany*) (Schäfer and Perl quoted in Rhodes, *Mystery in Philosophy*, 21). Michel Henry says appearance is "more essential" than being; "it is only because it appears that a thing is able to be" (Henry, "Phenomenology of Life," 242). Henry's preference for appearance is rooted in the principle, "Something is inasmuch as it appears [*Autant d'apparaître, autant d'être*]." Henry says he carries this "precedence of phenomenology over ontology one step further by saying that it is only if the appearing appears in itself and as such that something, whatever it may be, can in turn appear, can show itself to us." Marius Victorinus will be discussed at greater length, but his is a fine example of delineating the connection between light and being/substance. See Victorinus, *Against Arius IA*, 139.

actuality and intelligibility, leads back towards God in an ever intensifying degree. Nazianzen expresses delight that Plato—a heathen—discerns the fitting analogy between God and the sun: "the sun . . . [is] to all eyes like the leader of some chorus."[51]

Wedded with a notion of divine light, the doctrine of simplicity offers an opportunity, in light of Przywara's analogical principle (essence-in-and-beyond-existence), to conceive the possibility of holiness as "the" transcendental *of* the transcendentals. The five transcendentals—being, one, truth, goodness, and beauty—by nature transcend all limitations and categories; they exceed every conceivable object or method of inquiry. How then could the transcendentals be *transcended* by something else? The five transcendentals each contribute to every "moment" of existence, infinite or finite, by virtue of their convertibility with one another (their "sameness") according to simplicity. Because of their convertibility, one transcendental can never be isolated from the others. An exhaustive study of truth, for instance, would have to incorporate goodness, beauty, one, and being *to understand* truth. In other words: the "essence" of truth is found "in" it, but also "*beyond*" it. The other transcendentals also have their "essence-in-and-beyond-existence."

When Przywara discusses the tension between *a priori* and *a posteriori* approaches to metaphysics, he shows that one cannot reason purely "from" ("*a*") the first principles ("*priori*").[52] The metaphysician is not at one with ultimate being, but is a finite creature always reasoning *from* the perspective that "comes after" ("*posteriori*") the principles in question. The five transcendentals are considered *a priori* "principles" of existence. They are a part of the ground, and end, and definition in itself; they do not appeal to another source of goodness, truth, and beauty.[53] What is the nature

---

51. Gregory of Nazianzus, *Second Theological Oration*, 29:299. He says, "Have you considered the importance of the fact that a heathen writer speaks of the sun as holding the same position among material objects as God does among objects of thought? For the one gives light to the eyes, as the Other does to the mind; and it is the most beautiful of the objects of sight, as God is of those of thought" (Gregory of Nazianzus, *Second Theological Oration*, 30:300).

52. Przywara, *Analogia Entis*, 133.

53. While discussing Paul Ricoeur's "root metaphors," David Bentley Hart connects a Dionysian sensitivity to apophasis with the a priori nature of transcendental names in metaphysics: "Ricoeur is surely correct that there is a certain metaphorical 'depth' or intensity within language that, at particular points within a given discourse, governs, gathers, deploys, and enriches subordinate ranges of somewhat less expressive metaphors; and this depth or intensity is, in every instance, the effect of a certain impenetrability, or

of their interpenetration? How does one account for the "instability" of their essences? The scheme of the transcendentals is a form of relations determined by another vantage, namely that which simplicity confesses. The transcendentals, while taken as *a priori*, are actually intelligible only "*posteriori* to" another mode of existence. In other words, when we provide the list of five transcendentals that are convertible with one another, we recognize a singularity in their mode of existence that comes "before" the intellectual listing of them. This anterior singularity is intuited from the posterior transcendentals, and we can see that the transcendentals are themselves organized according to this inscrutable "beyond."

The transcendental "One" may seem to account for the anterior unity of simplicity, which would nullify an attempt to go "beyond" the transcendentals, its intelligibility (in others words its "essence"), appearance, and thus existence, are only known "with reference to" the others; and thus, it has its essence-in-and-beyond-existence. Discussing Maximus the Confessor, Balthasar says the one is not exactly a concept, nor substance or accident, but the "sign" by which we distinguish individuality.[54] Thus, every being in the world has two aspects, "that of its 'uniqueness,' through which it stands among other beings without reference to them, and that of its 'relatedness,' through which it stands towards others in a relationship."[55] These two aspects, uniqueness and relatedness, are "practically" inseparable in reality, but are distinguishable in thought.[56] Nevertheless, oneness remains *after* the fact, as "number accomplishes every affirmation of a particular being, in that it sets up a negative boundary against some other being, positing that other being implicitly as one that is 'other' than the first."[57] The

---

of a simultaneous impenetrability and suggestive figural fullness that always evokes—but is never exhausted by—the supplementation of other 'fitting' expressions. A phrase such as, for instance, 'God is love'—which is neither exactly predicative nor uncomplicatedly metaphoric—provides within the context of the discourse to which it belongs a moment of extreme semeiotic resistance, the richness of an irreducibility that calls out for a constant energy of addition and deferral, an eruption of analogical additions proportionate to and determined by its intensity. To say this differently, the 'successful' theological metaphor is one that is not analytic, but is, so to speak, a kind of synthetic a priori: it says more than can be said, it is somehow logically prior to all its efficient causes—or rather, it exhibits its final cause first" (Hart, *Infinite*, 303–4). See also Ricoeur, *Interpretation Theory*, 64.

54. Balthasar, *Cosmic Liturgy*, 109. See Maximus the Confessor, *Epistola 15*, 543.

55. Balthasar, *Cosmic Liturgy*, 109.

56. Balthasar, *Cosmic Liturgy*, 109.

57. Balthasar, *Cosmic Liturgy*, 110. Dionysius says "Its super-oneness, and Divine

nature of the one oscillates between intelligibility and obscurity, number and undelimited abyss, because while God is one, he is not of a singularity that could set him alongside other "ones" on a univocal or equivocal plane: God is not *that* one but Oneness beyond any one. By so oscillating, the "essence" of one runs into its antecedent, the holy.

While the depth of the divine nature is incomprehensible, one remains within the analogical pattern of divine names by considering the brimming totality of divine glories, raised and conjoined in supra-divine brilliance, the consequence of believing in divine simplicity. This revered mode of existence beckons the name reserved as the most contritely uttered superlative: "Holy." More than brightness, holiness is the purity of "white light," in which the refracted variety of "colors" adhere, and from which they emanate.[58] Gregory of Nazianzus says "God is Light: the highest, the unapproachable, the ineffible."[59] Symeon the New Theologian articulates how light analogically reveals the nature of simplicity, "He comes in a definite shape indeed, though it is a divine one. Yet God does not show Himself in a particular pattern or likeness, but in simplicity, and takes the form of an incomprehensible, inaccessible, and formless light."[60] This "light is supperessentially transcendent to all things" says Gregory Palamas, and it is the "light which surpasses light:" its being is unique and "mysteriously comprehends all in itself."[61] Palamas also says of that light that "the essence is one, even though the rays are many."[62] This reveals a longstanding pattern

---

generation, by the threefold and single name of God, we name the Deity, Which is inexpressible to things that be, the Superessential. But no Unit nor Triad, nor number nor unity, nor productiveness, nor any other existing thing, or thing known to any existing thing, brings forth the hiddenness, above every expression and every mind, of the Super-Deity Which is above all superessentially" (Dionysius, *Divine Names*, 981A). See also Rorem, *Pseudo-Dionysius*, 162.

58. Reflecting on the whiteness of Jesus' garment in the transfiguration, Origen says, "But since there are differences also of things white, His garment became white as the brightest and purest of all white things; and that is light" (Origen, *Commentary on Matthew*, 470).

59. Gregory of Nazianzus, *Oration on Holy Baptism*, 361.

60. Symeon the New Theologian, *Discourses*, 327.

61. Gregory Palamas, *Triads*, 36—38.

62. Gregory Palamas, *Triads*, 99. Gregory of Nyssa approaches the aspect of color refraction by advocating for the analogy of a rainbow: "Just as, therefore, in the illustration we distinguished clearly the different colours and yet cannot perceive by our senses any interval that separates the one from the other, conclude, I pray, that you may in the same way draw inferences from analogy regarding the divine dogmas. You may thus reason: that the individual traits of the Person, which may be compared with a particular

of thought that supports the consecration of one name to praise the complete coalescence of divine splendor. The transcendentals are like refracted colors that go up into the Holy. If a transcendental only "is-with-reference-to," we can now add that *only the Holy "is."* Consequently, everything else is "*of*" the Holy as "holies"; all is derived from the Holy, which itself is "all in all": as the face of simplicity, the name "Holy" is *sanctum sanctorum*.[63]

Like the good, being reverentially ascends into the holy. Aquinas says that being is the primary name of God and the first principle of metaphysics because the intellect recognizes it first.[64] Being, or existence, is the most elementary and evident reality. However, the way being discloses itself to the intellect is significant. As seen in Erich Przywara, the existence of the exterior world is never properly "outside" one's mind (or as Michel Henry would argue, outside "life").[65] Life and reality are nuptially wed in analogical

---

hue of the colours of the rainbow, flash their light upon each of those whom we believe to constitute the Holy Trinity; that, however, no difference can be perceived in the individual character of the nature of one as compared with another, although together with their community of substance the distinguishing characteristic traits of each shine forth" (Gregory of Nyssa, *Epistle 38*, quoted in Pabst, *Metaphysics*, 70).

63. Eric Perl rejects the idea that Dionysius's "God beyond being" could be explained by some form of hyper-being beyond being, a reading Perl calls "a more sophisticated and supposedly apophatic form which self-contradictorily identifies God as 'a being beyond being,' something which *is* albeit in a superior 'way'" (Perl, *Theophany*, 112). Although Perl's critique appears to attack the proposal that holiness is the hyperbolic and oxymoronic "Is," his subsequent explanation of Dionysius's true intent is unflinchingly analogical—especially when one considers it alongside Przywara's "essence-in-and-beyond-existence" formula: "Transcendence and Immanence are not opposed to each other, nor do they merely mitigate or even complement each other; they are, rather, strictly identical. Conceived Neoplatonistically, transcendence in no way implies separation or duality between God and the world, which would leave the world itself godless and hence unworlded and thus lead to nihilism. Rather, the transcendent is precisely that which is given through, in, and as the world. The more transcendent God is, the more—not the less!—intimately present he is to the world.... Thinking, therefore, must always look 'beyond' the being which it apprehends to that which is never merely 'present' either as a member of the world or as something separate from the world, but is always presented and so always equally and infinitely 'absent'" (Perl, *Theophany*, 112). See also Perl, "Pseudo-Dionysius," 772.

64. Aquinas says, "Now the first thing conceived by the intellect is being; because everything is knowable only inasmuch as it is in actuality. Hence, being is the proper object of the intellect, and is primarily intelligible; as sound is that which is primarily audible. Therefore in idea being is prior to goodness" (Aquinas, *ST* Ia.5.2.co).

65. Przywara, *Analogia Entis*, 120–21. Michel Henry is a Christian philosopher in the tradition of phenomenology. He has become known for his critique of phenomenology (and culture for that matter) for exchanging the basic human understanding of life for

suspension; Przywara says they are "to one another." If the intellect should perceive "being" (*esse* or "is"), that being will appear analogically stretched between "myself" and what is "other." Moreover, Przywara's "to one another" applies to the relation between one's mind and body (or returning to Henry, between life and flesh). The two are inseparably connected and proper to one another. Because the mind "leads" and defines the body (as the "essence" in-and-beyond one's existence), it has a priestly function in the corporation of one's flesh, gathering one's being in "holy *synaxis*."[66] The mind is the "head" of the body, which positions the self in a liturgical stance toward existence. Or as the Psalmist says, "Bless the Lord, O my soul, and all that is within me, bless his holy name" (Ps 103:1).[67]

The advent or disclosure of being by itself reveals the liturgical suspension of existence, and distinguishes the other in and beyond oneself, which is a consecrative gesture at the center of life and being named principally with "reverence." Przywara and Aquinas have well established that being analogically conceived inevitably points back towards God. However,

---

reduced mental processes in "consciousness." A living being, he insists, is not located in the "intentionality" of consciousness, but in what he calls the auto-affectivity of life. One of the implications is that life takes superiority over being; and thus when one perceives suffering, he or she is not discerning the essence of some-thing "outside" in the world of objects, but is *experiencing* a reality only fitting for the living (no suffering exists without some*one* suffering). Moreover, as life is more than "consciousness" phenomenologically conceived, the body is more than an external context of the intellect, and is rather the "flesh" which can only belong to life. Henry explains, "We must recognize between Word and flesh much more than an affinity—rather an identity of essence which is nothing other than that of absolute Life. As soon as flesh is given over to life, it ceases to be this objective body with its strange forms, with its incomprehensible sexual determinations, apt to arouse our anguish, delivered to the world, indefinitely subjected to the question 'why?' For as Meister Eckhart understood, life is without why. The flesh which carries in it the principle of its own revelation does not ask for any other authority to illuminate itself. When in its innocence each modality of our flesh experiences itself, when suffering says suffering and joy says joy, it is Life that speaks in it, and nothing has power against its word" (Henry, "Phenomenology of Life," 259). The two are nevertheless of the same mind: Henry insists that the relation between life and flesh is "an identity of essence" and Przywara says mind and body are inherently "to one another."

66. The special liturgical communion of the worshiping church (holy *synaxis*) empowers the soul to "unite by a spiritual kiss both the principles and ineffable modes of its own salvation and teaching through the symbol of faith," confessed with all thanksgiving. Maximus the Confessor, *Church's Mystagogy*, 205–7. Pabst argues that Dionysius sees even the human body manifests the "divine excess" which transforms "all language in a liturgical direction": "Each bodily sense not only registers sense impressions passively, but relates these back to their source" (Pabst, *Metaphysics*, 143).

67. Moreover, "All flesh will bless his holy name forever and ever" (Ps 145:21).

The White Light of Holiness

the "essence-in-and-beyond" formula penetrates even past the Creator-creation relation and dictates the order of God's transcendental names. As holiness is the "essence" in and beyond, it is holy-*of*-holies (*sanctum sanctorum*). Adding the formula *sanctum sanctorum* onto Przywara's, we can say that the "is" perceived by the intellect—which actually is a perception of the God named "being"—recedes back beyond being and into the holy, as only the holy "is." When the consecrative act goes the way of being, it is "obeying" the transcendental features of existence, but theologically speaking being is being-with-reference-to the holy, and is really a "hue" of divine holiness.[68] One sees "in and through" being toward the holy, as an allegorical "reading" of the holy in the narrative and text of existence.

The transcendentals, bracketed out from an awareness of the world as an awareness of God, are like a "raised place" (or *altaria*), and borrowing from Catherine Pickstock, they coalesce into "an infinitely receding place, always vertically beyond . . . the site where offerings are altered and transubstantiated."[69] Like the altar of the Roman Rite, the transcendental "altar" is not a fixed launching pad for vertical "apotheosis" but is always already an apotheosis, "already upwardly transfiguring before we could even have instigated such a movement."[70]

Describing the "holy soul," Clement of Alexandria connects natural knowledge with the consecration of the sacred.[71] Contra Hellenist cultus, God is not contained in or "localized" (ἵδρυσεν) by temples made by human hands.[72] God's "holy image," namely the human being, exhibits his glory, which is "made holy" by the "exceeding sanctity" of its archetype.[73] God

---

68. Michel Henry does not concede to Greek notions of being, but his description of good, beauty, and the sacred in his diagnosis of contemporary civilization is telling: "Beauty—which humans have elaborated and won over so patiently—is thus shown not only to be connected to the appearance of things but to be an inner condition of this life, one that is both exuded and required by it. Because life itself is attacked, all of its values also falter, not only aesthetics but also ethics and the sacred—and with them, so too the possibility of living each day" (Henry, *Barbarism*, 2). Moreover, "Like the swell of the ocean, all the productions of past civilizations rose and fell together, as if of a common accord and without being disconnected—knowledge produced the good, which produced the beautiful, *while the sacred illuminated everything*" (Henry, *Barbarism*, 3. Emphasis mine).

69. Pickstock, *After Writing*, 183.

70. Pickstock, *After Writing*, 183.

71. Clement of Alexandria, *Stromata*, 7.5:530.

72. Clement of Alexandria, *Stromata*, 7.5:530.

73. Clement of Alexandria, *Stromata*, 7.5:530.

cannot be localized, for he always "localizes" all beings by his transcendent act. Clement uses "localize" like Aquinas uses "actualize." Thus, as all things are "in a place," Clement calls the pathway to perfection (actualization) "being localized" and the destination "localized." He agrees with Aquinas, who says a thing is perfect in as much as it is actual (as God, the perfect one, is therefore pure actualization).[74] In the Gnostic, the true Christian, "God is enshrined," and "the true knowledge of God is *consecrated*."[75] Clement says "the righteous soul is the truly sacred altar, and that incense arising from it is holy prayer."[76] Such holiness is the end to which all human beings are "being localized." Consequently, one exists *only insofar* as he or she reveres the holy. Human beings find their place in space and time as living and intelligible beings *if* and *as* they instantiate their unique consecration of the holy.

David Schindler makes a similar connection between the analogical relation of being and the order of holiness. While not pursuing the question of what the holy "is" per se, he critiques trite opinions of the holy, and argues that to recover from secularity we must fortify an "onto-logic of holiness."[77] Therefore, Schindler says that our holiness is at once "a *way of being* ("onto") in relation to God and of *seeing* being ("onto-*logic*") in relation to God."[78] The "subjective" ("logic") *aspect* of holiness, which we would call consecration lifted to the fullness of *reverence*, discloses the ontological union between God and creation, understood according to the *analogia entis* and indicative of the "objective" relation of all things to

---

74. Clement says, "The non-existent is what is not localized" and "what exists cannot be localized by what does not exist; nor by another entity." Clement of Alexandria, Stromata, 7.5:530. Aquinas says, "Every being, as being, is good. For all being, as being, has actuality and is in some way perfect; since every act implies some sort of perfection; and perfection implies desirability and goodness.... Hence it follows that every being as such is good" (Aquinas, ST Ia.5.3.co).

75. Clement speaks of "the Gnostic" as the true knower, contra Gnosticism. Clement of Alexandria, Stromata, 7.5:530. Emphasis mine.

76. Clement of Alexandria, Stromata, 7.5:531.

77. He says "holiness" should be "thus understood as an onto-logic of relation to God" (Schindler, "Catholicity," 428). In his treatment of what the holy is, Schindler recognizes the potential for further discussion and simply says, "The term 'holiness,' however its meaning is further specified, is inclusive of relation to God, and in its etymological roots is associated with 'healing' and 'whole'" (Schindler, "State of Contemporary Theology," 427). On the need to recover holiness in response to secularity, see Schindler, "State of Contemporary Theology," 449.

78. Schindler, "State of Contemporary Theology," 428.

The White Light of Holiness

holiness ("onto").[79] Schindler's argument begs for a reconsideration of the holy in itself precisely because of the magnitude ascribed to it. He goes beyond saying that holiness is relevant to ontology, and argues that now ontology is *about* holiness. Because holiness comprehends "the order of being in its entirety," he appears to agree with the notion that only the holy "is," that everything is gathered up by this "all in all."[80]

THE ECLIPSE OF THE HOLY

This section will further explore the relationship between the holy and the other five transcendentals by modifying the traditional Christian analogy of God as light with the modern notion of color refraction, which will be used to develop "the eclipse of the holy." This concept will help relieve recurring issues regarding holiness, such as, if holiness is God's "otherness," then does it positively express or contribute anything to existence? If the holy is a transcendental, then why is it "preeminently" or uniquely transcendent? Also, how does holiness somehow transcend the dualities of truth and falsity, light and darkness, while encompassing both?

If the transcendentals go "up into" the holy, then what happens to them upon arrival? What is the relation between reality contoured by the five transcendentals and the hyper-transcendental existence of holiness? Are the two realities woefully irreconcilable? Is the holy detached from analogical expression? Indeed, it is not. Holiness is analogous to white light, which contains within itself the colors which are subsequently refracted into appearance. While "in" whiteness, the colors are present and make the original possible, but they are also phenomenologically "absent." The apex of refracted light is not a polychromatic compilation, but an emergent singularity that includes but also hides all colors. Likewise, the radiance of holiness has a singular appearance which phenomenologically includes but hides the transcendentals. This emergence is the eclipse of the holy.

The eclipse accounts for the way in which God's essence contains all opposites, while being beyond binary distinctions. Bearing the positive side of the transcendentals, light illuminates matters of truth, indicates moral

---

79. Schindler says "our key presupposition is that holiness, as inclusive of order, is thereby predicable analogously not only of (spiritual) subjectivity but of the objective structure and meaning of all entities in the cosmos" (Schindler, "Trinity, Creation, and the Order," 416).

80. Schindler, "Trinity, Creation, and the Order," 406.

dignity and purity, mediates aesthetic splendour, and derives from a single source as "one." However, the holy simultaneously eclipses these realities, and thus the holy is truth that blinds, goodness that condemns, beauty that terrifies, and the interminable one of being's abyss. Perennial issues in Christian theological history spring from this originary eclipse, the first (*arche*) paradox. Dionysius says that we see by "the superessential ray of the Divine darkness," as the wholly unseen fills our sightless minds with treasures beyond beauty.[81] He says God's essence is beyond the distinction of true and false, good and evil.[82] God's most remote self is what Marius Victorinus calls "the One before the One."[83] Moreover, the eclipse of the transcendentals exchanges Marion's interpretation of God "without" being, for a vision of God who super-essentially eclipses being, which is distinguishable from being-purely-manifest on the one hand and God without being on the other. The notion of eclipse is an acknowledgement of being-unrecognizable, that still admits the sphere of actuality, but does not make *hyper*-being contingent upon its opposite (non-being).[84] Meister Eckhart describes being this way, "in saying that God is not a being and is above being, I have not denied being to God; rather, I have elevated it in him. If I take copper [mixed] with gold, it is still present and is present in a higher manner than it is in itself."[85] Ever inscrutable, the holy has always evinced paradox. Otto speaks of the ominous grandeur of the holy, which grips its spectators in numinous fear, while Gregory of Nyssa looks on the dove-like serenity of the virgin and says "holy."[86] Holiness characterizes the compassionate nature of the church (cf. 1 Pet 1:15–16) and the condition of divine wrath, as the "holy place" of the Lord always threatens death (Ex 28:35; 43).

In *Moby Dick*, Herman Melville dedicates a chapter to "The Whiteness of the Whale," in which he attributes the whale's ominous quality to its whiteness: added to the more obvious reasons one might fear a gigantic whale, there is a "rather vague, nameless horror concerning him, which at times by its intensity completely overpowered all the rest; and yet so

---

81. Dionysius, *Mystical Theology*, 1000A.

82. Dionysius, *Mystical Theology*, 1048A-B.

83. Victorinus, *Hymn 1*, 315.

84. Marion quotes Dionysius's *Mystical Theology*: "Being returns to him, but he does not return to Being; Being is found in him, but he is not found in Being; he maintains Being, but Being does not maintain him" (Marion, *God Without Being*, 75).

85. Eckhart, "Sermon 9," 256.

86. Gregory of Nyssa, *On Virginity*, 1:343.

mystical and well nigh ineffable was it, that I almost despair of putting it in a comprehensible form. It was the whiteness of the whale that above all things appalled me."[87] Recounting the many good and beautiful things enhanced by whiteness, including the robes from John's revelation, "there yet lurks an elusive something, in the innermost idea of this hue."[88] From the pallor of the dead, we borrow the expressive hue of the shroud in which they are wrapped, and even in superstition we throw a snowy mantle on our phantoms; let us also add, says Melville, that the king of terrors rides on his pallid horse (Rev 19:11).[89] Because the essence of whiteness is not so much "a colour" as "the visible absence of colour; and at the same time the concrete of all colours," it emits a "dumb blankness, full of meaning" as "a colourless, all-colour of atheism from which we shrink."[90] "And of all these things the Albino whale was the symbol. Wonder ye then at the fiery hunt?"[91]

The "bi-polar character of the holy," says Debra Strickland, is rendered in a well-known image from a thirteenth-century English psalter, in which God appears as a three-headed monster.[92] Using Dionysius and Rudolf Otto

87. Melville, *Moby Dick*, 353.

88. Melville, *Moby Dick*, 355.

89. Melville, *Moby Dick*, 362. "Therefore, in his other moods, symbolize whatever grand or gracious thing he will by whiteness, no man can deny that in its profoundest idealized significance it calls up a peculiar apparition to the soul."

90. Melville, *Moby Dick*, 369. "Is it that by its indefiniteness it shadows forth the heartless voids and immensities of the universe, and thus stabs us from behind with the thought of annihilation, when beholding the white depths of the milky way?" (Melville, *Moby Dick*, 368). "And when we consider that other theory of the natural philosophers, that all other earthly hues—every stately or lovely emblazoning—the sweet tinges of sunset skies and woods; yea, and the gilded velvets of butterflies, and the butterfly cheeks of young girls; all these are but subtle deceits, not actually inherent in substances, but only laid on from without; so that all deified Nature absolutely paints like the harlot, whose allurements cover nothing but the charnel-house within; and when we proceed further, and consider that the mystical cosmetic which produces every one of her hues, the great principle of light, for ever remains white or colourless in itself, and if operating without medium upon matter, would touch all objects, even tulips and roses, with its own blank tinge" (Melville, *Moby Dick*, 368–69).

91. Melville, *Moby Dick*, 367–68. "But not yet have we solved the incantation of this whiteness, and learned why it appeals with such power to the soul; and more strange and far more portentous—why, as we have seen, it is at once the most meaning symbol of spiritual things, nay, the very veil of the Christian's Deity; and yet should be as it is, the intensifying agent in things the most appalling to mankind."

92. Strickland, "Holy and the Unholy," 109. Strickland further explains the image: "This particular divine monster communicates an important point of medieval Christian

to interpret the holy in the image, Strickland says that from an Ottonian perspective the monstrous figure is an appropriate representation of God insofar as the monstrous is the *mysterium* in a gross form.[93] Moreover, the image is an example of the "dissimilar symbolism" that Dionysius preferred for representing the holy, "because its shapes are so completely at variance with what it really is, the viewer through contemplation of dissimilar symbolism may come to discover how the holy transcends all materiality."[94] As a dissimilar symbol, the three-headed monster correctly portrays what the Godhead is not, while from an Ottonian standpoint, the image stirs the worshipper in both attraction and revulsion.[95]

Strickland's reading seems to agree with our thesis, namely that the holy stands in for the divine essence in Dionysius, which demands dissimilar symbolism. But this intuitive step—one for which we are arguing here—is nevertheless a step beyond Dionysius himself. Admittedly, no name is entirely comprehensive, but only the super-essential essence of God is properly "bipolar"; holiness hardly features, and when addressed in the order of names, it is quite a simple conception meaning purity, transcended by the good (which is subsequently transcended by the super-transcendent aspect of God).[96] This super-transcendent, bipolar, nature is accounted for by the eclipse of the holy.

John Milbank approaches the idea of the eclipse. He recognizes that Dionysius uses a unique formula for the divine essence that includes hyperbole and oxymoron, namely "super-luminous darkness" (*hyperphotos*

---

doctrine, in that its three heads correspond to the three persons of the Trinity and by attaching them to one body, the artist conveys their perfect unity. The caption indicates that the kneeling figure represents Abraham, which identifies the historical context of the image as the Old Testament episode of the three angels who came to dinner (Gen 18:1–16), widely understood as a typological parallel for the Trinity. As a representation of the Trinity, then, the three-headed monster is simultaneously a vision of God as Wholly Other. This, Abraham's attitude of reverence and awe before the Trinity may have had prescriptive value or have prompted viewers contemplating the image to recall their own experiences of the *mysterium tremendum*" (Strickland, "Holy and the Unholy," 108). For more on this image, see also Coakley, *God, Sexuality, and the Self*, 228; Mills, "Jesus as Monster," 40.

93. Strickland, "Holy and the Unholy," 108.
94. Strickland, "Holy and the Unholy," 108.
95. Strickland, "Holy and the Unholy," 108.
96. "These things, then, must be sung absolutely, respecting the Cause surpassing all, and we must add that It surpasses Holiness, and Lordship, and Kingdom" (Dionysius, *Divine Names*, 969C).

gnophos).⁹⁷ If we resign the mystery of God to contradiction, then paradox will be *merely* the impasse of necessary but irreconcilable propositions, in which case we will have only perpetuated a dualistic structure. If we absolutize the difference between God's essence and energies, then we risk either severing God himself between communicable and incommunicable polarities or postulating a "beyond" in which God is truly unpredictable or tragically unrecognizable. Mystery and paradox are not arbitrary or tragic but *profound*, which requires a certain internal harmony. With the eclipse of the holy, the transcendentals *are* at once present *and* absent (oxymoron) in a particularly intense mode of divine alchemy (hyperbole). Thus, David Bentley Hart can say Christian apophasis is born not from the poverty of the soul's knowledge of God, "but from the overwhelming and superconceptual immediacy of that knowledge," a "condition of insuperable unknowing."⁹⁸

Recently, Timothy Knepper has exhaustively shown that Dionysius's understanding of God's supra-transcendent nature accords with what Milbank called oxymoronic hyperbole, which negates those who posit an absolute apophatic abandon. Dionysius uses the "*hyper*" prefix to indicate that aspect of God that is most transcendent.⁹⁹ However, *hyper*-prefixed terms, like "preeminence" composed of "*hyper*" and "*echo*" ("hyper-having"), carry two meanings, what is utterly beyond (with superiority above) and

---

97. Milbank argues that it may appear that "Dionysius is more the mystic of the night than is Gregory [of Nyssa]. But in fact, just the opposite is the case. . . . Dionysius is supremely a mystic of light, and still more so than Gregory. For when Moses enters blindly into the darkness, he is at once overwhelmed by a divine excess of illumination. Thus whereas, for Gregory of Nyssa, the infinite darkness is said of itself to coincide with light, for Dionysius the infinite-finite darkness of the One is said to be also a 'super-luminous darkness'—*hyperphotos gnophos*, a linguistic hyperbole added to an oxymoron, where Gregory deploys *only* the oxymoron of 'brilliant darkness' (*lampros gnothos*). Dionysius's hyperbolically and asymmetrically augmented oxymoron represents rhetorically an inconceivable eminence of light that is the supereminence of all forms and not just, as with Gregory's mere paradox, a sort of positive counter-shining of indefinite obscurity" (Milbank, "Sophiology and Theurgy," 73).

98. Hart, "Hidden and the Manifest," 210. Hart further elucidates the role of speech and silence in theological discourse: "God's speech in creation does not, then, invite a speculative nisus toward silence—the silence of pure knowing or of absolute saying—but doxology, an overabundance of words, hymnody, prayer, and then, within this discipline of gratitude and liturgy, a speculative discourse obedient to the gratuity of existence and the transcendence of its source, or a contemplative silence whose secret is not poverty but plentitude" (Hart, *Infinite*, 298).

99. Knepper, *Negating Negation*, 48.

preeminently elevated (as excess).[100] Thus, divine predicates have a "lack of possession and preeminent possession, a sense of *both* the logical falsity or inapplicability of the predicate in question *and* the superabundant or excessive measure of that predicate."[101] The *hyper*-prefixed terms have a "bivocity," and sometimes mean one, sometimes the other, but rarely one to the exclusion of the other.[102] For example, Dionysius says "we cast ourselves, to the best of our ability, towards the superessential ray [τὴν ὑπερούσιον ἀκτῖνα], in which all the terms of every kind of knowledge *hyper*-expressively pre-exist [ὑπερρήτως προϋφέστηκεν]." Thus, one cannot adequately express his essence "on account of Its being pre-eminently [ἐξῃρημένην] above all things, and super-unknown, and Its having previously contained within Itself, superessentially, the whole perfections of all kinds of essential knowledge and power."[103] In this eclipse, God is "preholding [προέχον] identically in itself even things contrary."[104] While Dionysius may give the name "holy" a modest range of theological content in itself, he connects the formula "holy of holies" with bivocity. As Knepper says, "God is named holy of holies since God is '*hyper*-full of all according to one *hyper*-having *hyper*-throwing of all,' thereby implying divine preeminence; but it also goes on to say that God is '*hyper*-established all being,' thereby suggesting complete remove."[105]

Similarly, William Desmond argues that God, the unsurpassable beyond, confronts us with the "*hyperbolic dimensions* of disproportion," for which we require "reverence" to "read our place in being," as we search for

---

100. Knepper, *Negating Negation*, 48.

101. Knepper, *Negating Negation*, 48.

102. Knepper, *Negating Negation*, 50.

103. Dionysius, *Divine Names*, 592D–593A. Translation modified. Even more applicable to the analogy of light: "For the mindless, and the insensible, we must attribute to God, by excess—not by defect, just as we attribute the irrational to Him Who is above reason; and imperfection, to the Super-perfect, and Pre-perfect; and the impalpable, and invisible gloom, to the light which is inaccessible on account of excess of the visible light" (Dionysius, *Divine Names*, 869A). Moreover, "From Itself, and in Itself, as Cause, it preholds and pre-comprehends the notion and knowledge, and essence of all things; not approaching each several thing according to its kind, but knowing and containing all things, within one grasp of the Cause; just as the light, as cause, presupposes in itself the notion of darkness, not knowing the darkness otherwise than from the light" (Dionysius, *Divine Names*, 869A–B).

104. Dionysius, *Divine Names*, 912C.

105. Knepper, *Negating Negation*, 51; Dionysius, *Divine Names*, 972A–B.

"signs of the ultimate excess."[106] This reverence is transcendentally pervasive, equal to existence and desire, and thus integral to all forms of knowing and being. However, like all transcendental aspects, reverence in finitude is rooted in a "more *primal ontological reverence* [for God] out of which knowing as determinate cognition takes form."[107] If reverence is the proper means by which one recognizes and approaches the oxymoronic hyperbole of the divine eclipse, then the tradition itself fully anticipates that this *hyper*-aspect (in-and-beyond) should be conceived as the Holy because it metaphysically reveals itself to be holy through the reverence it commands (and thus *sanctum sanctorum*).

The Catholic theologian Klaus Hemmerle defends the anteriority of the holy, and even recognizes that the holy is like a transcendental, but finally rejects the possibility that it is a transcendental based on what must be considered modernist, or Ottonian, grounds. For Hemmerle, the holy is sublimely transcendent through its inexplicable, independent, and unconditional primacy and majesty with a freely-given *personal* weight. However, given that any ontological unity between "concepts" and personal divine being is ruptured—as concepts he argues are merely human constructs—Hemmerle argues that the holy is known only through inexplicable confrontation.[108]

Hemmerle admits that because the holy transcends all beings and yet pervades them all, it is close to the "universal notes" of being, namely truth, goodness, and beauty. These notes are communicated to beings, and, as he says, "tend to become predicates of beings and hence to become that which beings are."[109] Holiness is different. Beings are not holy of themselves, but only inasmuch as they point beyond themselves. The holy is *not* the comprehensive essence of being, it is not prior to beings, "but being's grateful memory of the hidden origin of all."[110] The transcendentals are "reflected" and "re-presented" in beings, but "the holy is merely commemorated there."[111] Hemmerle mixes a modern account of the holy, as a kind of supra-*a priori* value that, in Kantian-Ottonian style, *is* a vacuous phenomenon without any

---

106. Desmond, "Reverence," 284.

107. Desmond, "Reverence," 277. In others words, Desmond says "There might be root indeterminacies in the ontological situation" (Desmond, "Reverence," 269).

108. Hemmerle, "Holy I. 2–4, II," 640.

109. Hemmerle, "Holy I. 2–4, II," 640.

110. Hemmerle, "Holy I. 2–4, II," 640.

111. Hemmerle, "Holy I. 2–4, II," 640.

actual "being" or even cause, with a univocal scheme of transcendentals. The result is an incoherent, though also perceptive, vision of the holy. By recovering a thoroughly analogical vision of the transcendentals, the essence of which *is* the holy, we bolster the personal and mysterious aspects of holiness while addressing the legitimate philosophical issues that the holy engenders. To his credit, Hemmerle perceived quite accurately that holiness is like a transcendental yet somehow distinguished, it is also somehow anterior, and that a definition of holiness must account for its relationality.

The transcendental and summative nature of holiness relieves the polarizing issue in theology, namely whether or not one ever sees God's essence in the hereafter or otherwise. On the one hand, theologians distinguish the emanating glories or energies of God, known to creatures in varying intensities, from the "essence" which is wholly inaccessible.[112] However resplendent the presence of the Almighty, *what* God is remains "Incomprehensible," "Invisible," and thus one cannot comprehend or see *Incomprehensibility* and *Invisibility*.[113] The shape, profile, or features of God are hidden, as they would usually be given by his essence. Naming the essence of God with noun forms, such as "Inexpressible," demonstrates a qualitative understanding of essence; God is not something we deem inexpressible, but "*is*" inexpressibility in primordial secret.

On the other hand, Thomas Aquinas insists that one does come to know God's essence; what else could be the fullness of life and hope for now and always but the beatific vision of God? For indeed, "We shall see Him as He is" (1 John 3:2).[114] God is knowable, recognizable, even familiar, and one

112. For more on the eastern perspective see Golitzin, "Dionysius the Areopagite," 189–90; Flogaus, "Palamas and Barlaam Revisited," 4–8; Ware, "Praying with the Body," 6–35; Sinkewicz, "Doctrine," 181–242; Meyendorff, *Gregory Palamas*; Williams, *Ground of Union*; Lossky, *Vision of God*.

113. Gregory of Palamas can thus use "Inexpressible" as a noun when referring to God as he is in his essence. Gregory of Palamas, *Triads*, 36. On the invisiblity of the essence he says: "For each visible thing is visible, not in its inner being, but according to what surrounds it: It is not the essence of the sun which the eye perceives, but that which surrounds the essence." "For one applies the word 'sun' to the rays as well as to the source of the rays; yet it does not follow that there are two suns. There is, then, a single God, even though one says that the deifying grace is *from* God. The light is also one of the things that 'surround' the sun, yet it is certainly not the essence of the sun. So how could the light which shines from God upon the saints be the essence of God? Does the light of the sun appear only when one sees it, or does it exist before one has seen it?" (Gregory of Palamas, *Triads*, 108).

114. Quoted in Aquinas, *ST* Ia.12.1.s.c. Aquinas argues, "Some who considered this, held that no created intellect can see the essence of God. This opinion, however, is not

continuously plunges further into the treasury of wisdom and knowledge that is the divine horizon. Invisibility and incomprehensibility are adjectival, more quantitative, and thus describe the *inexhaustibility* of the essence we now know in part (1 Cor 13:9).[115]

Both perspectives have a fundamental unity if holiness is considered the transcendental *of* the transcendentals. As the originary eclipse of the transcendentals, the holy stands for inexpressibility variously expressed; while as transcendental, the holy is simultaneously thought as something *inexpressible* and "The Inexpressible." Transcendentals uniquely have this twofold nature. God is true and Truth, good and Goodness. Dionysius says the Cause (God) is beautiful and beauty.[116] Therefore, by offering up the name "Holy" amidst beatific excess, one recognizes that originary paradox, at once replete and depleted, in which the increase of ignorance is the increase of knowledge and the increase of knowledge is the increase of ignorance. The holy God has the name to which every knee shall bow and every tongue confess, yet which is also beyond every name, as God is he who must not be named. God's "Name" is holy, and his name is "Holy": "holy and reverend is his name" (Ps 111:9, KJV). His "Essence" is holy, and his essence is "Holy." Thus, Jean-Luc Marion says that "the icon can receive

---

tenable. For as the ultimate beatitude of man consists in the use of his highest function, which is the operation of his intellect; if we suppose that the created intellect could never see God, it would either never attain to beatitude, or its beatitude would consist in something else beside God; which is opposed to faith. For the ultimate perfection of the rational creature is to be found in that which is the principle of its being; since a thing is perfect so far as it attains to its principle. Further the same opinion is also against reason. For there resides in every man a natural desire to know the cause of any effect which he sees; and thence arises wonder in men. But if the intellect of the rational creature could not reach so far as to the first cause of things, the natural desire would remain void. Hence it must be absolutely granted that the blessed see the essence of God" (Aquinas, *ST* Ia.12.1.co).

115. Aquinas say, "Hence the intellect which has more of the light of glory will see God the more perfectly; and he will have a fuller participation of the light of glory who has more charity; because where there is the greater charity, there is the more desire; and desire in a certain degree makes the one desiring apt and prepared to receive the object desired. Hence he who possesses the more charity, will see God the more perfectly, and will be the more beatified" (Aquinas, *ST* Ia.12.6.co).

116. "But the beautiful and Beauty are not to be divided, as regards the Cause which has embraced the whole in one" (Dionysius, *Divine Names*, 701C). See Hart, *Infinite*, 177; Perl, "Pseudo-Dionysius," 775.

veneration only insofar as it visibly bears on its face the holiness of the Holy."[117]

Similarly, Sergius Bulgakov says that "the Name of God" contains divine energy and thus gives the presence of God; imprecisely, then, one can say that "practically and energetically, the Name of God is God."[118] More precisely, he adds, "the Name of God is present in the Power of God, which is inseparable from the Essence of God and in this sense is God himself."[119] Scripture introduces a real nuance when "the Name" is used in the place of God but not as a synonym, for the *Name* attests to the "touching of the Name of God, of God in His Name, through the photosphere of the Divine Name."[120] Bulgakov steps closer to the idea of the Holy as *sanctum sanctorum* when he says that God most easily and naturally addresses himself to his worshippers and "becomes accessible to them through His Holy Name."[121]

Though the East and West represented in Palamas and Aquinas respectively are often seen as antithetical to one another, particularly on the question of whether God's essence is knowable, some do see a fundamental agreement between them.[122] David Bentley Hart says "the true distinction

---

117. Marion, *Crossing of the Invisible*, 68.
118. Bulgakov, *Icons*, 159–60.
119. Bulgakov, *Icons*, 160.
120. Bulgakov, *Icons*, 143.
121. Bulgakov, *Icons*, 143. Bulgakov provides a number of biblical texts that almost exclusively emphasize the Holy: "'So will I make My Holy Name known in the midst of My people Israel; and I will not let them pollute My Holy Name any more: and the heathen shall know that I am the Lord, the Holy One in Israel' (Ezek 39:7); 'and will be jealous for My Holy Name' (39:25; 'and My Holy Name, shall the house of Israel no more defile' (43:7)" (Bulgakov, *Icons*, 143).
122. For views that emphasize the difference, see Milbank, "Christianity and Platonism," 158–210; "Ecumenical Orthodoxy," 160–61; Bradshaw, "In Defence of the Essence/Energies," 256–76; *Aristotle East and West*; Yannaras, "Orthodoxy and the West," 287; Loudovikos, "Striving for Participation," 122–49; Congar, *Nine Hundred Years*; LaCugna, *God For Us*, 197–98. Milbank says, "With Williams I wish broadly to criticise Palamas (though in a slightly more muted manner with which he himself now probably agrees). But with Bradshaw I wish to defend the theurgic tradition of both the pagans and of Dionysius. In order to sustain this opposite combination to either of them, I will argue that actually it is theurgic rather than Plotinian Neoplatonism which tends to urge towards a radical divine simplicity, incompatible with Palamas's famous or infamous distinction" (Milbank, "Christianity and Platonism," 161). Bradshaw argues that Aquinas's doctrine of God compromises key Christian convictions: his notion of divine simplicity eliminates the possibility of free will, and his division of nature and grace creates a rift between God and creation—which makes autonomous realms of natural knowledge possible while limiting God's influence primarily to efficiency—inconsistent

to be drawn is not one between two incompatible ways of naming God, peculiar respectively to West and East, but between two forms of the same name, corresponding to two distinct moments within what I would be content to call the 'analogy of being.'"[123] Hart affirms the two sided nature of God's transcendental being as the center of harmony between both traditions.[124]

Though Nikolaos Loudovikos disagrees with Hart and argues that the East and West are ultimately irreconcilable on this issue, he concedes to one important similarity between Aquinas and Palamas: "Thomas concludes with what Palamas started and tried to defend in his lifetime, namely the need for existential realization of participation."[125] By "conclusion" Loudovikos refers to Aquinas's "total silence" after his existential encounter with the divine light (6th December, 1273), which is the total silence of the remote cave of the Skete of Veroia where Palamas started his ascetic struggle. "In this sacred silence," he says, "Palamas meets Thomas and, after carefully listening to him expressing his unshakable conviction of the absolute essential unity of God in all his actions, he helps him articulate his conclusions."[126] The holy, an eclipse of truth and being which requires the proper proportion of speech and silence, harmonizes Aquinas and Palamas's narratives:

---

with the properly synergistic views of the Christian tradition (and the synergistic view for which Aquinas himself strove). See Bradshaw, *Aristotle East and West*, 257. Bradshaw summarizes the differences as such: If we were to "summarize the difference" between east and west in one word it would be "synergy": "For the East the highest form of communion with the divine is not primarily an intellectual act, but a sharing of life and activity.... It influences the entirety of the eastern outlook.... In the West synergy played a remarkably little role;" reasons for this may be that the West had no suitable word for *energeia*, and in place of synergy, Augustine supplied questionable ideas: the simple God, intrinsically intelligible, is known in two ways (through created intermediaries, or direct intellectual apprehension of the divine essence), and the highest end of human existence is such direct intellectual comprehension" (Bradshaw, *Aristotle East and West*, 264–65). His distinction between the physic synergy of the East and the intellectual encounter of the West are both harmonized if the essence is named Holy, the *sanctum sanctorum*, as transcendentals shape (or more precisely "are") noetic and ontic realities. Therefore, the distinction between intellect and embodied "soul" would be false, as each would disclose the singular transcendental value in question.

123. Hart, "Hidden and the Manifest," 198. For a critique of Hart on this issue essay, see Loudovikos, "Striving for Participation," 147.

124. See Bernard McGinn's multivolume set for the varieties of Christian mysticism. Bernard, *Presence of God*.

125. Loudovikos, "Striving for Participation," 147.

126. Loudovikos, "Striving for Participation," 147.

Gregory started on the ascetic path of silence, after which he was compelled to speak in exposition and defense of divine light; Aquinas, who began on the cerebral side, fell into silence upon his encounter with the divine light. Thus, they represent two sides of the same transcendental coin, saturated by the supra-luminous excess of the holy.

Additionally, the eclipse of the holy elucidates the issue of holiness and relation. D. F. Strauss's now notorious critique brought light upon a dormant conflict; he argues that the "ideas of the absolute and of the holy are incompatible."[127] Holiness implies relation, and thus requires something external against which God can so define himself. But if God is the absolute—who exists in pure aseity and repels every form of dependence on creation—he cannot be "holy," as that would be equivalent to saying God "*is*" his relation to finitude, which would nullify his place as the absolute. Strauss strikes a nerve. Theologians often depict holiness as the spectacle of God's moral superiority, or purity, but this depiction falls victim to Strauss's critique. Would the superiority of the spectacle be intelligible if lesser beings, against whom God could be compared, did not exist?[128]

Responding to Strauss's problematic, Wolfhart Pannenberg absolutizes God's relation to the finite. The holy, he argues, "is separateness from everything profane," and the infinite is defined as what "stands opposed to the finite"; thus the two ideas overlap.[129] However, the infinite cannot

---

127. Strauss, *Dogmatik*, quoted in Hodge, *Systematic Theology*, 1:316. He says, "The ideas of the absolute and of the holy are incompatible. He who holds to the former must give up the latter, since holiness implies relation; and, on the other hand, he who holds fast the idea of God as holy, must renounce the idea of his being absolute; for the idea of absolute is inconsistent with the slightest possibility of its being other than it is."

128. Charles Hodge, who has helped to popularize Strauss on this issue, makes his counter definition of holiness contingent on creation: on divine holiness, "This is a general term for the moral excellence of God. In 1 Sam 2:2, it is said, 'There is none holy as the LORD;' no other Being absolutely pure, and free from all limitation in his moral perfection" (Hodge, *Systematic Theology*, 1:315–16). Like John Webster, Jörg Splett denies that holiness is a kind of independent attribute or predicate, and rather defines the holy by absolutizing its connection to finitude: "To reflect on the holy is not to think of holiness as an attribute of God or of holy beings, places, times or things; what is in question, therefore, is not the meaning of the adjective holy as a predicate that can be applied to someone or something. Nor is the holy a neutralizing collective name for the different forms whether personal or impersonal in which the highest principle is conceived. Concern with the holy rather means seeking the domain or dimension proper to the divine encounter in which the supreme principle shows itself" (Splett, "Holy I. Phenomenology and Philosophy," 639).

129. Pannenberg, *Systematic Theology*, 1:397–98.

be merely a negation of the finite, as it would simply be another finite; for "as Hegel showed," the infinite is "truly infinite only when it transcends its own antithesis to the finite."[130] Similarly, the holy extends itself in love to the profane, that it might incorporate everything within the sphere of holiness.[131] Pannenberg begins in agreement with Strauss that holiness implies relation or separation, as the holy is defined as that which is separate from the profane. Holiness, seen in scripture and the logic of the infinite, goes outward to include its antithesis. While abolishing all profanity, the eschaton will fortify the holy difference between God and creation, which will be a realization via synthesis of the holy God who finally "is" the Infinite-finite totality. In the end, holiness is inconceivable without relation to finitude.[132] In Strauss's terms, Pannenberg chooses "holy" over "absolute."

On the contrary, the holy is "real." Holiness is not a relation God has with us, but a real divine quality that is *perceivable* in, though not constituted by, finite relation. Even if Christian thought has always, in some way, considered holiness to be substantial, it remains to be seen how this divine quality demarcates an immanent hierarchy: how is holiness "elevated," or separated, within God himself? The tradition has not explicitly resolved this problematic.

---

130. Pannenberg, *Systematic Theology*, 1:400. On the Infinite, Pannenberg says, "We have to think of the Infinite as negation, as the opposite of the finite, but also that it comprehends this antithesis in itself."

131. "The sending of the Son to save the world (John 3:16) aims at the bringing of the world into the sphere of the divine holiness" (Pannenberg, *Systematic Theology*, 1:399).

132. While Pannenberg is perceptive, one must admit that his theology makes God dependent upon creation. He argues that in the Nicene and Constantinopolitan tradition, "the thought of the eternal and essential Trinity broke loose from its historical moorings and tended to be seen not only as the basis of all historical events but also as untouched by the course of history on account of the eternity and immutability of God . . . then under the conditions of Hellenistic philosophical theology this Trinity had to be at an unreachable distance from all finite, creaturely reality. The immanent Trinity became independent of the economic Trinity and increasingly ceased to have any function relative to the economy of salvation" (Pannenberg, *Systematic Theology*, 1:332). On the contrary, argues Pannenebrg, "The unity of Father, Son, and Spirit certainly finds expression in the relations of salvation history which are determined by their mutual self-distinction, and especially in their joint working in manifestation of the monarchy of the Father in creation. . . . But this joint working of the persons and their mutual perichoresis must also be seen as an expression of the unity of the divine essence. The unity of the divine essence is a theme of its own in this regard. Discussion of it must show whether the one God can be viewed as so transcendent and yet also present in the process of salvation history that the events of history in some way bear on the identity of his eternal essence" (Pannenberg, *Systematic Theology*, 1:334).

Sanctum Sanctorum

Because of the inscrutability of the divine "supra-essential identity," Dionysius privileges "darkness" over light, or as with "dazzling darkness" modifies light with darkness. As light stands for the visible at a material level, so the "light" of goodness and beauty is conceivable, intellectually "visible" so to speak; the good is an overflowing radiance which removes the fog of ignorance from the eyes of the mind and the burdens of darkness.[133] Taking the contemplative from the darkness of ignorance (regarding the elementary things of God) to enlightenment is only half the journey; one must still traverse beyond the light of the good to darkness, into which Moses was plunged at Sanai.[134] Dionysius departs from the analogy of light because for him it was synonymous with (a certain) visibility, though he could never finally stop describing the cloud of unknowing as radiant. However, by qualifying the analogy of light as "white light," visibility is no longer taken for granted, because white light in and of itself, apart from being bent and refracted through a medium, can never be seen. Even the whiteness seen in nature—or made with paint and pixels—is a posterior, mediated blending of already refracted light; in other words, one does not—cannot—see light itself.[135] The white light analogy reinforces the ontological primacy of mediation, as light in itself is postulated from the "middle" of mediated light.[136] This allows one to develop the more traditional name of light, which Gregory Nazianzen, Maximus the Confessor, and Gregory Palamas tended to prefer. While John of Damascus said the "sweetest" names are a combination of affirmation and negation, like "super-essential essence," nevertheless "sun and light will be more apt names for Him than darkness."[137]

The eclipse of the holy offers an alternative vision of relation in keeping with the analogical metaphysics of the Christian tradition, primarily by appropriating two historic convictions. First, God's nature is simple

---

133. Dionysius, *Divine Names*, 700D–701B.

134. Dionysius, *Mystical Theology*, 1001A.

135. For more on Robert Finlay's breathtaking natural history of light, see Finlay, "Weaving the Rainbow," 383–431. See also Sloane, *Visual Nature of Color*, 52.

136. John Howe connects holiness with refracted light, but for him the beatific vision eradicates this mediatorial "between" that is essential: holiness "is an *entire* or *united* glory. We have something of the divine glory shining now upon us: but the many interpositions cause a various refraction of its light. We have but its dispersed rays, its scattered, dishevelled beams: we shall then have it perfect and full" (Howe, *Blessedness*, 80).

137. Nazianzen says God is "Light thrice repeated; but One Light and One God" (Gregory of Nazianzus, *Fifth Theological Oration*, 3:318). See also Palamas, *Triads*, 37; Maximus the Confessor, *Church's Mystagogy*, 206.

(uncreated) light, disseminated into rays. Second, the point *priori to* dissemination is a qualitatively different mode of divinity. To explicate this prior ineffable form, some departed from the analogy of light. However, the understanding of color refraction adds a slight nuance to the image of light. One can (*analogically*) see the difference between white light (in its own form of simplicity) and the subsequent array of colors that emerge. Thus, the analogy of light accounts for what the tradition often used darkness and light together to accomplish. Darkness is an important theological theme, but the analogy of God as light allows one to remain closer to the biblical witness, which is affirmed nowhere more clearly than in 1 John 1:5: "This is the message we have heard from him and proclaim to you, that God is light and in him there is no darkness at all." The Psalmist says, "O send out your light and your truth; let them lead me; let them bring me to your holy hill and to your dwelling" (Ps 43:3).

Moreover, the analogy of refraction expresses that the "white light" of God's holy essence is in one sense invisible and in another visible. The analogical difference between light in itself and the "appearance" of invisible light in the whiteness seen by the eye offers enough *qualitative* difference to maintain continuity with the school of Christian thought that upholds some distinction between God's essence and his expressions (or even energies). However, the difference still *logically* ensures inherent continuity between God's invisible self and his "appearance" as the invisible in creation. Thus, these two aspects of the analogy help to some degree bridge theological discourses between East and West.

The white light of holiness then radically reverses Strauss's terms. For Strauss, the essence of the holy requires relation to finitude. But because of the eclipse, the holy becomes the *only* thing, divine or otherwise, that *is not* borne from contingent relation. The holy is in some sense that which is not in relation but is *related to*. The qualitative difference between holiness and the transcendentals in the eclipse is analogous to the Creator-creature distinction, in which creatures have their essence and their existence contingently suspended by a "prior" reality, namely God whose essence is existence (who is "Is"). Heaven's beings cry out in the sanctuary, "you alone are holy" (Rev 15:4), "O Holy One, who is [ὁ Ὅσιος, ὁ ὢν]" (Rev 16:5). By naming God's essence (as existence) holy, we infuse the *analogia entis* with the holy: now, when considering the "essence of" something, holy is analogically present in every "essence" as "Essence" itself. The "essence of" something is always already participatory, as "essence" is holiness, the infinite treasury from which everything comes and to which everything (liturgically) stands.

CONCLUSION

"To sum up my discourse," as Gregory of Nazianzus says, "Glorify Him with the Cherubim, who unite the Three Holies into One Lord, and so far indicate the Primal Substance. . . . In Thy Light shall we see Light."[138] Because Dionysius preeminently *reveres* the superessential essence of God, and all names are predicated of God based upon the specific effect they cause in the contemplative, one can say that God's superessential essence *is* holy. Dionysius's ideal scriptural passages for naming God (Isaiah's vision, the transfiguration, and revelation) all doxologically distinguish the name holy. As everything is rendered intelligible according to the contours of the transcendentals, the theological emergence of the holy as the supreme divine name means that the transcendentals themselves emanate from and reverentially return to the holy. Therefore, the transcendentals *hallow* the holy. By qualifying the analogy of light with the aspect of colour refraction, holiness is metaphysically akin to white light, in which everything is at once present, though in a uniquely intense way, are phenomenologically absent. This "eclipse of the holy" is seen in John Milbank's description of the oxymoronic hyperbole of God's *hyper*-luminous darkness, which is at once utterly removed from all *and* pre-contains all in a hyper-unified modality. Przywara anticipates such a modality with his analogical formula "essence-in-and-beyond-existence," which I extend to the sphere of divine names in the form of *sanctum sanctorum*.

---

138. Gregory of Nazianzus, "Egyptians," 13:337.

2

The Invisible Father

"What appears . . . indicates neither a total absence nor a manifest presence of divinity, but the presence of a God who hides himself. Everything bears this mark."

—Blaise Pascal, *Pensées* [1]

"But the Lord of hosts, him you shall regard as holy; let him be your fear, and let him be your dread."

—Isa 8:13

INTRODUCTION

In *The Idea of the Holy*, Rudolf Otto deftly uncovers the holy from relative obscurity, like an archeologist brushing away debris and trusting an intuition that something lies below the surface. Otto not only discovered the phenomenality of the holy, but recognized that the holy occupies a *central*

---

1. Pascal, *Pensées*, 449/690.

place in the order of religion, and subsequently all existence as such.[2] In the previous chapter we considered holiness in itself, and argued that it is the transcendental *of* the transcendentals, which affirms much of Otto's work by relocating his intuitions within the greater Christian metaphysical tradition. However, since Otto has so successfully given to the holy its incomparable weight—as *mysterium tremendum et fascinans*—theologians must rethink how Otto's insights impact Trinitarian thought. Indeed, Christian history has always seen the Trinity as holy, but has little contemplated how the transcendentality of holiness definitively organizes the triune being, at least not in light of the aspects of dread and terror that accompany the holy for Otto. Humanity may well encounter the holy in fear and supra-rationality, but how does the Trinity experience holiness, or more precisely, how is the Trinity holy? This chapter will look primarily at the relation of the Son to the Father, and will argue that the Father is to the Son the holy (*of* holies) by appropriating the Trinitarian theology of Marius Victorinus in connection with Michel Henry and Jean-Luc Marion.

BEING IN REPOSE

Marius Victorinus was born in Roman Africa 280 CE. For his extraordinary achievements as a Roman state professor of rhetoric, Victorinus was honored with a statue in Trajan's Forum.[3] After converting to Christianity, he was forced to resign from his professorial career, and subsequently produced theological treatises on the Trinity, commentaries on select Pauline books, and a collection of hymns.[4] Victorinus offers a creative and learned treatment of philosophical theology, as he performs Latin metaphysical reflection on the Trinity, while integrating enduring neoplatonic motifs.[5]

---

2. Melissa Raphael explains: "The phenomenological thesis in *The Idea of the Holy* asserts that all religions are grounded not in theory or system, but on a universal, basically uniform numinous experience, historically and culturally variously expressed. Lastly, Otto's theological thesis asserts that the more fully a religion bases itself on numinous experience, the more profoundly it partakes of the essential nature of religion. Religion can begin only where there is immediate communion with the divine in the direct individual witness of the soul to the revelation of the will and presence of the divine in the *sensus numinis*" (Raphael, *Otto*, 65–66).

3. Cooper "Marius Victorinus," 538.

4. Cooper "Marius Victorinus," 538. See also Hunter, "Fourth-Century Latin writers," 305–9.

5. Mary Clark says, "No one can complete the reading of Victorinus's theological

Though not entirely well-known, Victorinus is nevertheless a formidable Christian theologian, who directly influenced Augustine.[6] His metaphysical style places him in the company of medieval scholastics, while his Nicene interests locate him squarely in the patristic milieu. His neoplatonic sensibility anticipates Aquinas's integration of Dionysius the Areopagite into a more realized Trinitarian vision.

In continuity with classic Christian metaphysics, Victorinus argues that God is transcendent being (*esse*), impassible and unchangeable, wholly eternal without boundary. Nothing can be added to or expanded in such an infinitely replete being of perfection, and thus the phrase "God 'has'" with regard to some attribute or quality is only a form of expression, for properly speaking "he does not have, but he is himself; indeed, up there all is simplified."[7] Likewise, divine being is neither lifelessly static nor an unceasing flux, but is in fact the still "higher" transcendence that is at once ceaseless movement and unchanging substance. Victorinus says, "True substance on high is movement and not only movement but first movement, which is a kind of movement which is also a state of repose, and for that reason is substance itself."[8]

Victorinus says that God gives *from* himself his "to be" (*esse*) to all beings as the substance (*ousios*) *of* all substances.[9] He recognizes that some say God is without substance (*anousios*), but in neoplatonic fashion, Victorinus argues that God is *anousios* only in the sense that he is not *a* substance among other substances. Rather, because God is superessential substance, or *hyper*-substance (*huperousios*), he is the ontological cause of all as the

---

treatises without coming to realize that the negative theology of Neoplatonism was recognized by Victorinus as inevitably correct. Victorinus the Christian clearly taught that only by an identification with Christ through the Holy Spirit who is the invisible Christ can man enter the eternal life of knowing the Father, that is, Trinitarian life" (Clark, "Neoplatonism of Marius Victorinus," 158).

6. In his *Confessions*, Augustine speaks at length about Victorinus's conversion. Augustine says that the errors of his philosophical ways had been "somewhat" straightened from reading "certain books of the Platonists, which Victorinus, sometime Professor of Rhetoric at Rome . . . had translated" (Augustine, *Confessions*, 8.2.3). After meditating upon Victorinus's courage and simplicity in faith, Augustine says "I burned to imitate him" (Augustine, *Confessions*, 8.5.10).

7. Victorinus, *Against Arius* IA, 117. "Ipsum autem, habet' secundum intellectum accipe: nonenim habet, sed ipsum est; simplicia enim ibi omni."

8. Victorinus, *Against Arius* IA, 138.

9. Victorinus, *Against Arius* II, 196–97.

one who "truly is."¹⁰ Moreover, Victorinus distinguishes between the essence (*what* a thing is) and existence (*that* a thing is) of beings, which are composite and contingently connected for creatures. Essence and existence *collide*, meet, or subsist as one in God alone. Thus, the God who "is substance and cause of substance" preexists all "existentially and essentially."¹¹ Victorinus calls essence and existence in God "*logoi*": for the divine being there are "two *logoi*, one through which each thing is, the other through which each thing has its mode of 'to be'"; and yet, since in God "the mode of 'to be' and 'to be' (*esse*) are identical as to their power, it . . . necessarily results that there is in God only one Logos, the form having the same power as the substance."¹²

Victorinus argues that the Father occupies an anteriority within the Godhead. If the Logos, or Son, is the cause, the Father is the "precause" (*praecause*).¹³ As "transcendent divinity," the Father is unknowable to us, beyond beatitude and for that reason he is "'to repose' itself" (*requiescere*).¹⁴ To be sure, the Father is one with the Son and Spirit, and indeed one in substance. However, the Father's mode of being is different. The Son is the movement of the Father. The divine Logos is intelligible being, *To On* (The Existent), and the Father is *Proon* (The Preexistent), "the unknown and incomprehensible . . . a sort of form without form."¹⁵ The Father is then *original To On* (The Existent), existing without origin, conceived by

---

10. Victorinus, *Against Arius* II, 196–97.

11. Victorinus, *Against Arius* IA, 136. "Deus enim et substantia et substantiae causa est, et omnibus quae sunt praeexsistit et universae exsistentialitati et universae essentialitati. Ab ipso enim omnia et ea quae sunt et nomina. Ex isto igitur deo, substantiae principium qui est et ideo qui sit substantia, ὁμούσιος filius, in ipso et cum ipso, quippe *forma eius qui sit et imago* et *character*, sine quibus deus non intellegitur nec intellegentia[m] ascendit."

12. Victorinus, *Against Arius* IV, 292. This distinction between essence and existence is an integral component of Christian metaphysics. Augustine says, a thing's "being at all [existence] and its being of such and such a nature [essence], arise from the intelligible and unchanging life, which is above all things." Augustine, *Trinity*, 3.8.15. Aquinas says of God, "His essence is His existence . . . that which has existence but is not existence, is a being by participation. But God is His own essence . . . [and] God is His own existence" (Aquinas, *ST* Ia.3.4.co). Erich Przywara adds that God is "essence-as-existence" (Przywara, *Analogia Entis*, 160).

13. Victorinus, *Against Arius* IA, 94.

14. Victorinus, *Against Arius* IA, 95.

15. Victorinus, *Hymn* III, 332.

a kind of "preknowledge" formed by the concept that he "preexists" as the "preprinciple."[16]

The previous chapter argued that the five transcendentals (being, one, truth, goodness, and beauty) refract from the holy, which therefore also has a kind of primordial anteriority in the divine nature. Like white light, the holy contains all the transcendentals (or colors) within itself, while the "hues" themselves may be "hidden" or phenomenologically absent, though actually present. This dynamic of the eclipse circumvents the theological problems of the relationship of intelligible being to what is "beyond" intelligible being. Marius Victorinus employs precisely the same techniques when faced with this problem, but he focuses on the Father as the unknowable, who is known in and through the Son.[17] The first "to be" [the Father] is so unparticipated that it cannot be called one or alone, but by "preeminence, before the one ... beyond simplicity, preexistence rather than existence, universal *of* all universals, infinite, unlimited—at least for all others, but not for itself—and therefore without form; it is understood by a certain intuition and is perceived, known, and believed by a preunderstanding rather than understanding."[18] Because he is indiscernible and unknowable, the Father is called *aoristia*, infinity and indetermination.[19]

However, the Father always remains one with the Son (*homoousios*). One of the key formulas Victorinus uses for the Trinity is the neoplatonic triad *esse-vivere-intelligere* (being-life-intelligence).[20] On one level, Victo-

---

16. Victorinus, *Against Arius* IA, 144–45. "This is God, this is the Father, preexisting preintelligence and preexistence keeping himself and his own happiness in an immobile movement" (Victorinus, *Against Arius* IB, 173).

17. Victorinus says, "Therefore, 'to be' we give to God, but 'form' to Christ because through the Son the Father is known, that is, through the form the 'to be' is known; and of this it was said: 'whoever has seen me, has seen the Father also'" (Victorinus, *Against Arius* II, 203–4).

18. Victorinus, *Against Arius* IV, 280–81. Emphasis mine. He adds, "It is not *on* (existent). For the *on* (existent) is something determined, intelligible, knowable. Therefore, if it is not *on* (existent), neither is it *Logos*." The Father is interior "to be," and "*agnosta adiakrita*, unknown and undiscerned" (Victorinus, *Against Arius* IV, 281–82).

19. Victorinus, *Against Arius* IV, 286. "He is called all-in-one or 'one that is all' or since he is called 'one that is all' or 'neither one, nor all,' it follows that he is infinite, that he is unknown."

20. This triad is derived from Plotinus, Porphyry, and Proclus. Plotinus, *Enneads*, 1.6.7; 6.6.15; Proclus, *Elements of Theology*, 101–3. For the neoplatonic roots of the Triad, see Hadot, "L'Image de la trinité," 411–24; *Porphyre et Victorinus*; "Etre, vie, pensee," 107–57; Edwards "Porphyry and the Intelligible Triad," 14–25; Edwards, "Being, Life, and Mind," 191–205; Edwards, "Marius Victorinus," 105–18; Majercik, *Chaldean Oracles*,

rinus matches this formula to the three triune persons directly: being (Father), life (Son), intelligence (Spirit). However, he makes no strict division between being, life, and intelligence in each person. Instead, all "moments" or degrees of divine *ousia* entail one another in simplicity.[21] The Father "is," the Son "is the form," and the Spirit "is the knowledge of the form." Thus, *all* three persons distinctly enact being-life-intelligence. Regarding being, the Father is "to be," the Son "being," and the Spirit is "knowledge of being." Regarding life, the Father is "to live," the Son "life," the Spirit "knowledge of life." Finally, regarding intelligence, the Father is "to know," the Son "the form of knowledge," and the Spirit "knowledge itself."

The significance of the being-life-intelligence formula is that Victorinus uses it to argue that even though the Father is *unknown* of himself, hidden or invisible, he is known in the form of the Son, and thus understood despite his secrecy. Or rather the Son discloses the Father *as* secret. Moreover, in continuity with the eclipse, Victorinus says the Father's enactment of "to be," "to live," "to understand," "*seems* not to exist, because it is above everything. That is why it is said that he is *anuparktos, anousios, anous, azon*, without existence, without substance, without understanding, without life, certainly, not by *steresin* (privation), but through transcendence," for all that "words designate are after him; that is why he is not *on* (existent),

---

8; Bell, "Esse, vivere, intelligere," 5–43; Boersma, *Augustine's Early Theology of Image*, 62.50. Dionysius replaces "Intelligence" with "Wisdom": "Let us now then pass to the name 'Being'—given in the Oracles as veritably that of Him, Who veritably is. But we will recall to your remembrance this much, that the purpose of our treatise is not to make known the superessential Essence—qua superessential—(for this is inexpressible, and unknowable, and altogether unrevealed, and surpassing the union itself), but to celebrate the progression of the supremely Divine Source of Essence, which gives essence to all things being. For the Divine Name of the Good, as making known the whole progressions of the Cause of all, is extended, both to things being, and things not being, and is above things being, and things not being. But the Name of Being is extended to all things being, and is above things being—and the Name of Life is extended to all things living, and is above things living; and the Name of Wisdom is extended to all the intellectual and rational and sensible, and is above all these" (Dionysius, *Divine Names*, 816B). Augustine uses the triad to describe human existence: "no one is blessed unless living, and no one lives who is not: one desires to be, to live and to have intelligence; but to be that one may live, to live that one may have intelligence." (Augustine, *Soliloquies*, 2.1.1. Translation altered). See also Ayres, *Augustine and the Trinity*, 135–37, 293–95.

21. Victorinus says, "Christ is life, but 'to live' is the *Logos*, and if life itself is 'to be,' and 'to be' is the Father, if again, life itself is 'to understand,' and this is the Holy Spirit, all these are three, in each one are the three, and the three are one and absolutely *homoousia* (consubstantial)" (Victorinus, *Against Arius* IB, 192).

but rather *Proon* ([προόν] Preexistent)."[22] Importantly, Victorinus adds that "all these things [namely words said of the Father] have been understood and named from secondary phenomena [*apparentibus secundis*]."[23] Victorinus anticipates Dionysius's understanding of divine names and how they relate in a hyperbolic and oxymoronic way to the superessential essence of God, yet locates this analogical distinction within the Trinity.

The Son is the movement or action of the Father, who himself is the silent unbegotten in repose.[24] The Father as "to be" is a kind of charged, or pregnant, potential towards being (*On*), which is begotten in an ineffable motion.[25] What is above *on* (existent) is the "hidden *on* (existent)," and for Victorinus, the manifestation of the hidden is begetting. Thus the existent comes into manifestation by the action of *on*.[26] The Father is the cause of "to be" in the *Logos*, but that is not reciprocal, and the property of the first "to be" is to remain tranquil. At the same time, the property of the *Logos* is to move and act, though not to move locally nor by change, but through a self-moving subsistence in itself.[27] As the "manifestation" or showing forth of the infinite, the generation of the Son is also the "manifestation of all things."[28] Thus, the *Logos* is not a single word, but the very power of creating and defining something.[29] Only the Son has "seen God," and we see God in Christ, for the Son is in the bosom and *metra* (matrix) of substance.[30] All

---

22. Victorinus, *Against Aruis* IV, 286–87. Emphasis mine. "Omnia enim quae voces nominant post ipsum sunt."

23. Victorinus, *Against Aruis* IV, 287.

24. Victorinus, *Letter to Candidus*, 74.

25. Victorinus, *Letter to Candidus*, 62. He adds, "This is the Son, the *Logos* who is 'with God,' this one 'through whom all things have been made,' this is the Son, the total filiation of the total paternity, he who is always Son and from eternity, but Son by a movement moved by himself. For, advancing from its power, and, as it were, from an immobile preexistence, where it was in repose, awakening itself to act, hastening to produce all kinds of movement, truly a life which is infinite, this movement in its vivifying action has, in some way, appeared outside. Necessarily therefore life has been born. But life is the Son, life is movement, life is substance which comes forth from vital preexistence for the establishment and the manifestation of all those universals which the Father is according to power so that preknowledge is made evident from the knowledge of the truly existents" (Victorinus, *Against Arius* IB, 174).

26. Victorinus, *Letter to Candidus*, 71.

27. Victorinus, *Against Arius* IA, 132.

28. Victorinus, *Against Arius* IA, 117.

29. Victorinus, *Against Arius* IA, 140.

30. Victorinus, *Against Arius* IA, 110.

created and uncreated reality is "in" the Son; he is the plentitude, "receptacle, and habitat" *of* the Father.[31]

Victorinus says the radiance of light is the "image" of the light, and the Son, eternal life, is the luminous manifestation of "preeternal life," yet life itself is perfected by knowledge.[32] He states, "for life is perfected when it will have recognized both who it is and from whom it comes, how it is from itself but by the will of the Father."[33] This manifestation has no appearance of otherness; that which is born, the image, is not born by division or emanation, but radiance, not by extension but appearance, not *duplicating* but activating the original.[34] As the splendor of the Father, the Son is in one sense "in" or "with" the Father, the light, but in another sense "outside," though never divided.[35]

The *Logos* delimits being from the infinite or ceaselessly renders the infinite intelligible, which is another way of saying that the Son makes it possible to praise the infinite. The fullness (*pleroma*) which *is* the Father "encloses" itself in the receptacle (*khorema*), the Son, who becomes "all from all," light from light.[36] Thus, "the *Logos* is both defined and defining."[37] The anterior Father is without measure and indistinct; however, Victorinus argues that this obscurity is not absolute (otherwise it would be purely unrecognizable *even as* the indistinct). On the contrary, the Father has the *Logos* "latent and hidden," and therefore, while the Father is God "above

---

31. Victorinus, *Against Arius* IA, 151. In an important summary, Victorinus says, "The son is 'form' of the Father. But here the form is not understood as outside the substance, nor as with us, as an appearance added to substance; but this form is a certain subsisting substance in which there appears and is shown that which is hidden and veiled in another. But God is as something veiled. For 'No one sees God.' Therefore the Son is the form in which God is seen. For if God is hidden existence, power, substance, movement, life, God is, as it were, without form. Therefore, if life is manifested and manifested through the power of movement, this life in its hidden movement is known, expressed, seen in the appearance, in the existence of movement . . . the Son, life of the Father, is the 'form of God,' in whom is contemplated the paternal power" (Victorinus, *Against Arius* IB, 178).

32. Victorinus, *Against Arius* III, 220.

33. Victorinus, *Against Arius* IB, 181–82.

34. Victorinus, *Against Arius* III, 221. "The Logos is therefore light, that which is the true." He is "the manifestation of the Father as 'to act,' which in the highest degree is *Logos*, the son, the Light, the Life" (Victorinus, *Against Arius* IA, 95). As "the shining of the light is not separated but is always in the light" (Victorinus, *Against Arius* IA, 141).

35. Victorinus, *Against Arius* IA, 146.

36. Victorinus, *Against Arius* IV, 294.

37. Victorinus, *Against Arius* IV, 281.

Nous, above truth,"[38] "since we say that he is unintelligible, by this we are in some way judging that he is intelligible."[39] Christ is the Whole whose depth is the Father.[40] Victorinus asks, What is form? That in which the Father is contemplated.[41] The Father is not an empty silence, but a silent voice, the Son already a voice, the Paraclete, the utterance of the voice.[42] Therefore, the Father is the fountainhead of the Trinity.[43] The Son has all things "by the gift of the Father," even as consubstantial (*homoousion*).[44] Because of simplicity, the movement of triune life is more like the "order of substance."[45]

THE REVELATION OF LIFE

Victorinus's Trinitarian theology may appear to be an eccentric take on orthodox themes, perhaps an over-indulgence in Greek philosophy, which was waiting to be fully Christianized in the following centuries. However, Victorinus's understanding of the Invisible Father more consistently accounts for the procession of the *Verbum*, the Son, than theologies that undermine the relative obscurity of the Father. The idea that the Father is invisible being in repose, undelimited and indeterminate, is necessitated by what has become metaphysical orthodoxy, namely that God knows himself through the *Logos*.[46] For Aquinas, the procession of the Son from the Father

---

38. Victorinus, *Against Arius* III, 231.

39. Victorinus, *Against Arius* III, 229.

40. Victorinus, *Hymn* I, 319.

41. Victorinus, *Against Arius* IV, 301. Victorinus says, "If God is silence, this action is called Word; if God is immobility, this action is called movement; if God is essence, this action is life, because, as we have taught, in that which is 'to be,' there is also 'to live,' in the silence the Word which keeps silent, and in that which is repose or immobility, there is present either a hidden movement or a hidden action. And so necessarily also movement or action is born from immobility, of the Word is born from silence, or life is born from essence" (Victorinus, *Against Arius* III, 231–32).

42. Victorinus, *Against Arius* IA, 106.

43. Victorinus, *Against Arius* IB, 180. "Since the Father is one reality, the Son another, indeed, since the Father is the source of the Son, the Son is like a river that flows from the source—but in the source the water remains and is in repose, pure, unpolluted, without appearance of springing forth, invisibly replenishing its fullness" (Victorinus, *Against Arius* IV, 298–99).

44. Victorinus, *Against Arius* IV, 297.

45. Victorinus, *Against Arius* IA, 124.

46. See Aquinas, *ST* Ia.27.2.

is analogous to the act of consciousness.[47] When the intellectual gaze is turned in upon itself, it creates or "generates" an image through which the intellect can see itself in a reflection. As the eyes cannot see themselves without a mirror, so the intellect cannot see itself without a mental "mirror," image, or *verbum* (word).

The French phenomenologist Michel Henry offers an account of life that makes us rethink how consciousness reflects upon itself, or sees itself. I will seek to show how Henry's understanding of consciousness as "auto-affected" life helps us theologically appropriate the all important *verbum* analogy. Picking up Edmund Husserl's diagnosis of the crisis of modernity, Henry provocatively argues that "We are entering into barbarism."[48] By so totally eliminating the human element in its procedures, "pure science" has allowed for no human remainder in life, but rather has secured the "brutal and progressive annihilation" of humanity as such.[49] Henry's phenomenological project prioritizes Life, and demands a break from the father of phenomenology himself, Edmund Husserl. In keeping with Husserl, Henry agrees that phenomenology is a proper philosophical discipline that investigates not any particular object, but the mode of givenness, phenomenally, or appearance of reality.[50] Contrary to the Greek legacy, Henry argues that appearance is "more essential" than being, as "it is only because it appears that a thing is able to be."[51] By privileging being over appearance, the West

---

47. Aquinas, *ST* Ia.27.2.co.

48. Henry, *Barbarism*, 1. For Husserl on the barbarism of modern Europe see Husserl, *Crisis of European Sciences*, 7.

49. Henry, *Barbarism*, 1–2. Henry works with the following general diagnosis: "with modern science, knowledge has made huge advances; to this end, it had to be divided into a proliferation of investigations, each with its own methodology, conceptual tools, and objects. It is no longer possible for anyone to master them all, nor some of them or even one of them. The unity of knowledge is at stake, and along with it, the discovery of a principle ensuring the agreement and thus the validity of experiments, assessments in all domains, and thoughts themselves. Our everyday behavior is significant in this regard: to deal with each specific problem, we call on a specialist. But, if this practice turns out to be effective for a toothache or repairing a machine, it still does not provide any broad view of human existence and its destiny" (Henry, *Barbarism*, 2).

50. Henry, *Material Phenomenology*, 2. Henry says, "One can confer various names upon this pure phenomenality: pure manifestation, showing, unveiling, uncovering, appearing, revelation, or even the traditional word: truth" (Henry, "Phenomenology of Life," 241).

51. Henry, "Phenomenology of Life," 242. Henry's preference for appearance is rooted in the principle, "Something is inasmuch as it appears [*Autant d'apparaître, autant d'être*]." Henry says he carries this "precedence of phenomenology over ontology one

has fallen into the trap of separating the "real world" outside, complete in and of itself, from the consciousness of the onlooker.[52]

For Husserl, consciousness is by nature intentional; one is always conscious-of-some*thing*. The mind is an invisible point of perception, or the transcendental location of "apperception."[53] The objects of intention are set off against the background, or horizon, of the world. Henry argues that intentionality so conceived reduces the human being to an impoverished faculty, namely the mind. Moreover, if consciousness is a oneway stream towards inert objects, guided by intention, how can one get "behind" their own intentional gaze, as it were, to perceive and thus know themselves as individuals with identity?[54] The intending mind is no more capable of producing identity, individuality, or ipseity than the human eye.

Henry carves an alternative path, which he calls "material phenomenology." Instead of dividing the being of an object from its mode of appearance, Henry inquires into "the substance, the stuff, the phenomenological matter of which it is made, its phenomenologically pure materiality."[55] Material phenomenology treats "invisible phenomenological substance."[56] What is the nature of this substance? It is not nothing, but rather affect, or the medium of every affect, affection itself.[57] Henry's reconceived substance has in view the "pathetic immediacy in which life experiences itself."[58] Life

---

step further by saying that it is only if the appearing appears in itself and as such that something, whatever it may be, can in turn appear, can show itself to us."

52. Henry, *Material Phenomenology*, 2. See sections 27 to 29 on the "natural standpoint" of the ego and the world. Husserl, *Ideas*, 51–55.

53. Henry, "Phenomenology of Life," 243.

54. Henry, "Phenomenology of Life," 243.

55. Henry, *Material Phenomenology*, 2. Henry's material phenomenology envisions reality anew, and Davide Zordan shows how Henry has impressed his mark upon phenomenology's favourite delicacy, the aesthetic. For Henry's philosophical next of kin, Maurice Merleau-Ponty, the canvas is a miracle, as it directs the soul to what is other, a concrete world beyond one's consciousness. True to form, Henry says, if intentionality divides oneself and the world, then a human being is equivalent to the surveillance camera monitoring the museum. Zordan explains: "The wonder itself of vision is not so much the power to see the beauty of various objects, but the revelation of subjectivity as a phenomenology ability to see." Zordan, "Seeing the Invisible," 83. For a critique of Henry's aesthetics which preferences Marion's, see Fritz, "Black Holes and Revelations," 415–40.

56. Henry, *Material Phenomenology*, 2.

57. Henry, *Material Phenomenology*, 2–3.

58. Henry, *Material Phenomenology*, 3.

is for Henry the new material starting point, the crisis of historic phenomenology, and the deprived theme of modernity. Life is that mysterious reality in which appearance and being coincide to reveal that "how" something is and "what" it is are one. Life is not a thing that reveals itself to the self, but "is" in its appearing, which is not *a* mode of existence but the principle form (the proper substance and material) of reality as a whole.[59]

Life founds being, not vice versa. Any concept of being outside of the auto-affected immediacy of life would be merely "dead being" or "nonbeing,"[60] a charge to which, Henry argues, historic phenomenology falls victim. By rupturing the primordial union between "the world" and life, phenomenology has made humanity a provincial, and even less real, instance within a cold world of objects, in which the "intangibles" like love and suffering inevitably disappear along with the individuals who made them possible.[61] When Henry says that life appears, he does not mean that an otherwise autonomous essence discloses itself, which would imply a radical difference between the "thing" in question and the occasion of its arrival or opening. Rather, life is an originary mode of phenomenality that "is" the revelation of itself. Life gives, or as Henry says "reveals" itself, and therefore is an "auto-revelation."[62] Like suffering and joy, life is invisible, and though these things disappear under the directed gaze, they nevertheless remain "immediate, incontestable, insuperable."[63] Suffering, for example, cannot exist "outside" the self, but always already is one's suffering; there is no distance between intention from the essence of suffering, as suffering is an experience only possible for life, the life in which human beings inexplicably find themselves.[64] Henry's axiomatic assertion then is this: "revelation and reality are one."[65]

Moving from the auto-revelation of the finite self to Absolute Life, Henry asks, "why there is a living being in life: why is no life possible that might be anonymous, impersonal, foreign to every individuality?"[66] Curi-

---

59. Henry, *Material Phenomenology*, 3. Life defines the "essence" of pure phenomenality and is coextensive with being.

60. Henry, *Material Phenomenology*, 3.

61. Henry, "Phenomenology of Life," 245.

62. Henry, "Phenomenology of Life," 247.

63. Henry, "Phenomenology of Life," 248–49.

64. Henry, "Phenomenology of Life," 249.

65. Henry, "Phenomenology of Life," 249.

66. Henry, "Phenomenology of Life," 249.

ously, he addresses what appears to be a very speculative question by saying the relation of life to the living being "is not a metaphysical one," nor an "object of speculative constructions or of indefinite debates."[67] This question must be at the heart of a phenomenology of life, and it is a question that forces one back towards the "Life" spoken by John.[68] Absolute life has the power to bring itself into life: "Life 'is' not, it happens and does not cease happening."[69] By constantly "reaching" into itself, delighting and experiencing itself, Absolute Life is "constantly producing its own essence." The "Word" of John's gospel is "consubstantial" with Life and an immanent condition of its "effectuation."[70]

Interestingly, Henry says the "strange analogy" between absolute life experiencing itself (in the "Self of the First Living Being") and our own auto-revealing becomes "less extraordinary than it seems at first sight if we first of all establish the distinction between them."[71] Moreover, Absolute Life comes into itself as life, auto-revelation in the most divine sense being the Word of God, and every particular is marked with a borrowed ipseity rooted in Life.[72]

Despite Henry's critique of metaphysics, his thought is remarkably metaphysical, especially when compared to Victorinus's vision. Henry may deny that appearance implies a preceding "object" in being, but Victorinus agrees wholeheartedly, as he argues that the Father's substance (*ousios*) and existence "*Is*" in the auto-revelation (to use Henry's term) of the Revelation

---

67. Henry, "Phenomenology of Life," 249.

68. Henry, "Phenomenology of Life," 249.

69. Henry, "Phenomenology of Life," 249.

70. Henry, "Phenomenology of Life," 250. Henry thoughtfully considers the possible objection: "doesn't this analysis of absolute life distance us from the phenomenology which seeks to confine itself to the concrete phenomena that we live through, does it not throw us back into speculation, if not into dogma or belief? Haven't we yielded to the 'theological turn of French phenomenology' denounced by Dominique Janicaud? And yet are we not, we too, living beings? Living being in the sense of a life which experiences itself, and not just a complex set of material processes which know nothing of themselves? Living being which are themselves also living Selves?" (Henry, "Phenomenology of Life," 250). See Janicaud, "Theological Turn," 16. For more on Janicaud's critique see, O'Sullivan, *Michel Henry*; Williams, "Gilles Deleuze and Michel Henry," 265–79; Rebidoux, "Given Life," 159–88.

71. Henry, "Phenomenology of Life," 250–51.

72. Henry, "Phenomenology of Life," 251. Thus, Cunningham says "our lives are themselves the auto-revelation of divine, transcendental ipseity" (Cunningham, "Suspending the Natural Attitude," 279).

of himself, namely in his Son. Fully intelligible *On* (being) is reserved for the one named "Life," "action," motion, or again as Henry would say, "happening."[73] Yet Henry never abandons or negates the substantiality of that happening. By so privileging appearance, the "stuff" question, namely the question regarding actuality, being, or "is," resurfaces within and as appearance. Victorinus candidly recognizes the relative obscurity of all "being" language: "existence, or substance, or 'to be' are used basically synonymously,"[74] and of the simplicity of that being he says there is a "fortunate ambiguity of meaning."[75] So whether we say ontology is phenomenological, with Victorinus, or phenomenality is substantial, with Henry, we emphasize one of two aspects of simplicity.

Moreover, Henry describes the relation between finite life and Eternal Life in terms that can only be described as analogical participation. Reflecting on Matt 25:40 and a "phenomenologically actual life, a real Self,"[76] he says, "It is impossible to touch this flesh without touching the other flesh that has made it flesh. It is impossible to strike someone without striking Christ. And it is Christ who says: 'Whatever you did for one of the least of these brothers of mine, you did for me.'"[77] This "is not a metaphor." It does not mean that striking a brother is "as if" one struck Christ: "Christianity has to do only with reality, not with the imaginary or with symbols . . . the me is not anchored in itself forever except by force of the essential Ipseity that, giving it to itself, binding it to itself in its *pathetik* embrace, has made of it this me that it forever is"; and, "before this me ever existed, the original Ipseity of the Arch-Son cast it into itself."[78] Human life, identity, and ipseity are actualized in direct substantial relation to Eternal Life, Identity, Ipseity. Thus, Henry admits the theological propriety of "analogy": that "strange analogy" between absolute life experiencing itself (in the "Self of the First Living Being") and our own auto-revelation becomes "less extraordinary," as he says.[79]

---

73. Victorinus says, "With the appearance of action, [the Son] both is and is called action" (Victorinus, *Against Arius* 1A, 94). Victorinus could equally say that "Something is inasmuch as it appears."

74. Victorinus, *Against Arius* IA, 136.

75. Victorinus, *Against Arius* IA, 152.

76. Henry, "Phenomenology of Life," 250.

77. Henry, *I Am*, 117.

78. "Without this Ipseity preceding it, no me would ever be" (Henry, *I Am*, 117).

79. Henry, "Phenomenology of Life," 250–51.

Henry not only shares certain participatory ideas, but helps reenvision the nature of life itself, and thus the Trinitarian "generation" of life. Particularly, Henry's critique of the intentional mind guides a proper interpretation of the classic analogy of the Son as a mental procession, as Word or *Verbum*. The picture of consciousness that Henry rejects depicts the mind as a capacity for perception that has a starting point, as it were, a fixed though invisible "location." In other words, Henry refuses to understand the mind as an intellectual "foundation." From this foundation, the intellectual gaze would extend towards external essences that are registered by the transcendental consciousness. On the contrary, Henry eliminates any strictly conceived starting point for consciousness, and argues that "consciousness" itself arises from or is the perfection of life, not a power incongruously and incidentally added to life. This idea of the intellect as the perfecting of life is a grace-perfecting-nature relationship, or more specifically, a development of perfections articulated by the Christian tradition in the being-life-intelligence triad (*esse-vivere-intelligere*).

Moreover, instead of separating a subject from an object which is mediated by appearance, Henry says that a "subject," or more precisely "a life," *is* in the appearance of the appearance that is life, namely auto-revelation, in which no such division between mind and image remains intelligible, for the "subject" (me!) is in the very appearing of *this* life. Not only does Henry detect a foundationalism in Husserl's intentional consciousness, but makes us aware that if this picture is ascribed analogically to God, then we anchor foundationalism in the Godhead itself. Thus, we can say that Henry considers consciousness not as a foundation, but as "suspended" in life, which directly connects to Erich Przywara's articulation of the *analogia entis* (analogy of being), and a dynamic William Desmond calls the "between" (*metaxu*):[80] Przywara says, "The 'in-and-beyond' has shown itself to be the

---

80. See his trilogy on the between: Desmond, *Being and the Between*; *Ethics and the Between*; *God and the Between*. The theme of "suspension" has become a key insight from the *ressourcement* reading of the *analogia entis*. Hans Ur von Balthasar used the phrase "suspended middle" to describe the character of de Lubac's theology: "De Lubac soon realized that his position moved into a suspended middle in which he could not practice any philosophy without its transcendence into theology, but also no theology without its essential inner substructure of philosophy. This center has been the vital environment of his thought from the beginning to the present, at the beginning in opposition to the modern dichotomy that Cajetan had projected into Thomas, today in opposition to a new form of Christian schizophrenia that yields so much to post-Kantian scientific rationalism and secularism (as 'opening to the world') that the only thing left for the sphere of faith is a groundless fideism" (Balthasar, *Theology of Henri De Lubac*, 11).

fundamental formal relation within this our principle of metaphysics as such. It is, firstly, a relation—that is, the suspension of a 'between'—as distinct from some demarcated position from which one could directly draw conclusions."[81]

The mental *verbum* analogy must be seen as limited in a very decided way. In light of Henry's arguments in which intelligence is no longer seen as a fixed or stable point of perception but rather "happens" in the "between" of the appearance of life, the "I" that generates the mental image (*verbum*) is not separable from the "appearance," nor does the "I" constitute the basis or foundation from which the *verbum* is defined.[82] Therefore, "the mind" is not the I in contrast to the image, but the I *as* image "is" in its own appearance of itself (again, what it is and how it is are the same). The analogy can no longer start with the stable mind that generates the mental word as a reflection, and insofar as we choose to use the analogy, we must recognize how fleeting and inaccurate it is because it makes us and our mode of cognition—and therefore all cognition as such—analogous to the Father, who is here thought as the "foundation" in eternity. However, our thinking is by nature appearance, and thus as "suspended intelligence" our thinking always has the quality of having *arrived*, having been brought forth without our involvement; in other words, we are inescapably those who have been *born*. The bottom of the *verbum* analogy falls out then, because the one who supposedly "generates" the *verbum* only "is" in the form of having been *born*, and thus the subject of the analogy opens out into the Infinite from which all consciousness arises and to which it returns.

As with Przywara, the "between" extends throughout everything, and thus the nonfoundationalist view of consciousness is exactly analogous to a metaphysics of the between, which for him is seen most clearly in the principle of noncontradiction.[83] This principle arises amidst the most unrelenting and savage denials of truth. Though I doubt everything, I cannot doubt *that* I doubt. While inescapable, the principle of noncontradiction does not

---

81. Przywara, *Analogia Entis*, 190.

82. Jean-Luc Marion, who will be discussed further below, fully agrees: "we admit that the image is as much as—indeed more than—the thing itself: what I am does not remain behind what I appear to be; on the contrary, what I appear to be (the look) invests my identity bit by bit and, in the end, completely, the deep strata of the person" (Marion, *Crossing of the Visible*, 52).

83. Przywara, *Analogia Entis*, 198. The principle of noncontradiction is that something cannot in the same respect simultaneously both "be" and "not be," nor can it be "validated" as true and untrue.

yield its own positive truth, but rather "suspends" one in the matrix of truth without content, which Przywara calls a "negative reductive formality."[84] Virtually any system of philosophy can abstractly confirm this principle, but as Przywara recognizes, the philosophical difficulty is to render the "negatively reductive" quality of the principle, which means construing the metaphysical reality that I am at once inescapably "happening" in the rhythms of absolute truth without any stake or claim or foundation therein.

Now, we must move, according to analogical reasoning, from individual consciousness through our relation to absolute truth to the way "knowledge" or consciousness or life is in God himself. Thus, by rethinking the mental *verbum* analogy, we are not just qualifying a *human* analogy for the Trinity, but grasping the very nature of life as such. This quality of appearing—having-been-born or suspendedness—is not only our mode of knowing, but is also the nature of knowledge as instantiated in the Trinity.[85]

The Father is not simply the "subject" or fixed gaze that perceives itself in the reflection of the Son, but rather "subjectivity" itself (ipseity), which is predicated upon life which is its own appearance (auto-revelation). Therefore, the inception of knowledge comes *after*, or more accurately *with*, the manifestation of life. But such knowledge, as attached to life, has the quality of having-been-born. In the Trinitarian life itself, "before" the awakening of hypostases, we already see the principles of "begottenness" and "paternity," generation and origin, and manifestation and hiddenness.

Without a division between "I" and the mental "image" (*verbum*), the "subjectivity" or auto-affection of God himself is, precisely like us, in the "middle"; in other words, God's Ipseity is with the Son. In the *verbum* analogy, the bottom of our consciousness falls out towards the Infinite. In other words, when we think about our own consciousness in light of the analogy, we have the phenomenal element of being finite or relatively posterior to the Infinite. Likewise, the divine *Verbum* as Life "opens out" into the Infinity of its superessential Origin. The posterior Infinite from which our consciousness springs, as it were, is not just a feature of finite consciousness, but consciousness, Life, Ipseity itself. Therefore, the name "Son" is completely appropriate to the second person of the Trinity. As both reality

---

84. Przywara, *Analogia Entis*, 199.

85. Victorinus describes the generation of the Son who is Life, "For, advancing from its power, and, as it were, from an immobile preexistence, where it was in repose, awakening itself to act, hastening to produce all kinds of movement, truly a life which is infinite, this movement in its vivifying action has, in some way, appeared outside. Necessarily therefore life has been born" (Victorinus, *Against Arius* IB, 174).

and word, the Son indicates generation, appearance, or begottenness. The name "Father," on the other hand, is itself an eternally proper name but a name that arises "after" the Son, or "with," the Son, as "Father" is meaningless without a Son. Thus, the name "Father" is a conjecture for God himself. Properly speaking, we do not occupy the Father's place in the *verbum* analogy. Rather, Christ is the kin of conscious beings, our brother. So he says, call none among you "father" (Matt 23:9), for "the one who sanctifies and those who are sanctified all have one Father" (Heb 2:11).

When Victorinus says no one has ever seen God in himself without his form, we take the Son to be the Form exactly in his motion, activity, and Ispeity (not as a static shape).[86] The "suspended middle" of human consciousness and metaphysics as such is an instantiation, or intonation, of the Trinity, which knows itself from the Son, whom Victorinus remarkably calls "the mid-angle of the Trinity; he reveals the preexisting Father and sends forth the Holy Spirit for the sake of perfection."[87] By rendering God's own knowledge in continuity with a Christian metaphysics of the "between," or the rhythms and oscillation of analogical being, we see how radically true the Trinitarian dictum really is: "the Father is known in the Son."[88]

Therefore, Life, which is proper *On* (being) (Victorinus) or phenomenological substance (Henry), is *born*, and thus we see the intra-divine basis of Przywara's analogical principle, as the Son who is Life has his "essence-in-and-beyond-existence" in the begetter. Moreover, God is himself and knows himself from this "suspended" mid-angle.

DIVINE REVERENCE

The eternal, only-begotten Son remains the divine *Verbum*, the Word of the Father, but now he must be seen as Art and Artist, Lyric and Poet at the same time. He is the image of the unbegotten in repose, *Proon* (Preexistent),

---

86. Victorinus says, "Therefore, the form of God, when understood to be in God, is God himself" (Victorinus, *Against Arius* IV, 293).

87. Victorinus, *Against Arius* IB, 181–82.

88. Victorinus, *Against Arius* III, 238. Victorinus says, "Although the Son is both in the Father and the Father in the Son, existence or substance in life and life in substance, nevertheless since substance is invisible, it is apprehended only in life. But Christ is predominantly life, although he is substance . . . When: 'Because you do not know me, neither do you know my Father. If you knew me you would also know my Father.' It is by 'me' that you 'would know' that that which is, exists, because I am also knowledge, which is the Holy Spirit."

whose dwelling is hiddenness, and as such, the Son does not mimic, imitate, or re-present a prior "image" or visible, but by his very living "makes visible what without him would have remained definitively invisible" thus "delivering the unseen from its anterior invisibility, its shapelessness."[89]

Jean-Luc Marion says the true painter "ushers something from the unseen into the visible."[90] Artists of every variety testify to the fortuitous nature of their gifts. Regularly, they credit the unknown with their ideas, and see themselves as "channels" of insight, conduits of revelation, or prophets. The artist is true to form insofar as he or she attends to the mystery of the beyond. One creates out of the chaos of Genesis, says Marion, before first light.[91] By going back before the separation of the waters, before the separation of light from darkness, even before the distinction between good and evil, the artist "descends to the undecidable frontier of the visible and the unseen only in order to cross it," and by so groping in the dark, "leads the unseens . . . from archaic obscurity to the light of visibility."[92] The artist dwells between the interstices of the *eclipse*.[93] The "Frame" or "Form" of the Son as Art is then the gate of the Underworld.[94]

For Marius Victorinus, the Son manifests what is "precontained" in the Invisible Father, but in keeping with Marion, the Artist does not "render real a 'preseen' [or previously seen] visibility," which would be reduced to a mere *re*production, but brings forth a new visible out of the invisible. By virtue of his begottenness, the Son knows himself as the appearance, image, or icon of the Father, and the "invisible visibility" of God himself.[95] The shape of the Son's life brings forth the invisible as invisible, and is authentic to the degree that it surrenders its own invisibility on behalf of the invisible. By enacting this "shape," by surrendering wholly to the Invisible, the Son "recollects" the divine *by* his "artistic" activity.[96]

---

89. Marion, *Crossing of the Visible*, 25–26.

90. Marion, *Crossing of the Visible*, 29.

91. Marion, *Crossing of the Visible*, 27.

92. Marion, *Crossing of the Visible*, 27.

93. See chapter 1 on the eclipse of the holy.

94. Marion, *Crossing of the Visible*, 27.

95. Victorinus says the Father is "Invisibly invisible," the Son "Invisibly visible," and the Spirit "Visibly Invisible" (Victorinus, *Hymn* III, 326–27).

96. John Milbank develops the idea that making (*poesis*) is our means of contemplating (*theoria*), which affirms the contingency of all cultural constructions with their metaphorical, or analogical, relation to the infinite. With Herder, Milbank argues that "expression" is only possible as a non-identical repetition: "'Expression' was for Herder

Without "being" underpinning the appearance, even if that being is eclipsed by the holy, the "beyond" of the invisible can only be an incongruous abyss of obscurity. The more one plunges into its depth, the more lost one becomes. But, by following the transcendentals up into the holy in kenotic surrender of invisibility for the Invisible as such (goodness), aesthetic recollection of what was previously unseen (beauty), and perceiving the paternal origin of knowledge itself (truth), the Son becomes *more* himself, or truly himself, the further he enters the holy. More mystery means more truth, goodness, and beauty, not less, which comes from the hierarchical, alchemistic, singularity of the holy which ontologically contains all, yet phenomenologically eclipses all. In his *Letter to Artists*, Pope John Paul II sees the creative act as similarly related to the beyond, for every genuine artistic intuition goes beyond the senses and reaches "beneath reality's surface, strives to interpret its hidden mystery. The intuition itself springs from the depths of the human soul, where the desire to give meaning to one's own life is joined by the fleeting vision of beauty and of the mysterious unity of things."[97] He adds that believers find nothing strange in this: "they know that they have had a momentary glimpse of the abyss of light which has its original wellspring in God."[98] If the "intimate reality of things is always 'beyond' the powers of human perception, how much more so is God in the depths of his unfathomable mystery!"[99] The Son then is the wellspring of an infinite depth.

But because the holy is oxymoronic, its "image" will be simultaneously irresistible, because of the "weight of glory," and terrifying because of the "power that it exerts in the name of the darkness from which it arises ... it still bears the marks of the forbidden, despite having renounced it."[100] For

---

ontologically irreducible, because what gets expressed is never just a prior 'content,' but always, in addition, something that only appears with the expression itself" (Milbank, *Made Strange*, 106). This "something" that "only appears with the expression itself" fits with Victorinus and Henry's understanding of the Son, who is the eternal expression of God as auto-revelation. Again, Milbank says, nonidentical repetition "indicates that what we do or make is not prescribed by a preceding idea; on the contrary, we have to discover the content of the infinite through labour, and creative effort" (Milbank, *Theology and Social Theory*, 306).

97. John Paul II, "Letter to Artists," 6.
98. John Paul II, "Letter to Artists," 6.
99. John Paul II, "Letter to Artists," 6.
100. Marion, *Crossing of the Visible*, 31.

The Invisible Father

"glory threatens, even when it saves."[101] Thus Marion says, the Christ who rose from the grave bore the marks of crucifixion, as every piece of art is a resurrection of sorts. The incarnation economically reveals the original return of the Son to the Father, who precisely at the moment of his greatest disclosure remains "unseen."[102] The Son became human, and again surrendered his invisibility. But he also gave up his visibility, as the guards maimed his image and dis-figured his face. Only his actions remained visible. And at the moment when he loses his human appearance, Christ became the figure of the divine will.[103] The book of Hebrews says that "In the days of his flesh, Jesus offered up prayers and supplications, with loud cries and tears, to the one who was able to save him from death, and he was heard because of his *reverence* [εὐλαβείας]" and "he learned obedience through what he suffered; and having been made perfect, he became the source of eternal salvation for all who obey him, having been designated by God a high priest" (Heb 5:7–10).[104] Christ's mangled non-form, irresistible and terrifying, creates a new visible that would have been impossible without the shrine of his body.[105]

Israel's Holy of Holies allegorically discloses Christ. Heavenly cherubim attend the sacred ark, and the high priest from a "nation of priests" (Exod 19:6; cf. 1 Pet 2:9), who can be called the priest *of* priests, represents the best of humanity because he represents God, and he represents God because he represents the best of humanity. The priest enters the spiritual house and images the invisible God. Similarly, the Apostle John sees into heaven where the slain Lamb of God, the new form of *reverence*, stands "between" (ἐν μέσῳ) the heavenly creatures and the Invisible "Holy" who is upon the "throne" and otherwise without determination. Again, in the new creation, John sees the Invisible on his throne alongside the Lamb (Rev 21:22–24; 22:1, 3–4). As the Priest *of* priests, Christ recapitulates all things and permits endless variations of a single prayer: "Our Father in heaven, hallowed be your name" (Matt 6:9). Said differently, "Holy Father [Πάτερ ἅγιε], keep them in your name, which you have given me" (John 17:11). The refracted brilliance of the holy gathers together again in the act of reverence, which cumulates and sums up all things in its return, its offering of

---

101. Marion, *Crossing of the Visible*, 31.
102. Marion, *Crossing of the Visible*, 31.
103. Marion, *Crossing of the Visible*, 61.
104. Emphasis mine. Translation altered slightly from NRSV.
105. Marion, *Crossing of the Visible*, 61.

itself in sacrifice to the holy. This is the most determinative formal quality of reverence: as Abraham Heschel says, "They who keep holy the things that are holy shall themselves become holy."[106]

Marion reiterates this exact principle regarding the Son and his relation to the Father. He says, "Christ himself holds his invisible holiness only by virtue of his return, permanent and total, to the invisible Father . . . who alone is holy."[107] Only by testifying to the unique holiness of the Father does Christ testify to his own holiness, and thus live up to his title "the Holy One *of* God" (Mark 1:24; John 6:69).[108] The Cross becomes a sacred symbol as it bears Christ's return of all holiness to the Father, and the common icon "can merit any fragment of the glory of the Holy" only insofar as it enacts this return.[109] In agreement with Heschel, Marion says every icon, whether an icon made by human hands or the Son who is the "icon of the invisible God" (Col 1:15), is qualified as holy by the "logic of this return," or as Heschel says, keeping "holy the things that are holy": Marion adds, "the icon finds its fulfillment in definitively relinquishing any claim to imitate the Holy One to which it returns and which returns in it."[110]

For Rudolf Otto, the human spirit encounters God properly in an awe-inspiring stance towards the Holy. This mystical awe, this "shudder," is reflected in self-consciousness as such by the release of the "creature-feeling" that he describes as the feeling of personal nothingness and abasement before the awe-inspiring object one experiences.[111] The creature-feeling may come sweeping like a gentle tide, pervading the mind with a tranquil mood of deepest worship, or remain as a lasting attitude of the soul. This feeling might suddenly erupt into frenzy or ecstasy, or more characteristically, become the hushed, trembling, and speechless humility of the creature in

---

106. Heschel, *God in Search of Man*, 78.

107. Marion, *Crossing of the Visible*, 75–76. In his discussion of Gregory of Nyssa, John Milbank articulates this principle with regard to the human being, namely the "notion of 'active reception' whereby in receiving we actively *become* what we receive: the triune God" (Milbank, "Force of Identity," 204).

108. Marion, *Crossing of the Visible*, 76. He says, "It is by never claiming his own holiness or his own glory, therefore it is only by giving back absolutely to his Father that he takes up that holiness that is given back to him in order to be glorified; Christ attains his holiness by coming undone . . . for the sake of the Father, by making sure that henceforth, all holiness finds its fulfillment in its transfer by itself toward the invisible Holy."

109. Marion, *Crossing of the Visible*, 76.

110. Marion, *Crossing of the Visible*, 76.

111. Otto, *Idea of the Holy*, 18.

the presence of "whom or what?"[112] Otto's observation cuts deeper than he realized. The holy fear of the *mysterium tremendum* belongs to Life, and not merely "creatures." The Psamist writes, "Holy and awesome is his name. The fear of the Lord is the beginning [ראשׁית] of wisdom" (Ps 111:9–10; cf. 1:7; Job 28:28). "Beginning" here means more than the starting point of knowledge for creatures, and indicates the founding principle, blueprint, or structure *of* Sophia. Christ himself is this Form, this Arche.[113] Therefore, Christ's "keeping holy" the Father, in other words the eternal *reverence* that "is" the Son, constitutes the formal principle of all knowledge: ἀρχὴ σοφίας φόβος κυρίου, which comes from "The fear of the Lord is the beginning of wisdom, and the knowledge of the Holy One *is* in-sight" (Prov 9:10).[114] The Son shows us how to "keep holy," both in the sense of keeping holy *what* is holy, and (thus) keeping oneself holy.

Clement of Alexandria says that the Son is the "Beginning of existences," by which he means the "timeless and unoriginated First Principle."[115] From this principle, we learn of the "remoter Cause, the Father" whom he calls the "most ancient."[116] Though the Father escapes expression by the voice, Clement says he is to be "reverenced with reverence, and silence, and holy wonder, and supremely venerated."[117] We know the Father only through the Son, as no one has seen God except the only-begotten God (μονογενὴς θεὸς), the one in the bosom of the Father (John 1:18). He says, we reserve paternal honor, and holy preeminence for the Father. Therefore, we learn from and participate in the reverential nature of the Son. The Father "alone" is the Almighty One, of incomparable perfection, "most holy," potent, kingly, and beneficent.[118] The Son orders all things according to the Father, and "holds the helm of the universe in the best way," tirelessly working all things while keeping in view its hidden designs.[119] Everything is in subjection to Christ, who subsequently exhibits the "holy administration for Him" who put all in subjection to Christ.[120] In the previous chapter, we

---

112. Otto, *Idea of the Holy*, 12–13.
113. For further discussion of Christ as Arche see Roberts, *Sacred Rhetoric*, 84–102.
114. Emphasis mine. Slight modification to the NRSV translation.
115. Clement of Alexandria, *Stromata*, 7.1:523.
116. Clement of Alexandria, *Stromata*, 7.1:523.
117. Clement of Alexandria, *Stromata*, 7.1:523.
118. Clement of Alexandria, *Stromata*, 7.2:524.
119. Clement of Alexandria, *Stromata*, 7.2:524.
120. Clement of Alexandria, *Stromata*, 7.2:524.

saw how for Dionysius every divine name "hallows" the superessential essence of God, the holy. Now we see that this same liturgy is carried forth in fullness by the eternal Son of God to the Father. The Apostle Paul says that because Christ is the Beginning (ὅς ἐστιν ἀρχή), he is "before all things, and in him all things hold together" (Col 1:17), and "all things have been created through him and for him" (v.16). Thus everything analogically repeats and performs the Son's liturgical, artistic, annunciation of the Holy One.

I argued that the transcendentals refract from the holy and are "made holy" by revering the *sanctum sanctorum* (Holy of holies). Because being is then a hue of holiness, only the holy "is." We see now that the Trinity—at this point the Son's relation to the Father—follows the *sanctum sanctorum* dynamic. As Ambrose says, "the source of generation is He Who is (ὁ ὤν)."[121] The Son is "begotten of the Eternal," and the one through whom we know that "the Father is eternal."[122] Through this dynamic, the attributes of the Father and the Son are in agreement. Regarding Christ, Ambrose says, "He is the radiance of the Father's glory, the expression of His substance, the counterpart of God, the image of His majesty; the Bounty of Him Who is bountiful, the Wisdom of Him Who is wise, the Power of the Mighty One, the Truth of Him Who is true, the Life of the Living One."[123] The Son is called the "image," "effulgence," and "expression" of God because these names "disclose the Father's incomprehensible and unsearchable Majesty dwelling in the Son."[124] The goodness and truth contained in the Father's bounty are "manifest" in the spotless counterpart of the Son, who by his person expresses "Eternal Bounty."[125] Augustine emphasizes the "*of*" connection (integral to the Holy *of* holies formula) in the Trinity: "For we call the Son God *of* God; but the Father, God only; not *of* God. Whence it is plain that the Son has another *of* whom He is, *of* his father, and is son to his father; but no father is what he is, *of* his son, but is father to his son."[126]

---

121. Ambrose, *On the Christian Faith*, 2.intro.3.

122. Ambrose, *On the Christian Faith*, 2.intro.3.

123. Ambrose, *On the Christian Faith*, 2.intro.3.

124. Ambrose, *On the Christian Faith*, 2.intro.8.

125. Ambrose, *On the Christian Faith*, 2.2.32.

126. Augustine, *Trinity*, 2.1.2. Speaking about this "of" relation, Przywara says, "The night of God as unknown, *Dues tamquam ignotus*, which for Thomas stands at the 'summit of our (earthly) knowledge,' is thus, on the one hand (at the limits of the philosophical), 'a darkening night' and, to this extent, induces that 'blindness' that alone leads into the theological (the *non videre* of the *credere*). But, on the other hand (at the limits of the theological), it is an 'en-compassing night' and therein that 'superluminous darkness' . . .

THE INVISIBLE FATHER

PRESENCE/ABSENCE

If we recover the invisibility of the Father, what do we make of mutuality or fellowship in the Trinity? Is the Father a phantom that looms over the tragically isolated Son? How can the Son see or know the Father, and thus have even the possibility of love? One can argue that the Trinitarian theology of Victorinus is susceptible to the charge of heresy. The "lower," visible, divinity of the Son is unequal to the Father's, and thus holds to a kind of subordinationism. However, Victorinus is fully within the boundaries of Nicene orthodoxy. The invisible-visible contrast is not between two competing deities, but is instead a distinctive of a single God, whose persons are *homoousios*. If we make unrestrained equality define orthodoxy, then the unique qualities of each person will become arbitrary. The Father, Son, and Spirit might then convene about which one should "incarnate," until the Son courteously volunteers. The proper, natural, differences make the incarnate *Logos* fitting, appropriate, and "convenient."[127]

The Preexisting One (*Proon*) manifests in the "self" of another, namely the only begotten. The two gaze upon one another, as "eyes or faces mutually seeing each other by a reciprocal look."[128] This reciprocity differs from the mutual gaze of human beings. When two people meet face-to-face, they gaze into each other's eyes. The invisible person, or we might tenuously say the soul, is no more in the eyes than the toes or fingers. However, the eyes form a gateway to the other's gaze through sight. We attempt to see their seeing and meet their gaze. Marion recognizes that the pupil is symbolic.[129] We are drawn to the pupil when we truly want to see someone, but the pupil is conspicuously absent of substance and light. The pupil stands for the invisible. The absence in the eye creates a new kind of visible that indicates the other's presence.

The finite gaze differs from the Son's. Human beings direct their gaze across time and space from a specific place. The Son's gaze is one with his bodiless, atemporal, person. The Invisible Father does not have eyes or another form through which he can be seen by the Son, that is, besides the

---

of the Areopagite, which announces the essence of the theo-logical: where, in the 'Word (of God),' the '(Word) of God' is revealed: the depth of his invisibility in the depth of his visibility" (Przywara, *Analogia Entis*, 182).

127. Aquinas, *ST* III.1.1.co.

128. Victorinus, *Against Arius* IB, 183.

129. Marion, *Crossing of the Visible*, 56.

Son himself. The Father is withdrawn.[130] We might say the Son's gaze is "crossed" all the way along. He does not locate the Father's gaze, but sees the Father's gaze in his own, or as his own. In other words, the Son encounters the Father's gaze not in any one place, but in his "being seen" by the Father. Contrary to Marion, the Father's withdrawal is not total. His presence is not solely marked by his absence. Rather, the Father is of a singularity that comprises and yet repels the terms presence and absence. His counter-gaze is full and intimate, but vast to the point of being vacuous. He escapes words as the pregnant abyss from which words are born, from which truth itself emerges.

The crossed gaze of the Son relieves the tension between the three hypostases and the one gaze of God, the three persons and the one Person.

130. Jean-Luc Marion identifies "withdrawal" as the form of the Father: "The permanence of distance as the highest revelation and manifestation of the divine in the form of the Father . . . our time will indeed have to attempt to possess if it does not want to miss the ultimate significance of its trial" (Marion, *Idol and Distance*, 131). Christ, he says, "manifests the irreducible anteriority of the Father, in his withdrawal" (Marion, *Idol and Distance*, 129). This "withdrawal" marks the entirety of Christian praxis. For example, "nothing indicates better the paternal provenance of Scripture than the withdrawal of its speaker, who disengages himself from it in order to leave it, hard and naked, amidst the words of men, as a silent, frightening, and derisory injunction . . . it is paternal discourse because the author detaches himself from it, and retires, in order to disappear—or rather to appear—in the figure of the Father. . . . Paternal through withdrawal, it becomes holy for us. . . . To be sure, He loves, the poet continues, that we respect the letter. But one must understand: the Father loves that we respect the letter only as a consequence of what the letter reveals—that the Father loves in and through his withdrawal. Because the Father loves, he entrusts to us the letter, in which he abandons himself" (Marion, *Idol and Distance*, 129–30). On the Eucharist, Marion says, "In the bread and wine, the Eucharist delivers to us a sacramental and therefore absolutely real presence only with the goal of a path and a journey. Bread and wine are blessed for us, because we endure the withdrawal of the Father, a withdrawal that puts us on the path of awaiting the return of the Son, in us. On this path, they become viatic for us: food for those who remain, and hence attempt to 'dwell' in withdrawal, respectfully—what we will henceforth call traversing distance" (Marion, *Idol and Distance*, 131). Of theology generally: "Can this God, whose withdrawal manifests his paternal figure, offer himself within an immediacy . . . through which he could become the object of a discourse, without being dissolved as the God of withdrawal? . . . To honor him with our silence, we must keep silent before God but not silence him. . . . The discourse should speak, without unsuitable predication, in order to express only the recognition of distance. Only the poet manages this, or rather the man who 'poetically dwells' in distance" (Marion, *Idol and Distance*, 132–33). Marion follows Dionysius as he thinks of divine names as hymns: "Thus above all, the speech rendered to God sings, that is, it *praises*. The divine names, which are lacking for any categorical statement, are valid only when taken up within a discourse of praise" (Marion, *Idol and Distance*, 133).

God has long since been seen as a transcendent gaze. Marius Victorinus says that in some way, God is seated at the center of all things (*ton panton onton*), and from there, "with his universal eye, that is, by the light of his substance" he sees the "radii of existents under an immutable aspect because he is repose, and from the center there is one sole look directed simultaneously upon all things. This is God."[131] Gregory of Nyssa finds "all-seeing one" in the etymology of the word "God." The Godhead, θεότης, includes the idea of "beholding" (from θέα).[132] God (θεός) is then the beholder (θεότης), and beholding is an act that belongs not to one of the divine persons but all three. If the Father's invisible counter-gaze is an inseparable part *of* the Son's, then the divine gaze is one with subsistent persons. We evade the problematic of how three gazes in turn also constitute one divine "seeing" because the seeing is by nature triune. Thus for Victorinus, the "reciprocal look" between the Father and Son "subsists" in a singular and perfect way, with "eyes everywhere, as faces . . . regarding each other."[133]

The Son is the mystic *par excellence*, insofar as the mystic experience participates in his eternal gaze upon the present/absent Father. What the "mystic" sensibility apprehends is the aesthetic measure of paradox that unveils the holy. Mystics know the intimate love of the bridegroom who is yet to arrive, yearn for the knowledge of God in the cloud of unknowing, and seek the uncreated light in the dark night of the soul. John of the Cross asks, "Why, if it is a divine light . . . does one call it a dark night?"[134] He gives two reasons why the divine wisdom is not only night and darkness for the soul, but also affliction and torment: first, because of the impurity of the soul; second, because of the height and excess of divine wisdom.[135] The more one looks into the sun, the more his or her faculty of sight is darkened and overwhelmed in its weakness. For him, such infused contemplation is

---

131. Victorinus, *Against Arius* IV, 289.

132. Gregory of Nyssa, *Not Three Gods*, 333.

133. Victorinus, *Against Arius* IB, 183. Scholarship generally credits Augustine with the creation of "subsistent relations," but one can clearly see it in Victorinus: the persons of the Trinity have "their own subsistence according to action in respect to divine relation" (all consubstantial, *homoousioi*). Victorinus, *Against Arius* IA, 111. Séjourné says the concept of subsistent relations is a creation of Victorinus; Hadot disagrees, showing its appearance in his opponent Candidus's writing (who may or may not be Victorinus incognito). See Victorinus, *Against Arius* 1A, 111.n.162. J. N. D. Kelly describes subsistent relations as Augustine's "own positive theory" (Kelly, *Early Christian Doctrines*, 274).

134. John of the Cross, *Dark Night*, 4.

135. John of the Cross, *Dark Night*, 4.

concerned with Dionysius's "ray of darkness," which is an enduring theme of "mystical theology."[136] This ray is recognizable by the way in which it is formless. The white light of holiness plays in the anterior of presence and absence, excess and poverty. Darkness accompanies the light because its vibrancy exceeds understanding and yet arrives with the kind of indeterminacy that can only come from the holy. This indeterminacy is not simply the non-presence of light travelling at too high a frequency, (in which case it becomes entirely unrecognizable). Rather it is the signature of an originary paradox that comes at once as light and darkness, over-saturation and withdrawal, but is exactly neither.[137]

The Apostle Paul felt this tension. He writes to Timothy of him "who is the blessed and only Sovereign, the King *of* kings and Lord *of* lords. It is he alone who has immortality [ἀθανασίαν] and dwells in unapproachable light [φῶς οἰκῶν ἀπρόσιτον], whom no one has ever seen or can see" (1 Tim 6:15-16).[138] The anonymous author of *The Cloud of Unknowing* says that when one seeks the divine light, "thou findest but a darkness; and as it were a cloud of unknowing."[139] This cloud of darkness hovers between "thee and thy God." It is not any cloud, or darkness as such, that romances the mystic, but *this* darkness, God. For, "thou mayest neither see Him clearly by light of understanding in thy reason, nor feel Him in sweetness of love in thine affection," but one should nevertheless "bide in this darkness as long as thou mayest, evermore crying after Him that thou lovest. For if ever thou shalt feel Him or see Him, as it may be here, it behoveth always to be in this cloud in this darkness."[140] Richard of St. Victor says that the divine light pours out upon the world, "at one time to pour the ray of its light on the eyes of the mind, and at another time to hide itself by withdrawing. . . . At one time it lifts it to a high place and at another time presses it down to a low place and

---

136. John of the Cross, *Dark Night*, 4.

137. St. John speaks of the presence/absence dynamic of the light: "In striking the soul with its divine light, it surpasses the natural light and thereby darkens and deprives individuals of all the natural affections and apprehensions they perceive by means of their natural light. It leaves their spiritual and natural faculties not only in darkness, but in emptiness too. Leaving the soul thus empty and dark, the ray purges and illuminates it with divine spiritual light, while the soul thinks it has no light and that it is in darkness, as illustrated in the case of the ray of sunlight that is invisible even in the middle of the room if the room is pure and void of any object of which the light may reflect" (John of the Cross, *Dark Night*, 7).

138. Emphasis mine.

139. *Cloud of Unknowing*, 53.

140. *Cloud of Unknowing*, 53-54.

abandons it to itself. But it returns again unexpectedly, and when it was not hoped for, it appears and shows itself merry."[141] The Catholic theologian and spiritualist Pierre Teilhard de Chardin speaks of the presence/absence dynamic in terms of the *"inner tension"* and *"deep brilliance"* of the divine milieu: "Nothing is more consistent or more fleeting—more fused with things or at the same time more separable from them—than a ray of light. If the divine milieu reveals itself to us as an incandescence of the inward layers of being, who is to guarantee us the persistence of this vision? None other than the ray of light itself."[142]

As Richard and Chardin describe, God eludes our powers. When we are overcome by a sense of his glory, and when we cry out in loneliness, he is the one saturating the withdrawal. This can take the form of either his being totally immanent in the isolation or, inversely, "beyond" even in the fullness of his glory. The condition of "darkness" is due partly to sin and finitude as such. But primarily, darkness goes along with that sacred and entirely inscrutable brilliance. Moreover, the mystic's inability to comprehend this brilliance is not due to his or her finitude, but because Life himself, intelligible in truth, goodness, and beauty, is "contemplative." The mystic is crossed by the Father's gaze as is the Son, and both return reverence to the ever-elusive though singular holy.

Desiring that Israel would "learn to fear me," the Lord told Moses to assemble the people at the foot of Mount Sinai (Deut 4:10; cf. Exod 19:9). The mountain was blazing "up to the very heavens" and was "shrouded in dark clouds." When the Lord spoke out of the fire, the people "heard the sound of words but saw no form [ותמונה]; there was only a voice" (Deut 4:12). This formless appearance of God is the rationale of laws against

---

141. Richard of St. Victor, *Mystical Ark*, 192. For an in-depth treatment of Richard's theology see, Coulter, *Per Visibilia ad Invisibilia*. Though Richard's theology of light is quite different than Dionysius's, he nevertheless evinces the phenomenon in question, namely the dual aspect of light as in one sense absent and in another present.

142. Chardin, *Divine Milieu*, 130–31. He says, "Like those translucent materials which a light within them can illuminate as a whole, the world appears to the Christian mystic bathed in an inward light which intensifies its relief, its structure and its depth. This light is not the superficial glimmer which can be realised in coarse enjoyment. Nor is it the violent flash which destroys objects and blinds our eyes. It is the calm and powerful radiance engendered by the synthesis of all elements of the world in Jesus. The more fulfilled, according to their nature, are the beings in whom it comes to play, the closer and more sensible this radiance appears. . . . No power in the world can prevent us from savouring its joys because it happens at a level deeper than any power; and no power in the world—for the same reason—can compel it to appear."

idolatry: "Since you saw no form when the Lord spoke to you at Horeb out of the fire, take care and watch yourselves closely, so that you do not act corruptly by making an idol for yourselves, in the form [תמונה] of any figure" (Deut 4:15–16). However, one of the ten occurrences of this word "form" suggests that Moses had seen it, for the Lord said, "With him I speak face to face—clearly, not in riddles; and he beholds the form [ותמנת] of the Lord" (Num 12:8). But Moses beheld only a kind of formless form. "Show me your glory," asked Moses, and the Lord said he would make all his goodness pass before Moses, and he would proclaim his name "the Lord"; but, he said, "you cannot see my face; for no one shall see me and live" (Exod 33:18–20). The Lord continued to say that he would cover Moses with his hand until he passed by, and then after he removed his hand, he would only reveal his back (Exod 33:21–23). Israel remembers the formlessness not as a lack of form, but as proper to the very form or face of God.

These mystic tropes—including mountains, fire, and clouds—are the aesthetic features that, through choice arraignment, unveil the holy. Why else summon the fire, the clouds, and the darkness if only to say the Lord is not in them? Elijah encountered God in a similar vision. Standing upon a mountain, the Lord passed by and a great wind rent the mountains, breaking the rocks to pieces, followed by an earthquake and fire (1 Kgs 19:11–12). However, the Lord was not in the wind, the earthquake, or the fire. Elijah heard a still small voice, and upon hearing it, he wrapped his face in his mantle and sought the voice (1 Kgs 19:12–13).

Even after the incarnation in which God revealed his form, the exact imprint of his nature, the mystic paradox still prevails. In John's vision, the heavenly creatures likewise cover their faces in the presence of the Invisible Father and cry "Holy, holy, holy," and the intelligible Lamb remains between the creatures and the one upon the throne (Rev 4:1–5:5). Like the prophets before him, John sees God suffused in grandeur, including a raised throne, torches of fire, storm clouds with thunder and lightening, and a sea like crystal reflecting a spectacular and multicoloured light. But as we know by now, God is not "in" the fire, the clouds, or the sea. Again, a lone voice emerges amidst the grandeur. Who speaks? The unseen One whose name is Holy, who is enthroned above every name, creature, or power.

The Father remains a mystery *after* the full revelation of God's image in Christ, and this precise mystery orchestrates the cosmos. The various beings live, and move, and have their being in direct proportion to the invisible one. The eschatological harmony of God's kingdom obeys the holy, first and foremost. The artistic creations of this heavenly, cosmic temple are not incidental, for their beauty, truth, and goodness are genuine revelations of the invisible holy, and thus a means or medium of praise and delight, but as such these creations are what they are in virtue of their explicit, transparent, reverence to the Father.

This originary mystery further accounts for the unique holiness of Mary, Mother of God (θεοτόκος). She is revered as preeminently holy because of her exemplary faith, and because she is the temple of the Holy Spirit, the sanctuary in which the Word became flesh.[143] But in light of the inscrutable nature of the Father, Mary receives an unrepeatable formal quality that forever distinguishes her as *Panagia*, All-Holy, or Mother of All-Holiness. She bears the only-begotten Son of the Invisible Father. Through the gift of Christ, Mary is structurally established to encounter the holy in a more efficacious and paradigmatic way than any other member of the church.

Mary was told she would bear the Son of the "Most High" (Ὑψίστου), who "will be holy" (Luke 1:35). The recurring biblical commands to take care of the word of the Lord, heed it, abide with and even love it, receive new levels of profundity in Mary, who weaned the infant Christ, the Word of the Lord. She knows the presence of God, and what is more, she gives birth to the presence of God in the world, flesh of her flesh. As a response of gratitude, Mary prays to God and says, "holy is his name . . . his mercy is for those who fear him" (Luke 1:49–50). While Mary knows the intimacy of God through the love of his Son, his image, she is also acquainted with God's absence. Mary rears her son alone, without the immediate presence of his father. The excess of paternity leaves Christ fatherless. He is suspended between Joseph, the non-father who raised him, and the heavenly Father who remains unseen. There is no greater symbol of divine intimacy and presence than the Son of God growing in a woman's womb, so when that

---

143. The *Lumen Gentium* of the Second Vatican Council distinguishes Mary with reverence: "Joined to Christ the Head and in the unity of fellowship with all His saints, the faithful must in the first place reverence the memory 'of the glorious ever Virgin Mary, Mother of our God and Lord Jesus Christ'" (Second Vatican Council, *Lumen Gentium*, 8.1.52). As "the beloved daughter of the Father and the temple of the Holy Spirit . . . [and because] of this gift of sublime grace she far surpasses all creatures, both in heaven and on earth . . . she is hailed as a pre-eminent and singular member of the Church, and as its type and excellent exemplar in faith and charity. The Catholic Church, taught by the Holy Spirit, honors her with filial affection and piety as a most beloved mother" (Second Vatican Council, *Lumen Gentium*, 8.1.53).

symbol also carries with it the mysteriously withdrawn Father, we have to consider his absence as paradoxically tied to his presence.

Because the terms presence and absence follow an anterior mystery, neither are comprehensive. Jesus exhibits precisely this dynamic. In both Joseph and his Father, presence and absence collide in inverted but complimentary ways. While the Father is unseen, and thus in a sense absent, he nevertheless makes his presence known. He visits the Son with the Holy Spirit and pronounces: "a voice from heaven said, 'This is my beloved son with whom I am well pleased'" (Matt 3:17).[144] And by willing that Mary and Joseph care for their son, the Father shows his love and mercy through them, as those who have his "favour." Though Joseph is physically present throughout Christ's childhood, he has no natural paternity. The "absent" Father bears certain marks of presence, and thus these marks of presence qualify his withdrawal as not-truly-absent. The "present" Joseph bears certain, fundamental, marks of filial absence as not-truly-present. Thus, the terms presence and absence are each inaccurate and hyper-accurate, which is signalled by Christ's family relations.[145]

Through Mary's unique maternal form, she interrupts or dislodges any absolute claim of the natural family (through the Invisible Father), and knows her natural family as a gift and creation of God (namely through the miraculous Christ-child) that is structurally bound as family only through the transcendent God. Mary mediates a sacramental grafting into the body and family of Christ through the Spirit. She also mediates God's family ties to the entire world, and thus she is the Patron Saint of all humanity.[146]

---

144. Translation altered.

145. In this way, Dionysius's formula for divine names resurfaces in paternity. Names, such as good and true, are paradoxically "false" (as an *oxymoron*, because the super-essential essence of God is "beyond" such names) and supra-accurate (as a *hyperbole*, for God's essence is true beyond truth, good beyond good, actual in a more transcendent way).

146. "The Church indeed, contemplating her hidden sanctity, imitating her charity and faithfully fulfilling the Father's will, by receiving the word of God in faith becomes herself a mother" (Second Vatican Council, *Lumen Gentium*, 8.3.64). She is the model and exemplar of holiness: "the followers of Christ still strive to increase in holiness by conquering sin. And so they turn their eyes to Mary who shines forth to the whole community of the elect as the model of virtues. Piously meditating on her and contemplating her in the light of the Word made man, the Church with reverence enters more intimately into the great mystery of the Incarnation and becomes more and more like her Spouse" (Second Vatican Council, *Lumen Gentium*, 8.3.65).

Mary's unique place in salvation history is remarkable, but for our purposes, it is important to recognize that the holy is the transcendental *of* the transcendentals, which eclipses all in its originary paradox. Understanding the holy in this way contours eternal paternity and filiation as such, and reveals Mary's formal relation to the Invisible Father to be of incomparable stature. Because she is so situated, by pure gift, Mary has the most profound opportunity to revere, and as our principle dictates—those who "keep holy" the things that are holy shall themselves become holy— Mary becomes the most holy creature by the unsurpassable degree of her reverence. Thomas Aquinas says that if *dulia* is the veneration accorded to angels and saints, Mary is *hyperdulia*.[147]

God the Father reveals through Mary why he has always had an affinity for orphans and widows, for a "father to the fatherless, a defender of widows, is God in his holy dwelling" (Ps 68:5; cf. 146:9; Job 29:12, NIV). Because Mary is the preeminent form of the church, true religion "that is pure and undefiled before God, the Father, is this: to care for orphans and widows in their distress" (Jas 1:27). Moreover, in the same way that Jesus said one must be blind in order to see (John 9:41), give away everything to become rich (Matt 19:21; cf. 13:44), and die in order to live (Matt 10:39), one must in a sense become fatherless in order to be adopted as an orphan by the Father into the household of Mary. Paul says, God reconciled the world "so that we might receive adoption as children. And because you are children, God has sent the Spirit of his Son into our hearts, crying, 'Abba! Father!'" (Gal 4:5–7; cf. Eph 1:5; 1 John 3:2).

CONCLUSION

The *mysterium tremendum* of the holy—with its accompanying play between intimacy and withdrawal, attraction and dread—contours not only creaturely existence but Life as such. Reverence constitutes the formal structure of the triune being, which knows itself only through the Ipseity of the Son, who is made holy by returning all holiness to the Father, the only one who "is" Holy. The Trinitarian theology of Marius Victorinus explicates the ineffable Father as hidden being in repose, and the eternal Son as the

---

147. "Consequently the worship of 'latria' is not due to any mere rational creature for its own sake. Since, therefore, the Blessed Virgin is a mere rational creature, the worship of 'latria' is not due to her, but only that of 'dulia': but in a higher degree than to other creatures, inasmuch as she is the Mother" (Aquinas, *ST* III.25.5.co).

manifestation, being (*On*), and determination of the pre-existent (*Proon*) Father. Victorinus uses the same concepts of excess and absence for the Father that were established in chapter 1 for the holy, namely that the holy ontologically contains and phenomenologically eclipses all. Likewise for Victorinus, the Father is of such a hidden nature as to "seem not to exist." This apparent or phenomenological absence is also disclosed in the life and form of the Son. Based on the eternal invisibility of the Father, Mary deserves preeminent veneration among creatures (as the *hyperdulia*), as one who is hypostatically related to the Invisible Father, and thereby becomes the foremost symbol of creaturely reverence.

3

The Holy's Spirit

"[T]he Father, when he kisses the Son, pours into him the plenitude of the mysteries of his divine being, breathing forth love's deep delight."[1]

—BERNARD OF CLAIRVAUX, *SONG OF SONGS*

"Let him kiss me with the kisses of his mouth!"

—SONG OF SONGS 1:2

INTRODUCTION

THE PREVIOUS CHAPTERS HAVE intentionally remained quiet on the the Spirit of God. In part, this is simply due to the necessity of covering other important issues, such as the proper form of the *Logos* as reverence. However, this silence is also meant to allow the void of the Spirit to make itself felt so that we gain a more tacit feeling for what the Spirit "adds." As John Milbank has correctly argued, we lack the rationale for the *necessity* of the Spirit's hypostasis. This chapter proposes such a rationale, and

---

1. Bernard of Clairvaux, *Song of Songs*, 8.6.

shows how the holy is integral to the Trinitarian subsistence of the Spirit. It also responds to the question, if the Spirit is a "second difference" in the Godhead, then in what way is he "holy." Additionally, this chapter shows how the Spirit, in this understanding, further explicates the nature of the transcendentals, encompasses the entire cosmos as a sanctuary, and renders touch through flesh as our only means of becoming holy.

THE CONSECRATOR

Thus far, the discussion of being has been quite abstract. A certain reading of Victorinus and Aquinas could give the impression that reality is grounded upon "substance," the terrain of which metaphysics investigates. This abstraction is akin to the way we recognize the laws of physics. We can consider how the starry hosts adhere to and thus disclose principles of astrophysics, or how music can be further understood and thus more sublimely rendered through mathematical concepts. Similarly it is easy to forget the reality from which "substance" is discerned.

For, *what* God is is Spirit. Substance is an intellectually discernible aspect of Spirit. Substance—or "being"—is an aspect of Spirit that lives. Victorinus says "if you wish to know what is God, the term Spirit designates his 'to be,'"[2] and the "substance of God is light, spirit, God."[3] He thus decenters the concept of substance. Speaking of the Father and Son, Victorinus says, "subsistence is more properly said of these two than substance, since that which is original 'to be' with a form is called subsistence. But this is also called substance. And that is why it was said: 'From one substance there are three subsistences,' so that that itself which is 'to be' subsists in a triple manner."[4] Christ himself says to the Samaritan woman at the well, "true worshipers will worship the Father in spirit and truth, for the Father seeks such as these to worship him. *God is spirit*, and those who worship him must worship in spirit and truth" (John 4:23–24).[5] Perhaps the most explicit

---

2. Victorinus, *Against Arius* IB, 181.
3. Victorinus, *On the Necessity*, 307.
4. Victorinus, *Against Arius* II, 205.
5. Emphasis mine. Basil of Caesarea says, "Who on hearing the titles of the Spirit is not lifted up in soul, who does not raise his conception to the supreme nature? It is called 'Spirit of God,' 'Spirit of truth which proceeds from the Father,' 'right Spirit,' 'a leading Spirit.'; Its proper and peculiar title is 'Holy Spirit'; which is a name specially appropriate to everything that is incorporeal, purely immaterial, and indivisible. So our Lord, when teaching the woman who thought God to be an object of local worship that the

argument for this point comes from the Apostle Paul: "Now the Lord is the Spirit, and where the Spirit of the Lord is, there is freedom. And all of us, with unveiled faces, seeing the glory of the Lord as though reflected in a mirror, are being transformed into the same image from one degree of glory to another; for this comes from the Lord, the Spirit" (2 Cor 3:17–18).

Thus, insofar as metaphysics investigates the principles of being, it will inevitably find itself tracking the elusive though intimate Spirit God, whose comings and goings are like the wind (cf. John 3:8). "Being" in the broadest sense means "the being *of* Spirit." This simple assertion clarifies the distinction between that brand of rationalist metaphysics—along with its postmodern critique—and a genuinely Christian *scientia*. The "bottom" of reality (so to speak) is not a neutral substance upon which God lives and creates, but as unrivalled, boundless spirit, it is *the* Spirit.[6]

If God is Spirit, which includes Father and Son, why is *the* Spirit hypostasized into another subsistence or person of his own? John Milbank was quite right when he said there is a gulf between the confident proclamation of the Spirit as a Trinitarian person, and the lack of *rationale* for this separation.[7] If the Spirit is understood as "applying" the benefits of Christ, then he is in danger of being reduced to the power of Christ's person.[8] The immanent Trinity is no less problematic. The necessity of God's self-reflection

---

incorporeal is incomprehensible, said 'God is a spirit.' On our hearing, then, of a spirit, it is impossible to form the idea of a nature circumscribed" (Basil, *On the Spirit*, 9.22).

6. David Bentley Hart says of the impact of Trinitarian dogma on the concept of substance, "Of course, to talk of difference in terms of the Trinity must necessarily inspire distrust: Is this not just another metaphysics of the one and the many, an attempt to subdue difference by 'grounding' it in a transcendent substance or ideal structure of differentiation as such? But this is a somewhat tedious—if perhaps inevitable—question, and one moreover that altogether misses what is genuinely of interest in the matter. Theologically there is no value in speculation about ideal or metaphysical *causes* of difference, ontic or ontological; the triune *perichoresis* of God is not a *substance* in which difference is grounded in its principles or in which it achieves the unity of a higher synthesis, even if God is the fullness and actuality of all that is; rather, the truly unexpected implication of trinitarian dogma is that Christian thought has no metaphysics of the one and the many, the same and the different, because that is a polarity that has no place in the Christian narrative. . . . Created difference 'corresponds' to God, is analogous to the divine life, precisely in differing from God; this is the Christian thought of divine transcendence, of a God who is made inconceivably near in—whose glory is ubiquitously proclaimed by—creation's infinity of difference from God, its free, departing, serial excess of otherness" (Hart, *Infinite*, 180).

7. Milbank, *Made Strange*, 172.

8. Milbank uses "she" for the Holy Spirit here.

in the Father and Son may be understandable, namely a reflection in difference and relation, but what of a "second difference"?[9] This still "smacks of the arbitrary, the incantatory."[10] It is extremely fortuitous for our purposes that at the crux of the resolution, he appropriates Marius Victorinus, who is otherwise scarcely employed throughout Milbank's corpus. He says that Victorinus provides the most compelling rationale for why the hypostasis of the Spirit is essential: "Still more emphatically than Basil, Marius Victorinus with his *esse–vivere–intellegere* model for the Trinity, proposed a connection of the Spirit with the perfect emergence of the understanding . . . Victorinus posits a single substantial manifestation of active life which becomes 'form' in the Son but is not thereby exhausted. Understanding *presupposes* form, yet form is only completed through understanding."[11] Thus for Milbank, the Spirit is demonstrably necessary because of his defining role as understanding, without which neither Father nor Son would be comprehensible even to themselves.

Moreover, Victorinus offers an even more definitive rationale for the Spirit's personality. To discover the "necessity" of the Spirit as a hypostasis, we must retrieve Victorinus's understanding of the Father as the Unbegotten in repose, the *Proon* (Preexistence) withdrawn *in* his form, the *Logos*. Chapter 2 showed how this account of the Father radicalizes the theological dictum that the Father is known in the Son. The Father is entirely indeterminate and thus inconceivable apart from the Son. The Father is not a locatable counter-gaze upon which the Son may set his own gaze. Rather, I argued that the Son's gaze is "crossed" all the way along. He sees the Father's invisible gaze in his own, or rather as his own. In other words, the Son

---

9. Milbank, *Made Strange*, 172.

10. Milbank, *Made Strange*, 172.

11. Milbank, *Made Strange*, 187. "Thus Victorinus secures a dynamism in the Trinity which is not based on the 'fontal plentitude' of the Father. Precisely *because* the Spirit is adequately established as a separate *hypostasis* it is also *regressio* in the sense that it renews fundamental being which characterizes the Father. Somehow, because the divine *actus* is *infinite*, and therefore 'interminably terminated' it comprises a non-temporal dynamic or mutual 'play' between an infinite 'conclusion' of expression in the Son, and an endless 're-opening' of that conclusion by the desire of the Spirit which re-inspires the paternal *arche*. What may be recovered from both Basil and Victorinus is the idea of a receptive comprehension or judgement constituted through the comprehended image, yet 'retroactively causal' for the form of that image itself" (Milbank, *Made Strange*, 187). Victorinus says, "Christ is life, but 'to live' is the *Logos*, and if life itself is 'to be,' and 'to be' is the Father, if again, life itself is 'to understand,' and this is the Holy Spirit, all these are three, in each one are the three, and the three are one and absolutely *homoousia* (consubstantial)" (Victorinus, *Against Arius* IB, 192).

encounters the Father's gaze not in any one place, but in his "being seen" by the Father. Thus, the Son's every intuition and insight of the Father is a vision of himself. Insofar as the Father is determined, he is already logized, which itself gives occasion for reverence towards the Invisible Holy.

If the Father is indeterminate without the Son, he is irretrievably absent without the Spirit. We are left with the problem of the Spirit's hypostasis when we neglect the invisibility of the Father and assume he is fully intelligible and present independent of the other two Trinitarian persons. With Victorinus, the Father is *Proon* (The Preexistent), "the unknown and incomprehensible . . . a sort of form without form,"[12] who is "'to repose' itself" (*requiescere*).[13] Therefore, every indication of his presence, every moment of communion, and indeed every movement of the Father, is already the presence, communion, and movement of some *other* that must have been "sent" from the very depths of the Father himself. This insight also already recognizes the determining role of the *Logos*, who discloses the Father as repose. The shift here is that we can no longer assume that the Father is present, but must begin with his inscrutability, after which we can then fully recognize that every encounter with him is by *necessity* an encounter with that which is strictly speaking not the Father, namely the Spirit.

Additionally, we can also see that this present "other" *of* the Father requires personality or hypostasis. If this other was not personal, then it would merely be an inanimate form of correspondence that would only make the distance between the Father and Son tragic. Rather, the Father can be present *only* by the Spirit that goes forth from himself, which means that if the Father is to be meaningfully engaged in the Trinitarian life, and creation for that matter, then the Spirit must be so entirely *of* the Father or one with the Father (*homoousios*), that his presence is seen as the acceptable form of the Father's presence.

In what way is this third hypostasis holy? We saw with the Son that one is made holy by keeping holy the things that are holy. Thus the Son receives his holiness by revering the Father. As the *Logos*, the Son is the originary form of reverence as such. But before this form is even possible, it must be begotten, which creates the intra-Trinitarian distance that allows the Son to "see" the Father and thus revere him. The Father, however, is wholly reposed. Therefore the idea of begetting as a movement must, from the outset, be considered the act of another hypostasis. Victorinus makes

---

12. Victorinus, *Hymn* III, 332.
13. Victorinus, *Against Arius* IA, 95.

it clear that the Spirit is the movement of the reposed Father. He says the Spirit is "power in movement; for that principle of begetting is movement," and thus "The Holy Spirit is then the first interior movement."[14] The Holy Spirit "both precedes, if he is the Spirit of the Father, and follows, if he has his being from the Son."[15]

The Spirit's original act of distancing coincides with the "setting apart" aspect of consecration. Thus, the Spirit's movement is consecrative in nature. But because the Son is begotten from the Father through the Spirit, one might have the impression that the Spirit begins with the Father and then consecrates the Son as the most holy. To repeat, the Father is unintelligible apart from the *Logos*. The begetting of the Son is synonymous with the awakening of reverence to the Father. Therefore, the first consecrative act is from the Son to the Father which *is* the Father begetting the Son. This act of consecration is the Spirit, the Consecrator. But because the Spirit is movement as such, he is not simply a being that consecrates, but transcendent conservation in which every other instantiation participates. The Son can only "set apart" the Father by the Spirit who himself *is* setting-apart, and already comes from the Father.

We distinguish here the difference between the Son as the form of reverence and the Spirit as the consecrator. The Son is the *Logos* that makes the richness of reverence intelligible, while the Spirit is the movement of the Father that actively opens the distance at which reverence can "see." While distinguishable, the Spirit and Son are of one nature, and thus the Son is the form of the Spirit's act, and the Spirit is the act of the Son's form. The Spirit is *of* the Father, or we might say is the Holy's Spirit. Therefore, he is made holy by "setting apart" the Father. Gregory of Nyssa says "the Holy Spirit is, to begin with, because of qualities that are essentially holy, that which the Father, essentially Holy, is; and such as the Only-begotten is, such is the Holy Spirit."[16] Thus, the Father is to the Spirit, along with the Son, the Holy *of* holies (*sanctum sanctorum*).

---

14. Victorinus, *Against Arius* IB, 184–85. Thomas Weinandy makes a similar argument: "The Holy Spirit goes forth from the Father as the one in whom the Father begets the Son. Thus the Spirit proceeds from the Father of the Son because it is in the Spirit that the Father, by begetting the Son in the Spirit, also constitutes himself as the Father of the Son. The procession of the Spirit, then, does not just presuppose the begetting of the Son, but is also simultaneous with and constitutive of the begetting of the Son" (Weinandy, *Father's Spirit*, 90–91).

15. Victorinus, *Against Arius* IA, 111.

16. Gregory of Nyssa, *On the Holy Spirit*, 323.

The Son is *Life*, and because the Spirit begets the Son through the consecration of the Father, we can say at a fundamental level that if the Son *is* Life, "the Spirit *gives* life" (2 Cor 3:6; cf. John 6:63; 3:16).[17] As we saw, Life is formally oriented by reverence, and the Spirit gives this reverence. He gives birth to life, he activates or vivifies that life, and he fulfills life. The Spirit is always "arriving" from the Father *in* our reverence back to the Father. Thus Life is fulfilled as it *receives* excess and grace in the form of its creative *reaching* towards the Father.[18]

If the Spirit is the only access to the Father's depth, then the truth that emerges from the Father in the Son is by nature revelation. The Spirit who searches the depths of God goes forth from the Father to give testimony to the Son. But this testimony is only given through that creative plunging of the Son into the Father. Basil says, "The revelation of mysteries is indeed the peculiar function of the Spirit."[19] In light of the Father and Son, the access to and presence of the Father's depth is paradoxically a *plunging* of the *Logos* that is simultaneously the Spirit's *revealing*. This paradox is rooted in the begetting of the Son, for the Son is begotten by the Spirit which *is* the awakening of reverence to the Father. When I say "begotten by the Spirit," I do not mean to fundamentally change the classical understanding that the Father is the one who begets. Rather, because of the uniquely reposed and inscrutable nature of the Father, the very *means* by which he acts and reveals *is* the hypostasized "other" of his own Spirit. Though, the Spirit only really comes into his own and completes the triune life subsequent to the Son's begetting.

While the Son is the form of knowledge, that form is begotten, vivified, and returned to the holy, and thus the act of knowing (*intellegere*) is the Spirit. Moreover, the dual aspects of the Spirit's revealing and the Son's plunging is the Trinitarian basis for the relationship between revelation (faith) and reason. To be sure, the Trinity is intelligible according to

---

17. Emphasis mine.

18. Basil says, "As the art in him who has acquired it, so is the grace of the Spirit in the recipient ever present, though not continuously in operation. For as the art is potentially in the artist, but only in operation when he is working in accordance with it, so also the Spirit is ever present with those that are worthy, but works, as need requires, in prophecies, or in healings, or in some other actual carrying into effect of His potential action" (Basil, *On the Spirit*, 26.61). Moreover, speaking of heavenly powers Basil says, "But their sanctification, being external to their substance, superinduces their perfection through the communion of the Spirit."

19. Basil, *On the Spirit*, 16.38.

a definite *Logos*, which affirms reason and the philosophical task. But that *Logos* is born out of and only fulfilled by its returning to the inscrutable holy revealed by the Spirit, which means that reason is by nature reverential to the holy. Gregory of Nyssa says "every intellectual nature is governed by the ordering of the Holy Spirit."[20]

Because the Spirit's activity is so all-encompassing, Basil says he is like a *place*.[21] We live, and move, and have our being in this "place." Victorinus says of the Spirit, "It is itself for itself both the place and the inhabitant, dwelling within itself, alone in the alone, existing everywhere and nowhere."[22] The Spirit is not a neutral, void place, but that which is variously rendered though singularly focused, namely a place of consecration. In other words, the Spirit is a sanctuary. But keeping with the paradox above, there is no sanctuary without the creative forms of reverence. When Moses instructed Israel to build the tabernacle, he said, "you shall make holy garments for Aaron your brother, for glory and for beauty. You shall speak to all the skillful, whom I have filled with a spirit of skill, that they make Aaron's garments to consecrate him for my priesthood" (Exod 28:2–3, ESV). The sanctuary is *constructed* under the prompting of the Spirit and fulfilled by the subsequent indwelling of the Spirit, or his "arrival," as the created forms are activated (which echoes the Trinitarian dynamic).

The extent of the Spirit's sanctuary is not confined to the temple walls. Rather the cosmos as a whole is intended to be rendered a sanctuary. The Edenic atmosphere of the tabernacle helped Israel to interpret the world itself as God's tabernacle. When the Spirit overshadowed Mary, the eternal

---

20. Gregory of Nyssa, *On the Holy Trinity*, 329. Regarding this argument, Gregory asks, "If the gift of the Holy Spirit is principally a grace of the soul, and the constitution of the soul is linked by its intellectuality and invisibility to the angelic life, what person who knows how to see a consequence would not agree. . . . For since it is said 'the angels do always behold the Face of My Father which is in heaven,' and it is not possible to behold the person of the Father otherwise than by fixing the sight upon it through His image; and the image of the person of the Father is the Only-begotten, and to Him again no man can draw near whose mind has not been illuminated by the Holy Spirit."

21. Basil says, "It is an extraordinary statement, but it is none the less true, that the Spirit is frequently spoken of as the *place* of them that are being sanctified. . . . This is the special and peculiar place of true worship. . . . Now what is a spiritual burnt offering? 'The sacrifice of praise.' And in what place do we offer it? In the Holy Spirit" (Basil, *On the Spirit*, 26.62). Also, "when we think of the grace that flows from Him operating on those who participate in it, we say that the Spirit is *in* us. And the doxology which we offer 'in the Spirit' . . . we shew that we are not sufficient to glorify Him ourselves, but our sufficiency is in the Holy Spirit" (Basil, *On the Spirit*, 26.63).

22. Victorinus, *Against Arius* IB, 172.

Son of the Father became flesh and tabernacled among us (John 1:14; cf. Matt 1:18; Luke 1:35). This Christ was raised to resurrected life and is now the *Arche* of a new creation, which finds its fulfillment in the eschatological new heaven and earth that is the true temple and *thus* the true cosmos (Rev 21). God is bringing the world to this determined end through Christ's body, the church, in which the Holy Spirit dwells. The Apostle Paul says, "Do you not know that you are God's temple and that God's Spirit dwells in you? . . . For God's temple is holy, and you are that temple" (1 Cor 3:16–17, ESV). In Ephesians, Paul says that those who were "far off" have been brought near, for through Christ we all "have access in one Spirit to the Father" (Eph 2:17–18). So then, "you are no longer strangers and aliens, but you are fellow citizens with the saints and members of the household of God, built on the foundation of the apostles and prophets, Christ Jesus himself being the cornerstone, in whom the whole structure, being joined together grows into a holy temple in the Lord," moreover, "In him you also are being built together into a dwelling place for God by the Spirit" (vs. 19–22, ESV).[23] Here we see that the many roles of the Spirit collide. Giving life to the forms of reverence establishes sanctuary and characterizes the Spirit's work in creation, reconciliation, and sanctification.[24] All these works are of a kind.[25]

---

23. Paul says, "For we are the temple of the living God. . . . Since we have these promises, beloved, let us cleanse ourselves from every defilement of body and spirit, bringing holiness to completion in the fear of God" (2 Cor 6:16, 18, ESV).

24. Basil says, "There is no sanctification without the Spirit" (Basil, *On the Spirit*, 16.37).

25. Therefore, the telos of the cosmos, and all therein, is to become a sanctuary. This telos is not limited to the "religious" aspects of life. Rather, we see in the New Testament that all aspects of socio-political life are rethought in light of the holiness of Christ's new temple. Husbands and wives are to love one another, and plunge into the "profound mystery" of marital union for the sake of holiness (Eph 5:22–33). Children ought to obey their parents, while those parents ought to love and nurture their children in the way of the Lord (Eph 6:1–4; cf. Luke 18:15–17). One is to do their work with all their heart as if working for God himself, whatever that work may be (Col 3:23); even masters and slaves are to treat one another well for the sake of God (cf. Eph 6:5–9; 1 Peter 2:18–25). We ought to pray for and submit to the government, which is God's very means of ruling (1 Tim 2:1–2; Rom 13:1). Our relationship to civil law is altered in light of the charity and holiness of God's new temple (1 Cor 6:1–20). Participation in even suspect cultural practices is evaluated according to what "builds up" the temple in which God is at work (1 Cor 10:23–32).

ON THE ONE WHOSE NAME IS DISTANCE

The Spirit's original consecrative act between the Son and the Father, his primordial act of distancing, is also the basis of the five transcendentals. Distance is at the center of all the transcendentals and creates the very possibility of their logic and appearance. This transcendent distance is what allows anything to appear. It is the ontological equivalence to the distance that makes reading the words on a page possible. This distance is not a void or gap across which one sees, but in light of the Trinitarian dynamic, the originary distance is an infinite vista, a superabundant *Spirit* that "is" and "reveals" the infinity of God.[26] In other words, the intra-Trinitarian relations are predicated upon a primordial distance that is realized according to the contours of the transcendentals.

If truth is not imposed arbitrarily, it is nevertheless tied to intellect. Aquinas says that "the truth of things consists in their *relation* to the divine intellect."[27] Truth is the judgement of how near something is to its own essence or nature.[28] This is logically different from the being of something, which establishes *that* a thing is. Truth is concerned with *what* a thing is. Only intellect can so discern *what* a thing is. Aquinas says that while we might think that sight can see perfectly well what something is, only intellect can measure the relationship between what is seen and the intellectually perceived essence that progressively reveals itself through things. This

---

26. On distance, Hart says, "Because the difference between God and creation is not a simple metaphysical distinction between reality and appearance, but the analogical distance between two ways of apprehending the infinite—God being the infinite, creatures embracing it in an endless sequence of finite instances—the soul's ascent to God is not a departure from, but an endless venture into, difference. The distance between God and creation is not alienation . . . but the original ontological act of distance by which every ontic interval subsists, given to be crossed but not overcome, at once God's utter transcendence and utter proximity" (Hart, *Infinite*, 194).

27. Aquinas, *ST* Ia.16.1.co. Emphasis mine. He says, "Truth resides, in its primary aspect, in the intellect," or "the true adds relation to the intellect" (Aquinas, *ST* Ia.16.2.co).

28. Aquinas says, "The being of the thing, not its truth, is the cause of truth in the intellect. Hence the Philosopher says that a thought or a word is true "from the fact that a thing is, not because a thing is true" (Aquinas, *ST* Ia.16.1.ad.3). This includes not only objects, but the truth of even the intellect itself: "Now since everything is true according as it has the form proper to its nature, the intellect, in so far as it is knowing, must be true, so far as it has the likeness of the thing known, this being its form, as knowing" (Aquinas, *ST* Ia.16.2.co).

measurement is truth itself, and therefore, strictly speaking, truth is not "in" things, but in the relation of things to the intellect.[29]

Already with these few comments we can elaborate a number of invaluable insights. Essences are progressively revealed through intellectual work. But because things are not really static, universal items of data, but functioning essences, we discover the nature of something through our putting it to use. Because essences are part of everything, we are always at work creating new essences. Moreover, if we create essences in response to our context, then essences (and truth) are inescapably historical. And because truth is the radiance of harmony and perfection and tells how a thing is in relation to its own essence, we employ a discourse of beauty to comprehend the nature of truth in the first place.[30]

One might suspect that we have not overcome the value-object distinction, because we still differentiate between the being of a thing and its relation to the intellect. The key here is that objects are not merely related to some finite intellect, but are always already intelligible to the infinite God. Aquinas says, "truth is found in the intellect according as it apprehends a thing as it is; and in things according as they have being conformable to an intellect. This is to the greatest degree found in God. For His being is not only conformed to His intellect, but it is the very act of His intellect," and thus "it follows not only that truth is in Him, but that He is truth itself, and the sovereign and first truth."[31]

The Son is the image of the Father and thus the truth. As image, the Son is that which is perfectly realized, and the Father is the invisible essence discovered in the image, if still revealed by the Spirit. Again, the Son is more than *a* truth, but as the image of being as such, the Son's own nature is truth itself. We can see that the logic of truth is predicated upon a prior

---

29. "For although sight has the likeness of a visible thing, yet it does not know the comparison which exists between the thing seen and that which itself apprehends concerning it. But the intellect can know its own conformity with the intelligible thing; yet it does not apprehend it by knowing of a thing 'what a thing is.' When, however, it judges that a thing corresponds to the form which it apprehends about that thing, then first it knows and expresses truth. This it does by composing and dividing" (Aquinas, *ST* Ia.16.2.co).

30. Aquinas says that beauty appears in integrity/perfection, proportion/harmony, and brightness/clarity. Aquinas, *ST* Ia.39.8.co. See also Aquinas, *ST* Ia.5.4.

31. Aquinas, *ST* Ia.16.5.co. "His act of understanding is the measure and cause of every other being and of every other intellect, and He Himself is His own existence and act of understanding."

distance, which establishes that which has being and the intellectual judgement of its truthfulness (i.e., whether it is "true to form").

If being is *what* makes something actual, and truth is the judgement of whether or not that thing is true to form, goodness "presents the aspect of desirableness, which being does not present."[32] Insofar as anything exists at all, it is already in progress towards the perfection of its form. This movement is predicated upon the lure of the good, which is thus an end.[33] But in order for something to take to motion, it must initially have some formal understanding of the perfection it seeks to reach. Therefore, while the good is an end, it is also a formal cause prompting even the first movement.[34]

The Trinity shows the dynamics of the good. Even prior to divine intellection, and wholly outside temporality, the Father begets the Son through the Spirit. The Father so begets because of the formal cause of the good. We cannot say this begetting was yet a "conscious decision" but instead was that basal moving of the will towards what is ineffably understood to be the good, namely the Son. The possibility of such movement requires an inherent understanding of what is desirable. The desirable is only perceptible from a projected *distance*, which prompts the original self-exteriorizing movement.[35]

---

32. Aquinas, *ST* Ia.5.1.co.

33. Aquinas says, "For goodness has the aspect of the end, in which not only actual things find their completion, but also towards which tend even those things which are not actual, but merely potential. Now being implies the habitude of a formal cause only, either inherent or exemplar; and its causality does not extend save to those things which are actual" (Aquinas, *ST* Ia.5.2.ad.2).

34. "Since goodness is that which all things desire, and since this has the aspect of an end, it is clear that goodness implies the aspect of an end. Nevertheless, the idea of goodness presupposes the idea of an efficient cause, and also of a formal cause. For we see that what is first in causing, is last in the thing caused. Fire, e.g., heats first of all before it reproduces the form of fire; though the heat in the fire follows from its substantial form. Now in causing, goodness and the end come first, both of which move the agent to act; secondly, the action of the agent moving to the form; thirdly, comes the form" (Aquinas, *ST* Ia.5.4.co). This is a movement of the appetite: "For everything is good so far as it is desirable, and is a term of the movement of the appetite; the term of whose movement can be seen from a consideration of the movement of a natural body. Now the movement of a natural body is terminated by the end absolutely; and relatively by the means through which it comes to the end" (Aquinas, *ST* Ia.5.6.co).

35. Victorinus says, "The Holy Spirit is then the first interior movement, which is the paternal thought, that is, his Self-knowledge. Indeed, preknowledge precedes knowledge. Therefore through this natural mode of knowledge understanding was externalized" (Victorinus, *Against Arius* IB, 184–85). Also, "This same movement, when it looks to the external—to look to the exterior is to be movement or motion which is precisely

Beauty is that which pleases when seen. The good lures the will or appetite towards what is desirable, and when that desirable thing is "seen," the good causes pleasure, which is known as beauty.[36] David Bentley Hart says, "This presence of distance within the beautiful, as primordially the *effect* of beauty, provides the essential logic of theological aesthetics," namely an aesthetics "that does not interpret all distance as an original absence, or as the distance of differentiation's heterogenous and violent forces, but that sees in distance, and in all the series and intervals that dwell in it, the possibility of peaceful analogies and representations that neither falsify nor constrain the object of regard."[37]

We see that distance is integral to the transcendentals. The Holy's Spirit creates this distance as an act of "setting apart" or consecration. Therefore, all the transcendentals are born out of a more original act of consecration, and all in their own way contribute to the reverence that beholds the singularity of the holy. Truth *perceives* the distance, being *is* the distance, the good *lures* at a distance, beauty *traverses* the distance, the one *demarcates* the distance, and the holy *creates* the distance (through the act of consecration, in the register of reverence).

---

to will to see oneself, to think of and to know oneself; but the one who sees himself exists as double, and there is known the seeing and that which is seen, the one who sees being himself the one seen, because he sees himself, this turning toward the exterior is, therefore, being begotten or being toward the exterior order to know what one is—therefore, if this movement is toward the exterior, it is begotten, and if begotten, this is the Son, the only begotten, because he is alone, he who is total act and total movement, universal and unique" (Victorinus, *Against Arius* III, 223).

36. Aquinas says, "Goodness is praised as beauty. But they differ logically, for goodness properly relates to the appetite (goodness being what all things desire); and therefore it has the aspect of an end (the appetite being a kind of movement towards a thing). On the other hand, beauty relates to the cognitive faculty; for beautiful things are those which please when seen. Hence beauty consists in due proportion; for the senses delight in things duly proportioned, as in what is after their own kind—because even sense is a sort of reason, just as is every cognitive faculty. Now since knowledge is by assimilation, and similarity relates to form, beauty properly belongs to the nature of a formal cause" (Aquinas, *ST* Ia.5.4.ad.1).

37. Hart, *Infinite*, 18. On distance he also says, "A proper understanding of beauty's place in theology may show how . . . more primordial than the difference between the same and the other, the transcendent and the immanent, or even Being and beings—is the thought of the distance that opens up all differences, the interval between their terms, the event of their emergence; and in asserting that distance is originally the gift of the beautiful—rather than the featureless sublimity of will, or force, or *différance*, or the ontological Nothing—theology interprets the nature and possibility of every interval within being" (Hart, *Infinite*, 18–19).

The implications of so including the holy among the transcendentals, as the transcendental *of* the transcendentals, are extensive. Really, this book can only be seen as an introduction to the transcendentality of the holy. Further elaborations of this thesis will have to be the topics of future work. If this argument is granted, then there is absolutely nothing that cannot be directly explicated according to its measure of holiness, for holiness is coextensive with being and therefore everywhere "is" is. Nevertheless, among those whose work is relevant to the issue of reverence and the holy, William Desmond is remarkable. Particularly, the chapter called "On the Betrayals of Reverence" in his book *Is There a Sabbath for Thought?* raises reverence to the level of truth, goodness, and being, though he never introduces holiness as such.[38] His chapter shows what damage has been wrought in the absence of reverence, but also begins to re-envision what difference reverence makes.

Desmond says that the very desire to know is rooted in a more primal ontological reverence, a reverence that escapes the confines of fixity and determination "in attunement to the good of being, the glory of creation, the gift of the 'to be.'"[39] He asks, is this "reverence not our being in *the spirit of truth?*"[40] Reverence transcends the flat univocity that underpins modernity and the radical equivocity that underpins postmodernity.[41] Reverence

---

38. Desmond, *Reverence*, 262–88. Dietrich von Hildebrand also has not only included reverence among the antique philosophical "values" but has raised it to the highest seat: "Reverence is *the* attitude that can be designated as the mother of all moral life, for in it man first takes a position toward the world that opens his spiritual eyes and enables him to grasp value" (Hildebrand, *Art of Living*, 3).

39. Desmond, "Reverence," 268. Reverence "offers itself as a porous attunement to what gives itself as worthy to be admired, indeed to be loved, an attunement that cannot be made completely determinate, though it provides something essential to the context or ethos within which our more determinate fixations of finite life take place. In that respect, it is a source of more determinate formations that come out of it . . . because reverence has *love* in it, it is also a yielding of the fixed boundary of one's affirmed integrity."

40. Desmond, "Reverence," 271.

41. On univocity, he says, "Reverence moves in a different direction to the spirit of this univocalization. It lives in ambiguity. It also lives in a milieu in which there are excesses to determination . . . the excess asks to be let as excess" (Desmond, "Reverence," 270). Desmond says, against equivocity, that "There must be an unknowing knowing, or a knowing unknowing, in the complex intermediate character of our desire and ignorance. My suggestion is that there is a more *primary ontological reverence* out of which knowing as determinate cognition takes form; and it is with reference to this reverence that the double condition can be approached, the equivocal condition of being in relation and yet not being cognitive master of it" (Desmond, "Reverence," 277).

challenges the modern myth of neutrality, for all scientific procedure is born out of an original wonder and builds towards deeper reverence. Without such ordering, "Neutrality mutates into indifference, indifference into contempt, contempt into hostility, hostility into aggression, and then we have the full assault that will subject being, as an other to be dominated."[42] Moreover, Desmond says, "Kill reverence and intellectual curiosity *undergoes a mutation*."[43] Methodologically, science simply is not a question unto itself, in other words it is not a phenomenon explainable to itself. Reverence gives signs about a superior source that transcends self-production.[44] Also, reverence undercuts the primal suspicion of nihilism, and the inevitable tyrannies that follow upon its success.[45] Thus for Desmond, reverence is an ontological reality that can be avoided only at great cost, for ultimately "There is no higher cognitive state in which reverence is dispelled or overcome."[46]

---

42. Desmond, "Reverence," 279.

43. Desmond, "Reverence," 279. "The loss of reverence is at the source of such ontological tyranny wherein the human being is not at all one neutral being among others, but rather is the autocrat of the neuter."

44. On the scientific quest, he says, "The desire to know is a source of the scientific quest, but what is the source of the desire to know? . . . When we wonder about the sources of the desire to know, our question is not any straightforward scientific question. In asking the question, we show ourselves already to participate in that which is the 'object' of our inquiry, hence we can never stand objectively outside it. In that regard, science is not a question to itself, though it questions everything else, and even though at moments of limit and crisis the question of its own nature and methods does come alive for it. *But this perplexity about its own sources* is not the element in which it lives, or wants to live. It is carried by the desire to know, which it takes for granted as its enabling power, without astonishment or perplexity about what grants this power at all" (Desmond, "Reverence," 274). In response, "Reverence, properly understood, can give signs about the source that further comes to determinate form, as the extraordinary desire to know that is our native endowment. These signs suggest that this source cannot be contained within the circle of thought that thinks itself. For again the release of reverence to a superior otherness is a granting that is not self-produced by us; it is a happening, in which we are as much gifted as we are carried by a transcending beyond ourselves" (Desmond, "Reverence," 276).

45. "In religious reverence, it is to be beyond oneself in devotion to the superior, the supreme other. Yet this being beyond is a strange intimacy with what as mysterious is strange, and what as strange is in deepest community with us. Reverence is related to wonder, where this shows a free contemplation of worthy otherness: the ontological value of its otherness as other, and the aura of the source that plays around its givenness" (Desmond, "Reverence," 279).

46. Desmond, "Reverence," 287.

HOLINESS AND TOUCH

If Desmond shows how reverence applies to such large-scale philosophical visions, I would also stress that holiness is there at the most basic levels of existence. The phenomenologist Maurice Merleau-Ponty says philosophy arises *after* life, *after* thought, and "questions this antecedent being and questions itself concerning its own relationship with it."[47] Here, we already see an affinity between this suspended conjecture upon an anterior mystery and the posteriority of truth in relation to the holy. While the philosophical quest returns upon itself and all things, it does not return to immediacy. If philosophy approaches the mystery in question in order to fully fuse with it, then that mystery will vanish altogether. For "it is only by remaining at a distance that it remains itself."[48] Even with the most apparently immediate object, Merleau-Ponty says that our flesh "lines and even envelopes all the visible and tangible things with which nevertheless it is surrounded."[49]

At the cusp between myself and the world is flesh. My eyes can see and thus can be seen, my body can touch and thus be touched, and therefore I see and touch the world *from within*.[50] The world and I are within one another. When I find the actual world as it is, "under my hands, under my eyes, up against my body, I find much more than an object: a Being of which my vision is a part."[51] Again, this does not mean that the world and I are fused together. On the contrary, this reveals a duality about my flesh. For "my body looked at and my body looking, my body touched and my body touching, there is overlapping or encroachment, so we must say that the things pass into us as well as we into the things."[52] This duality Merleau-Ponty calls "double reference," which is the "identity of the retiring into oneself with the leaving of oneself, of the lived through with the distance."[53]

---

47. Merleau-Ponty, *Visible and the Invisible*, 123.
48. Merleau-Ponty, *Visible and the Invisible*, 123.
49. Merleau-Ponty, *Visible and the Invisible*, 123. He then says, because the world and the "I" are really one, that radical autonomous "anteriority" does not exist. The object that appears to pre-exist vision is constituted by vision (e.g., color and light). This is consistent with what has been said about the holy in connection to the Father and his *Logos*, for while the Father is anterior, he is only such as articulated by the Son, his image.
50. Merleau-Ponty, *Visible and the Invisible*, 123.
51. Merleau-Ponty, *Visible and the Invisible*, 123.
52. Merleau-Ponty, *Visible and the Invisible*, 123.
53. Merleau-Ponty, *Visible and the Invisible*, 124.

The Holy's Spirit

This duality, of retiring into oneself and leaving oneself, has already been established in our discussion of the divine *Logos*, which yielded the paradox that the Son becomes himself (is begotten) by plunging into the Father. Even more profoundly, Merleau-Ponty gives us an understanding of flesh as that which *distances* on our behalf. This distancing is, as he says, dual. The distance *reveals* the world to me and is the means through which I *enter* the world. We already saw that the Holy's Spirit *is* revealing distance, and I argued that all such instantiations participate in this operation of the Spirit. Therefore, the flesh is *spiritual* through and through. It distances and thereby consecrates what is other.

Here we have a connection between the most basic act in existence (touch) and the abstract formula for sanctification (that which keeps holy the things that are holy shall become holy). I appear because I touch, which can now be interpreted as such: I exist and thus possess integrity, being, and holiness as and because I distance (consecrate) what is other (holy). This basic consecrative act is constitutive of being itself, and is reflected in the nature of the transcendentals. Touch is that medium of encounter through which something becomes itself through distancing, namely a distancing that is increasingly "intelligent" by an increased feeling for reality as other. Everything from biological organisms to human beings *touches* the holy, and is matured and perfected, evolved and sanctified, to the extent that the sensitivity of its touch increases.[54] Acute sensitivity becomes sensibility, and develops a more apt "feeling" for what is holy. In the end, all knowing, seeing, and acting is a form of touch.[55] Therefore, we only become holy through our habits of touching.

---

54. One might say that inanimate objects are omitted from this principle, but that is not the case. Even a rock maintains a certain substantial integrity through its distancing of the world around it, which sets apart the objects that surround it and thereby establishes its own dwelling (or sanctuary).

55. John Milbank describes the relationship between touch and distance: "Since touch is mediated by the flesh, there is also a distance, a transparency involved in touch, as much as with vision. But this is now much more emphatically an inner-reflected, psychic transparency. Inversely, however, Aristotle declares that *all* sensation involves the immediacy of touch, since even the transparencies of light and air are mediated by a series of contiguous bodies. And through the transparent medium of light, the eye really does touch the visible object. Therefore, all sensation is touching and occurs only by the medium of the flesh. Therefore again, the visible medium collapsed as touch into immediacy regains mediation as the inner psychic distance. Merleau-Ponty also affirmed that touch is mediated vision, and vision is mediated touch. He regarded this as yet another instance of reciprocal intertwining—noting that all touching falls within the field of the visible, while all that is seen is what can potentially be touched" (Milbank, "Beauty and the Soul," 17).

Sanctum Sanctorum

The very basis of orthodox Christian faith is an apostolic tradition of touch: "We declare to you what was from the beginning, what we have heard, what we have seen with our eyes, what we have looked at and touched with our hands, concerning the word of life" (1 John 1:1).[56] This word, Jesus Christ, became flesh in order that all flesh might fully live. This he demonstrated through touch, whether giving sight to a blind man by touching his eyes (John 9:6), cleansing a leper by touching him (Luke 5:13), or healing the severed ear of the man who arrested him by touching his ear (Luke 22:52). Eventually, as word spread about the Christ, people from every city brought the sick to him that he might touch and heal them (Mark 6:56; Luke 8:47), while others brought their babies to receive his blessing (Luke 18:15). Of all his triumphs, the resurrection was his greatest as it was a triumph over the grave. There also he invites us to be fully healed: "Look at my hands and my feet; see that it is I myself. Touch me and see; for a ghost does not have flesh and bones as you see that I have" (Luke 24:39). The growth of the early church was connected to the continuation of such signs: people were healed when Peter's shadow touched their garments (which is in continuity with the woman who was healed by touching Jesus' cloak [Luke 8:47]). Paul was converted and anointed an apostle of Jesus Christ through touch. When Paul was temporarily blind after encountering Christ, Ananias was sent by Christ in a vision to find Paul and lay his hands on him that he might regain sight and be filled with the Holy Spirit (Act 9:12-19). After this, Paul was immediately baptized.

The apostolic legacy is the transmission of sacred, even sacramental traditions. Jesus Christ himself was immersed in the waters of baptism, to the horror of John the Baptist. Jesus insisted that he partake of, *touch*, our somatic reality in order to consecrate it *by* his touch, which is really an anointing. The touch of baptism is a symbol of redemption. Christ "touches" and heals our wounds by receiving his own wounds. Our death has been anointed with the touch of Christ's death, which leads to resurrection. Thus the apostles are themselves anointed to pass on such holy means. Jesus says to them, "Go therefore and make disciples of all nations, baptizing them in the name of the Father and of the Son and of the Holy Spirit" (Matt 28:19). We touch Christ by entering the *same* anointed waters

---

56. The passage continues: "This life was revealed, and we have seen it and testify to it, and declare to you the eternal life that was with the Father and was revealed to us—we declare to you what we have seen and heard so that you also may have fellowship with us; and truly our fellowship is with the Father and with his Son Jesus Christ. We are writing these things so that our joy may be complete" (1 John 1:2-4).

of baptism that he did. We eat the same bread and drink the same wine that he anointed, "'Take, eat; this is my body.' And he took a cup, and when he had given thanks he gave it to them, saying, 'Drink of it, all of you, for this is my blood of the covenant, which is poured out for many for the forgiveness of sins'" (Matt 26:26–28). The apostles "received" such anointed practices that they would "deliver" them to the church (1 Cor 11:23).

Though Christ's physical body is gone, he passed on these "means" so that we can continue to "touch" him. In worship, we are made holy by keeping holy the things that are holy (through touch). This spread of holiness through touch, this chain of holiness, was true of Israel's holy place. The law says of the items in the tabernacle, "You shall consecrate them, that they may be most holy. *Whatever* touches them will become holy" (Exod 30:29; cf. 29:37). Thus the church hears Christ's word spoken, consumes his body and blood, and is touched by him through the laying on of hands and anointing with oil. Even the gesture of "lifting up holy hands" has the visual queues of "touching" the Invisible Holy.[57] We can see that the spread of holiness has its causal link through touch. Something is made holy by touching what is holy, and that very thing can then make others holy by *being touched*.

But this begs the question, what *kind* of touching makes one holy? If we make no further clarifications, then we have only affirmed unthinking superstition, which inevitably leads to tyranny and virtueless indulgence. We can immediately affirm that nothing is holy "in itself," that is, outside the sphere of habit and intention. While Paul says that we must touch no unclean thing (2 Cor 6:17), he also says, "I know and am persuaded in the Lord Jesus that nothing is unclean in itself, but it is unclean for anyone who thinks it unclean" (Rom 14:14). Christ himself taught us to extend our love through touch to those who are "unclean," many of whom he healed through touch. Paul even says that an unbelieving spouse will be sanctified by the believing spouse in the sacred unity of marriage, and the children will be "holy" (1 Cor 7:14). This is part of the church's (spiritual) work, which is to extend the reaches of God's sanctuary through touch.[58] Inversely, Paul condemns those who "touch" the Eucharist in an unholy way, by committing the errors of neglecting to give food to some and then

---

57. Psalm 134 says, "Come, bless the Lord, all you servants of the Lord, who stand by night in the house of the Lord! Lift up your hands to the holy place, and bless the Lord" (Ps 134:1–2).

58. "Spiritual" is parenthesized because all work, as en-fleshed work, is spiritual, and everything is teleologically oriented towards the holy.

getting drunk on the sacramental wine (1 Cor 11:20–22). Consequently, Paul says, "it is not the Lord's supper that you eat" (v. 20). The manner in which they touched the elements disrupted the teleological chain to the holy, and therefore defiled the meal through their unholy touch.

While clean and unclean are still viable categories, they are re-envisioned according to the broader scope of holiness revealed through Christ. If the law, as a temporary "tutor," drew stark lines between clean and unclean objects, the new covenant of freedom in the Spirit releases the inner dynamism of sacred cleanliness.

An impoverished vision of Christian asceticism refrains from certain embodied pleasures because they are seen as carnal and therefore unholy. Paul quips, "Why do you submit to regulations, 'Do not handle, Do not taste, Do not touch'? ... These have indeed an appearance of wisdom in promoting self-imposed piety, humility, and severe treatment of the body, but they are of no value in checking self-indulgence" (Col 2:20–23). Paul is not denying the validity of those who consecrate their lives to God in ascetic forms. Rather, he is saying that true Christian asceticism introduces practices of restraint precisely because such embodied goods are holy. Paul himself says that a married couple should only abstain from sexual intimacy for a specific duration so that the couple can return more *fully* to sexuality, and thus return upon its sacredness (1 Cor 7:1–5). Restraint is never simply a matter of denying what is good, but of cultivating one's sensitivity to what is good.

Touching creates a teleological chain to the holy. All the days of creation are sanctified by their teleological "reverence" to the Sabbath. Time is oriented towards the eschaton when God will be fully revealed in holiness, and thus our time here reveres that end and thereby "touches" the end (especially in the Eucharist), and thus becomes holy. We are what we touch. As creatures called to holiness, everything we touch should be explainable according to how it aids the end of holiness. In this way, the essences of even everyday objects take on a "keeping holy" nature, or consecrative nature. All our habits and goods are to "touch" or consecrate the holy. Money and material goods are not lords over us, but gifts that must be rendered in service to the cosmic temple. The same is true for government, family, and work. Everything is to be sanctified by consecrating what is holy according to its own means and nature.

If this chain is hierarchical, it does not present a hierarchy plain and simple. A Dionysian theology sees all names as inherently fragile and ultimately inadequate. Holy is the name that *hymns* God's nature to the greatest extent possible while simultaneously, and overtly, communicating the inscrutability of that nature, which consequently destabilizes all our cultural-linguistic constructions. This theology of the divine names informs the way in which we consider things, practices, and people holy. The very dynamic of the holy itself purposefully undercuts all our attempts to demarcate and define what is holy. Jesus, the Holy One of God, playfully disrupts the holy standards established in his time. For example, he picks grain on the Sabbath. His rationale exposes the teleology beneath this chain of holiness, as he says "The sabbath was made for humankind, and not humankind for the sabbath; so the Son of Man is lord even of the sabbath" (Mark 2:27–28).

This disruption is not anarchy or cynicism, but the holy disruption of love. Jesus "works" on the Sabbath to give food to the hungry, just as anyone would go looking for their lost sheep or coin on the Sabbath. He also forgives and "touches" scandalous women, for the sick are in the greatest need of a physician, the hurting in greatest need of a comforter. After being caught picking grain on the Sabbath, Jesus places his actions in continuity with David, who took the consecrated bread from the tabernacle so that in a time of need he would have food (1 Sam 21:6). Therefore, the holy always undercuts its own manifestations with love, which only re-instates its presence more fully. This is the holy disruption of hierarchy, if still a restatement of hierarchy in a new form. For the greatest will be least, and the least greatest. While Jesus, being holy, makes others holy by being touched, like the woman who anointed his feet (Matt 26:10), he also *is* holy in washing others' feet (John 13:1–11). And if one is to be made holy, they cannot be "too humble" to receive his gesture (v. 8).[59]

As was argued, the flesh is likened with the spirit, because in its "double reference" flesh is the very cusp between the soul and the other, and thus distances through its touching, thereby consecrating what is other. Therefore it is fitting that the fullness of holiness should find itself in the

---

59. C. S. Lewis says of humility and touch: "We must not think Pride is something God forbids because He is offended at it, or that Humility is something He demands as due to His own dignity—as if God was proud. He is not in the least worried about His dignity. The point is, He wants you to know Him: wants to give you Himself. And He and you are two things of such a kind that if you really get into any kind of touch with Him you will, in fact, be humble—delightedly humble, feeling the infinite relief of having for once got rid of all the silly nonsense about your own dignity which has made you restless and unhappy all your life" (Lewis, *Mere Christianity*, 107).

most sensitive, tender, form of touch, namely a kiss. Throughout the New Testament, Christians are encouraged to greet one another with a "holy kiss" (Rom 16:16; 1 Cor 16:20; 2 Cor 13:12; 1 Thess 5:26) or the "kiss of love" (1 Pet 5:14). When the Song of Songs says, "Let him kiss me with the kisses of his mouth!" (Song 1:2), we ought to think of the "flesh" of the kiss itself as the Spirit. As Bernard of Clairvaux says, "[if] the Father is he who kisses, the Son he who is kissed, then it cannot be wrong to see in the kiss the Holy Spirit, for he is the imperturbable peace of the Father and the Son, their unshakable bond, their undivided love, their indivisible unity."[60]

CONCLUSION

This chapter began by making the important assertion that "being" or "substance" is not an autonomous entity in which and through which the three persons of the Trinity emerge and relate. Rather, being is an intellectually discernible aspect of Spirit. We saw with Victorinus that God *is* Spirit, and

---

60. Bernard of Clairvaux, *Song of Songs*, 8.2. He says, "We are to speak of the supreme kiss, that of the mouth. You must listen with more than usual attention to a theme that is sweet to the spirit above all others, that is so rare an experience and more difficult to understand. I think I should begin by considering the higher truths, and it seems to me that a kiss past comprehension, beyond the experience of any mere creature, was designated by him who said: "No one knows the Son except the Father, just as no one knows the Father except the Son and those to whom the Son chooses to reveal him." For the Father loves the Son whom he embraces with a love that is unique; he who is infinite embraces his equal, who is eternal, his co-eternal the sole God, his only-begotten. But the Son's bond with him is not less affectionate, for it led him even to death, as he himself testifies: 'That all might know that I love the Father, rise, let us go.' And he went forth, as we know, to his passion. Now, that mutual knowledge and love between him who begets and him who is begotten—what can it comprise if not a kiss that is utterly sweet, but utterly a mystery as well?" (Bernard of Clairvaux, *Song of Songs*, 8.1). Augustine says of the Spirit and the kiss: "It behoved the Holy Spirit to be manifested when coming upon the Lord, that everyone might understand that if he has the Holy Spirit he ought to be simple as the dove, to have true peace with his brethren, that peace which the kisses of doves signify. Ravens have their kisses too; but in the case of the ravens it is a false peace, in that of the dove a true peace. Not every one, therefore, who says, 'Peace be with you,' is to be listened to as if he were a dove. How then are the kisses of ravens distinguished from those of doves? Ravens kiss, but they tear; the nature of doves is innocent of tearing. Where consequently there is tearing, there is not true peace in the kisses. They have true peace who have not torn the Church. Ravens feed upon carrion, it is not so with the dove; it lives on the fruits of the earth, its food is innocent. This, brethren, is really worthy of admiration in the dove. Sparrows are very small birds, but yet they kill flies at least. The dove does nothing of this sort, for it does not feed on what is dead. They who have torn the Church feed on the dead" (Augustine, *Gospel of John*, 6.4).

that "subsistence" is more properly said of the three persons than substance. We saw that the Spirit is not only God, but that (again) God is Spirit (John 4:23–24). Therefore, insofar as metaphysics studies the nature of being, it will inevitably find itself tracking the Spirit of God.

We then probed the question of why the Spirit is hypostasized as another Trinitarian subsistence or person. John Milbank recognized that our confidence about the personality of the Holy Spirit is disproportionate to the rationale we have for this "second difference." Granted, the Christian tradition, rooted in the apostolic legacy, is fully justified in worshipping him. The New Testament and the practices of early Christians are sufficient to validate the Spirit's integrity and divinity as a person, but as Milbank argues, we have not reached the logical place of perceiving the utter *necessity* of the Spirit's hypostasis.

For Victorinus, the Spirit is demonstrably necessary because of his defining role as understanding, without which neither Father or Son would be comprehensible even to themselves. As valid as this point is, Victorinus offers an even more definitive explanation, with his understanding of the Father as the wholly Invisible Unbegotten in repose, who is *Proon* (Preexistence). If the Father is indeterminate without the Son, he is irretrievably absent without the Spirit. Therefore, every indication of his presence, every moment of communion, and indeed every movement of the Father, is already the presence, communion, and movement of some *other* that must have been "sent" from the very depths of the Father himself. The shift here is that we can no longer assume that the Father is present, but must begin with his inscrutability, after which we can then fully recognize that every encounter with him is by *necessity* an encounter with that which is strictly speaking not the Father, namely the Spirit.

Since the Father is silent, invisible, being in repose, his presence in the Spirit must be an "other" *of* the Father, which speaks to the additional hypostasis of this other. At the same time, this other must be personal. If the Father is to be meaningfully engaged in the Trinitarian life, and creation for that matter, then the Spirit must be so entirely *of* the Father, one with the Father (*homoousios*), that his presence is seen as the acceptable form of the Father's presence.

Victorinus clearly articulates that the Spirit is the movement of the reposed Father. The Spirit's original act of distancing coincides with the "setting apart" aspect of consecration. The Spirit's movement is thus consecrative in nature. There is a difference between the Son as the form of reverence and the Spirit as the consecrator. The Son is the *Logos* that makes the richness of reverence intelligible, where the Spirit is the movement of the Father that actively opens the distance at which reverence can "see." While distinguishable, the Spirit and Son are of one nature, and thus the Son is the form of the Spirit's act, and the Spirit is the act of the Son's form. Thus, the Father is to the Spirit, along with the Son, the Holy *of* holies (*sanctum sanctorum*).

Basil and Victorinus recognize how the Spirit is like a place (and the inhabitant). The Spirit is not a neutral, void place but that which is variously rendered though singularly focused, namely a place of consecration. In other words, the Spirit is a sanctuary. Thus, all of the Spirit's operations (e.g., giving life, redemption, sanctification) are teleologically oriented to extend the reaches of sanctuary to encompass the entire cosmos. By explicating the Spirit's sanctifying work (which is synonymous with sanctuary-building), we saw how the distance presupposed by the transcendentals is an original act of consecration. Truth perceives the distance, being is the distance, the good lures at a distance, beauty traverses the distance, the one demarcates the distance, and the holy creates the distance (through the act of consecration, in the register of reverence). Finally, this ontological basis of distancing is operative in the flesh through touch, which thus makes flesh inherently "*spiritual*." This leads to an understanding of the Christian tradition as implicitly maintaining that we only become holy through our habits of touching.

4

Nosferatu, A Symphony of Horror

"That Name rings like the cry of a bird of prey. Never speak it aloud."[1]
—*The Book of the Vampires*

"Serve the Lord with fear, and rejoice with trembling."
—Ps 2:11

INTRODUCTION

THIS BOOK SEEKS TO demonstrate that holiness is the transcendental *of* the transcendentals (*sanctum sanctorum*). This entails showing how holiness is a part every conceivable aspect of existence. Chapter 1 considered the divine names and argued that holiness is co-extensive with being. Chapter 2 showed how *Life* itself adheres to the transcendental dynamics of the holy, namely its mode of being as reverence. Chapter 3 argued that the Holy's Spirit is the Consecrator and Sanctuary *of* the Holy. If these three arguments are sound, then we are well on our way to establishing the transcendentality

---

1. Quoted in *Nosferatu*, 14:15.

of holiness. From a theological point of view, the theoretical basis of the transcendentality of holiness has been established. Because *everything* is now in some measure holy, then *anything* can be further investigated for its measure of holiness. However, recent theological discussion has well understood how holiness permeates the "mundane" and the socio-political sciences, among other things. While this book might give way to further work in such areas, they are not *theoretically* problematic to the very idea of the holy as the transcendental *of* the transcendentals. Thus, because of the limited space, I would like to skip to what might be the greatest problem for this thesis, namely in what sense can we consider obscene atrocities and insidious horrors to be holy?

This chapter argues that sanctity is the basis of horror, and thus even the most grotesque realities revere the holy. Moreover, the grotesque has a qualitative and structural affinity to the holy, and thus the latter half of this chapter will offer an *apologia* for a committed retrieval of the grotesque as an aesthetic genre or mood.

THE PLAY OF THE ABSURD

In his essay "The Corpse of Beauty," Sergei Bulgakov says that "when one enters the room where Pablo Picasso's works are collected, one is surrounded by an atmosphere of mystical fear amounting to terror."[2] This darkness, he says, is the "Night" of Tyutchev's poem "Day and Night": "the abyss is laid bare before us with its fears and mists, and there are no more barriers between us and it. This is why night is fearful to us."[3] Bulgakov sees in Picasso's work a disincarnate, sterile, and ultimately evacuated view of human flesh. Picasso depicts femininity as unutterably hideous, heavy, shapeless, and the very "corpse of beauty."[4] Though amazed, Bulgakov remains mostly hostile towards Picasso's artwork.[5] For him art is the most subtle form of

---

2. This essay was written after visiting a Picasso exhibition. Bulgakov, "Corpse," 67.

3. Tyutchev, "Day and Night," quoted in Bulgakov, "Corpse," 67.

4. Bulgakov, "Corpse," 69. Bulgakov gives the following examples: this is seen in "God-defying cyncism (*Nude in a Landscape*), in diabolical malice (*After the Dance*), as a decaying astral corpse (*Seated Woman*), or with the snake-like leer of a witch (*Woman with a Fan*)."

5. David Borgmeyer addresses Bulgakov's hostility towards Picasso, who is otherwise praised by art critics, and says it is understandable in light of "Russian Orthodox culture, in which the image is (or at least can be) not merely an image, but an icon: a direct reflection of a spiritual, transcendental reality. To the extent that there is something

"Luciferian infection" in the human spirit. Additionally, Picasso's art is a religious trial to be exorcised by the sobriety of faith and the togetherness of the church, although Picasso remains a trial that the church must willingly face.[6]

Even in Bulgakov's analysis we see something altogether spiritual about Picasso, the spiritual content of his artwork is permeated from beginning to end by one feeling the ever increasing horror of life.[7] He is frightening because he is demonically genuine, which is why after one views Picasso everything else in the gallery falls flat and seems insipid.[8] His artwork is "mystical throughout."[9] It is spiritual, Bulgakov says, but has the "spirituality of a vampire or a demon."[10] Because an "uncanny" power flows from them, Picasso's pieces are like miracle-working icons of a demonic nature.[11] Even ordinary objects bear the same "mystic dread and anguish."[12] The dark force that one feels emanating from these works is almost "tangibly felt," as if coming from black icons.[13]

Bulgakov appears to see nothing redeemable about the demonic in Picasso's work. However, from the standpoint of the Christian tradition, one might challenge such a one-sided, wholly negative reading of this darkness. Bulgakov testifies to the recognizable and overwhelming power of spiritual dread, but we might ask, with whom does this power ultimately lie? The demonic conjures within us not merely fear but dread; in the presence of the demonic, one feels not only overpowered but haunted. We recognize the demonic by a distinctly frightening quality, one which instills the sense that something astral and terrifying looms. Rudolf Otto's work has established this distinctive as the "numinous," which is an ominous spiritual power

---

profoundly disturbing about the *zeitgeist* of the first half of the twentieth century, and to the extent that these paintings really are icons of their times, both as representatives and influences, then Bulgakov might not be so wrong. . . . Bulgakov saw in Picasso's artwork something masterful, but still a herald of something both seminal and terrible: and in hindsight, perhaps he was right" (Borgmeyer, "Modernism," 168).

6. Bulgakov, "Corpse," 71.

7. Bulgakov, "Corpse," 67–68.

8. Bulgakov, "Corpse," 70–71.

9. Bulgakov, "Corpse," 67. He says, "The mystical nature of art is here laid bare and made self-evident" (Bulgakov, "Corpse," 70).

10. Bulgakov, "Corpse," 68.

11. Bulgakov, "Corpse," 69.

12. Bulgakov, "Corpse," 69.

13. Bulgakov, "Corpse," 69.

Sanctum Sanctorum

(*numen*).[14] But is the demonic an alternative spiritual power, separate from the God of light and beauty to whom Scripture bears witness? The demonic is also dazzling, majestic, and attractive, which is seen in its enduring relevance to painting, poetry, film, literature, music, and fashion. If the demonic has an independent vivacity of its own, which operates autonomously from the spiritual realm of God, then one would have to re-construe the cosmos according to absolute ontological dualism. Or, one must consider evil to be an actual, positive substance that God created. Both alternatives disrupt the participatory ontology of the Christian tradition that understands evil as pure privation and creation as brought forth out of nothing (*ex nihilo*).

Moreover, the numinous belongs properly to the holy. Nothing is more frightening than God. Therefore, in light of the incomparably ominous, awe-inspiring, dread-inducing register of the holy, it is clear that the demonic is the idolatrous distortion of numinous fear. The terror of the demonic is nothing less than a participation in the holiness of God. The demonic is not in opposition to the holy, but can only be demonic—terrifying, frightening—because of the holy.

The relative fear conjured by demons is superseded by the terror of holy angels. At the birth of Christ, angels appear to shepherds in a field, "Then an angel of the Lord stood before them, and the glory of the Lord shone around them, and they were terrified" (Luke 2:9; cf. Exod 23:27, "I will send my terror in front of you"; 15:16, "Terror and dread fell upon them"; Acts 10:4). Then at Christ's tomb there was an earthquake, and "an angel of the Lord, descending from heaven, came and rolled back the stone and sat on it. His appearance was like lightning, and his clothing white as snow. For fear of him the guards shook and became like dead men" (Matt 28:2–4). When a demon saw Jesus, it begged of him, "Let us alone! What have you to do with us, Jesus of Nazareth? Have you come to destroy us? I know who you are, the Holy One of God" (Luke 4:34). When Jesus was called "Good Teacher," he said "No one is good but God alone," displaying the participatory flow of all goodness back to the original Good (Luke 18:19). Christ envisions the same flow with regard to fear: "do not fear those who kill the body, and after that can do nothing more. But I will

---

14. Otto, *Idea of the Holy*, 7. Otto says that the gothic in Western architecture draws upon primitive magic, but exceeds the power of magic: "The impression Gothic makes is one of magic; and, whatever may be said of his historical account of the matter, it is certain that in this at least he is on the right track. Gothic *does* instil [sic] a spell that is more than the effect of sublimity. But 'magic' is too low a word: the tower of the Cathedral of Ulm is emphatically not 'magical,' it is *numinous*" (Otto, *Idea of the Holy*, 70).

warn you whom to fear: fear him who, after he has killed, has authority to cast into hell. Yes, I tell you, fear him" (Luke 12:4–5). Thus, this unique fear belongs properly to the holy, which also fits with the Christian *mythos* that demons are fallen angels, and therefore exercise their power not because of their fallenness but in virtue of their holiness, however corrupted (Luke 10:18; cf. Matt 25:41; Rev 12:9). The holiness of the demonic is analogous to the good of Hitler. Though Hitler committed atrocious sins, one cannot say that Hitler acted entirely apart from the horizon of the good as such. Rather, Hitler acted according to *misconstrued* ideas about what the good is, i.e., gaining acceptance, security, and legacy through the horrors of the Nazi regime. Likewise, demons do not have access to some special power inaccessible to God. On the contrary, demons live, and move, and have their being through participation in God's holy being, and exert terror by the qualitative dread of a supernatural aura (shining forth from the holy) and the possibility of physical harm. Both means of terror are contingent, while misused, gestures categorically akin to God.

Bulgakov insists that Picasso induces a kind of nightmare, and that there "is not a single ray of light in this arid and sorrowful desert."[15] However, the super-luminous ray of darkness (Dionysius), the white light of holiness, is exactly responsible for this recognizable dread. Remarkably, he says that the veil of day with its "reassuring multiplicity of colours is blown away, and one is encircled by horrible formless night, full of dumb, evil phantoms and shadows."[16] The white light of holiness contains and eclipses the variously refracted "colors" (as the transcendental *of* the transcendentals), and thus the holy "is" in the rupture of truth, goodness, beauty, being, and unity. Thus, the primeval power that spills out through Picasso's grotesqueries achieves monumental effect because of the play of form and formlessness, proportion and oblivion, boredom and horror. Bulgakov recognized how similar the demonic is to the holy. He observes that light and darkness have a mysterious rhythm, a certain musical correlation. The unknown architect of the Norte Dame was obedient to this rhythm when he constructed his *chimères*, those ghastly architectural figures (and gargoyles, which evince great artistic power and profound mystical reality).[17] Are Picasso's paintings not *chimères* on the spiritual temple of modernity?[18]

15. Bulgakov, "Corpse," 70.
16. Bulgakov, "Corpse," 67.
17. Bulgakov, "Corpse," 71.
18. Bulgakov, "Corpse," 71.

We can see a qualitative affinity between the demonic and the holy, which is grounded in a participatory ontology of holiness.

Wolfgang Kayser concludes his authoritative work *The Grotesque in Art and Literature* with a section entitled, "An Attempt to Define the Nature of the Grotesque."[19] Kayser's final observations on the grotesque align remarkably well with the arguments posited about the holy. For Kayser, the word "grotesque" applies to three different realms: the creative process, the work of art itself, and its reception.[20] Though artists reuse certain techniques and tropes, the grotesque is not reducible to any particular form, but often appears as "nightmarish and ominously demonic, that is, the medium through which some horror, anguish, or fear of the incomprehensible is expressed."[21] If no single form captures its essence, Kayser still insists that the grotesque is a "structure."[22] He says the nature of the grotesque can be summed up in a phrase: "the grotesque is the estranged world."[23] By estranged, he means more than simply "strange." He means an ominous tension, or a "pregnant moment," that disrupts and surprises. An elaborately told fairy tale can be perfectly strange without instilling dread, while the continuously morphing and estranged world of nature can be profoundly frightening.[24] The encounter with the grotesque presents to us a world in which we are unable to live, a world that would consume us. We are so strongly affected and terrified because our world ceases to

---

19. Kayser, *Grotesque*, 179–89.

20. Kayser, *Grotesque*, 180. He says, "The decisive changes in the connotation of the word occurred in the first few centuries of its history, when the technical term became a 'significant' word, an esthetic category referring to certain creative attitudes (dreamlike, for example), contents, and structures, as well as to effects upon the beholder" (Kayser, *Grotesque*, 179).

21. Kayser, *Grotesque*, 181.

22. Kayser, *Grotesque*, 184.

23. Kayser, *Grotesque*, 180.

24. One can find the grotesque almost anywhere in nature—plant life, microscopic creatures, or insects. But the paradigmatic creature for the grotesque is the bat: Kayser explains, "The grotesque animal incarnate, however, is the bat (*Fledermaus*), the very name of which points to an unnatural fusion of organic realms concretized in this ghostly creature. And strange habits complement its strange appearance. An animal of the dusk, the bat flies noiselessly, has exceedingly subtle senses, and moves so rapidly that one could easily suspect it of sucking the blood of sleeping animals. It is strange even in the state of repose when its wings cover it like a coat and it hangs, head down, from a rafter, more like a piece of dead matter than a living thing" (Kayser, *Grotesque*, 183).

be reliable.[25] Kayser rightly says, the grotesque instills "fear of life rather than fear of death."[26] The categories that once applied to our world become "inapplicable."[27]

But who, asks Kayser, "effects the estrangement of the world, who announces his presence in this overwhelming ominousness?"[28] This question brings us to the "final depth of horror" that is conjured by the absurd, namely that this question remains unanswered.[29] The depth remains unnamed, for if we could name these powers and relate them to the cosmic order, the grotesque would lose its essential quality.[30] This is for Kayser the world of the demonic that intrudes upon us from an abyss.[31] What intrudes remains "incomprehensible, inexplicable, and impersonal."[32] For Kayser, this unknown, objectified by the grotesque, is an "It," the ghostly "It" in contrast to the psychological "It" (it pleases me = I am glad) and the cosmic "It" (it rains).[33] Kayser gives the following quotation from Karl Philipp Moritz: "by means of the impersonal 'it' we seek to express that which exceeds the sphere of our concepts and which language cannot name."[34]

25. Kayser, *Grotesque*, 184–85.
26. Kayser, *Grotesque*, 185.
27. Kayser, *Grotesque*, 185.
28. Kayser, *Grotesque*, 185.
29. Kayser, *Grotesque*, 185.
30. Kayser, *Grotesque*, 185.
31. Kayser, *Grotesque*, 185. Kayser says that we take it to be "characteristic of the grotesque that it does not constitute a fantastic realm of its own (for there is none such). The grotesque world is—and is not—our own world. The ambiguous way in which we are affected by it results from our awareness that the familiar and apparently harmonious world is alienated under the impact of abysmal forces, which break it up and shatter its coherence" (Kayser, *Grotesque*, 37).
32. Kayser, *Grotesque*, 185.
33. Kayser, *Grotesque*, 185.
34. Moritz, *Magazin*, quoted in Kayser, *Grotesque*, 209n5. Referring precisely to this point in Kayser, Wolfgang Stechow says, "Kayser's book contains a conscientious chronicle of the vicissitudes of the term *grotesque* throughout a long span of time, but it seems to me that with the 'it' quality its author has indeed hit upon the most important bond between almost all those meanings. Even a Raphael grotesque, that harmless Renaissance resuscitation of an antique ornamental device, contains some germs of a substance which will not fit into the normal cosmic order, and as Raphael's basically gay and unproblematic ornament was taken over and transformed by his Mannerist followers such as Agostino Veneziano, that gaiety is rapidly replaced by a quality which even we ... still sense to be weird and deeply disturbing: the nameless takes over from the well defined, and we are at once transposed into an ambience" (Stechow, "Bosch," 113–15).

Kayser argues that "the grotesque is a play with the absurd."[35] The creator of the grotesque must not and cannot suggest a meaning, nor distract us from the absurd. Other genres such as comedy and tragedy also use absurdity, but they situate it within a larger, overarching, scheme. Comedy uses the absurd for the purpose of laughter, while tragedy for the purpose of displaying the inevitability of destiny. The grotesque is not concerned with any particular plot or even the destruction of moral order (though both aspects may be involved), rather, it is primarily an expression of our failure to orient ourselves towards the physical universe.[36] Consensus suggests that the grotesque gives an "unimpassioned view of life on earth as an empty, meaningless puppet play or a caricatural marionette theatre."[37] Kayser appears to suggest that absurdity is grotesque insofar as horror is the principal theme. In such grotesque creations, horror does not serve a higher purpose, nor is it overcome or redeemed. The grotesque induces horror as horror and makes no attempt to justify, obfuscate, or evade it, however unsightly it is.

If horror is the primary word, it is not the only word. When the artistic creation succeeds, a "faint smile" passes across the scene or picture, with "slight traces" of "playful frivolity."[38] Within the play, all of the helplessness and horror inspired by "dark forces which lurk in and behind our world and have power to estrange it, the truly artistic portrayal effects a secret liberation."[39] The darkness has been seen, the ominous discovered, the incomprehensible challenged.[40] And thus, Kayser argues, we arrive at a final interpretation of the grotesque: "an attempt to invoke and subdue the demonic aspects of the world."[41]

We have already seen the qualitative affinity between the holy and the grotesque, or the demonic, but Wolfgang Kayser brings us towards a structural affinity. First, the expressed fear of the incomprehensible, the grotesque fits directly within a discourse of the holy, that supremely inscrutable other. The holy is more than inscrutable; it is recognizable by an originary fear, a primordial reverence, which is also the signal of the

---

35. Kayser, *Grotesque*, 186.
36. Kayser, *Grotesque*, 185–86.
37. Kayser, *Grotesque*, 187.
38. Kayser, *Grotesque*, 188.
39. Kayser, *Grotesque*, 188.
40. Kayser, *Grotesque*, 188.
41. Kayser, *Grotesque*, 188.

grotesque itself. Kayser speaks profoundly when he says the grotesque has to do with the fear of life, rather than the fear of death.[42] For the special horror that accompanies the grotesque is not merely a contingency, a fear predicated upon the inevitable peril of all mortal life. This definite dread is of a singular, enduring nature and accompanies life itself. The link between ominous fear and life complements our previous modification of Rudolf Otto, which entailed making numinous awe not only an aspect of "creature-feeling," but of the eternal reverence of the Son (Life itself) to the Holy Father (Πάτερ ἅγιε).[43] Second, Kayser says that the grotesque presents a world (or realm) that would consume us, which is precisely the threat of the holy face/form (essence) of God. Likewise, God's holiness threatens in its very brilliance. Third, the grotesque emerges from an absolute depth as a "pregnant moment," which reflects Marius Victorinus's idea that the Father is like a "pregnant abyss" from whom the Son is inexplicably begotten, and to whom he inevitably returns (or who is returned in the Son).

Fourth, because of the anterior, incomprehensible depth, Kayser recognizes the limits of language to render the other of the grotesque. Categories that once applied to our world are ruptured, fractured, and crossed by the grotesque, and thus reveal the tenuous nature of our concepts and names. Dionysius the Areopagite's understanding of the fragility of language was covered in chapter 1. For him, divine names are invariably tenuous and incomplete, and they cumulate in the super-essential essence of God, which I have argued must be named "holy."[44] For Kayser, the "who or what" that lies behind the grotesque is unknown and unnamable, which is what the divine name "holy" declares on its surface, by explicit proclamation.[45] Due to the eclipse of the holy, God may "appear" in withdrawal, or remain "withdrawn" even in appearance. Therefore, the anonymity of the grotesque is a natural feature of the holy as such. As Kayser argues, the grotesque is born of excess that is again a key aspect of the holy, because in the holy all the transcendentals (and thus all things) are super-essentially alchemized.[46]

42. Kayser, *Grotesque*, 185.
43. See chapter 2.
44. See chapter 1.
45. Kayser, *Grotesque*, 185.
46. Kayser, *Grotesque*, 209n5. In *Rethinking the Concept of the Grotesque*, Shun-Liang Chao also sees the grotesque as an aesthetic entryway, characterized by the play of contradiction, into absolute excess: "Indeed, grotesque *trans*-formation is an *excessive* pursuit of incompleteness and contradiction: it transgresses the natural order of things

Fifth, Kayser is led by his observations to unwittingly employ our central metaphysical formula: "dark forces" he says, "lurk *in and behind* our world," which is a slight variation on Przywara's "in-and-beyond."[47] We have re-envisioned Przywara's formula according to the preeminence of holiness, and thus rendered the same idea within "*sanctum sanctorum.*" As Kayser devotes almost sacred status to the Unnamable Beyond of the grotesque, the only moderately accurate (non)name is "It."[48] We addressed this when it came to the unnamable essence of God in negative theology. Like theology's "It," Kayser's is not entirely unknown otherwise *it* would pass by without notice. Moreover, much can be, and is, truthfully said about it, insofar as we continue to "revere" its ominous quality. Thus, I argued that the holy is the "It" in "It cannot be named" (which is a variation on the ontological statement that God is the "Is" in both "it is" and "it is not").[49]

Sixth, Kayser envisions the grotesque as a play of contradiction, excess, and absurdity. In other words, Kayser sees the grotesque as the estranged world.[50] I argued that the "mystic" sensibility apprehends the aesthetic measure of paradox that unveils the holy, which is what Kayser sees in the nature of the grotesque itself.[51] The structural affinity between the holy and the grotesque shows that the grotesque is mystical on a formal

---

and produces within itself a self-contradictory (or in-between) physical structure, one that, as we shall see, displeases classicists because of its ability to feed the feelings of (dis)pleasure and to obscure the borderline between life and death, beauty and deformity, the central and the peripheral. With this in mind, I propose to weave together the thread of *furor poetics*, of the uncanny, and of the sublime, into an aesthetics of *excess* which defines the irrational nature—both in work and in response—of the (antique/Mannerist) grotesque and which marks the critical role of the grotesque in the pursuit of the marvellous" (Chao, *Rethinking*, 26). Chao says, "To conclude, the grotesque, as we have seen, em*bodies* the pursuit of incompleteness and contradiction which carries within itself an aesthetics of *excess*, namely an aesthetics that exceeds our sense of order by (con)fusing *fantasia* and *mimesis*, the central and the peripheral, death and life, and so forth. The grotesque . . . runs off the rails of reason, penetrates the orderly empirical world, and unveils the penetralia of being in which objects are not perfectly defined and designated but melt into and permeate one another, or contraries exists side by side without cancelling each other out" (Chao, *Rethinking*, 40–41). Finally, the grotesque "is the (con)fusion of (bio)logical categories that carries within itself two emotional poles; whilst one of them prevails, the other, *still present*, retreats into the background" (Chao, *Rethinking*, 134).

47. Kayser, *Grotesque*, 188. Emphasis mine.
48. Kayser, *Grotesque*, 185.
49. See also Przywara, *Analogia Entis*, 159–60.
50. Kayser, *Grotesque*, 180.
51. See chapter 2.

level—something Bulgakov reluctantly acknowledged—and participates in the eternal gaze of the Son upon the Invisible Father.[52] In such an estranged world, the grotesque must contain the right proportions of the familiar and the alien. Otherwise, the strangeness will be so entirely strange as to be irrelevant or unrecognizable. However, it cannot be too familiar, as this would diminish its shock-value.[53] Only by a judicious measure of paradox can estrangement take effect. Moreover, this aesthetic measure is another way of signifying the suspended middle (or between) that has been discussed at length. Between concepts and the unknown, natural and supernatural, fear and attraction, one is "suspended" by the grotesque as an expression of the holy.[54]

52. Justin Edwards and Rune Graulund on the paradoxical sensibility of the grotesque: "The grotesque provokes conflicting responses: fascination and repugnance, compassion and disgust, sympathy and confusion. Grotesque bodies might rouse disgust and/or attraction insofar as they offer insights into the limits of the body and human experience. Authors, artists and filmmakers have long celebrated the strange body as a site of production: its repulsive qualities can be attractive to those seeking modes of transgression that challenge normative forms and behaviours. In this, the grotesque is disturbing because it incites seemingly incompatible emotions through its representations of abjection and possibility, limitations and becomings, compassion and rejection, attraction and repulsion" (Edwards and Graulund, *Grotesque*, 78).

53. In *The Sense of Beauty*, George Santayna says, "What appears as grotesque may be intrinsically inferior or superior to the normal. That is a question of its abstract material and form. But until the new object impresses its form on our imagination, so that we can grasp its unity and proportion, it appears to us as a jumble and distortion of other forms. If this confusion is absolute, the object is simply null; it does not exist aesthetically, except by virtue of materials. But if the confusion is not absolute, and we have an inkling of the unity and character in the midst of the strangeness of the form, then we have the grotesque. It is the half-formed, the perplexed, and the suggestively monstrous" (Santayna, *Sense of Beauty*, 256–58).

54. On the similarity between theology and the grotesque at the point of mystery, Roger Hazelton says, "The art of the grotesque is peculiarly open and congenial to theological reflection. By showing us incongruity and even monstrosity in a great variety of forms, grotesque art can induce reflection upon elements of distortion and disorder in our experience. . . . Both theology and grotesque art, in fact, serve to remind us of the mystery of being human in a world that has always left something to be desired by way of practicability and clarity. Hence I would suggest that the grotesque is an 'appropriately odd' disclosure of that mystery, whether forbidding or benign, with which theology is also and necessarily concerned" (Hazelton, "Grotesque," 75). Moreover, Hazelton rightly argues that mystery is not a synonym for residual ignorance, dispelled through science. Neither is it equated with the unknown as such: "A secular culture wants of course to neutralize and minimize the horizon of mystery in human life as much as possible, and so tends to regard it as threatening but surmountable. Theology and grotesque art, on the other hand, the one in terms of propositions and the other in terms of images, find a

Sanctum Sanctorum

HORROR WITHOUT REMAINDER

When the Baroque artist Peter Paul Rubens (1577–1640) painted *Saturn Devouring His Son*, he captured something of the horror in Hesiod's *Theogony*, which describes Great Cronos (Saturn) who "swallowed as each came forth from the womb to his mother's knees with this intent, that no other of the proud sons of Heaven should hold the kingly office amongst the deathless gods. For he learned from Earth and starry Heaven that he was destined to be overcome by his own son, strong though he was, through the contriving of great Zeus. Therefore he kept no blind outlook, but watched and swallowed down his children: and unceasing grief seized Rhea."[55] Rubens paints Cronos according to the measures of physical perfection found in antiquity. Cronos stands amidst the clouds, gripping a scythe in one hand, and the naked body of his son, a baby cherubim, in the other. Before a starry night, Cronos is seen with his teeth still sunken into the baby's chest, as it collapses lifelessly in his arms. By so rendering the scene according to classical proportion, Rubens's genuinely disturbing image makes no protest against his subject. Rubens gives no signal of an inherent conflict between divinity and this heinous cannibalism. The painting believes in these gods, and bestows upon Cronos the dignity he would demand. In other words, Rubens creates a world in which this horror "fits."

Nearly two hundred years later, Francisco Goya (1746–1828) used the same Greek myth to create one of the defining images of the modern age. Goya's *Saturn* differs from Rubens's in nearly every way. Rather than starry heavens, Saturn dwells in what appears to be the darkness of a pit. He is a lanky, disproportionate creature, whose skin drapes over his bones. With two hands clutched around the torso of his son's headless body, Saturn stuffs his gaping mouth with what remains of a bloody arm. Rubens's Saturn is reasoned and determined in his intentions, while Goya's is incapable of reason. However, Saturn is not of a lower nature and thus indifferent, like a lion devouring its prey. Goya creates something "more." Saturn's eyes betray trauma, which is only possible of a creature who has a certain awareness, a degree of intellect, morality, and aesthetics, but however he came to acquire his consciousness, he remains wholly consumed by savagery. Rubens's Saturn is proud, Goya's is desperate.

---

certain affinity in a common persuasion that mystery remains a real and radical feature of our existing the world" (Hazelton, "Grotesque," 75–76).

55. Hesiod, *Theogony*, 460–69.

The difference between the two approaches is seen perhaps most clearly in the sons. In Rubens, the son is healthy, vibrant, even heavenly, and while lifeless, we at least see his face. In Goya, what is left of the son's body is mannequin-esque, and not only do we not see his face, but the face, along with the rest of his head, has been eaten. And while Rubens's son is short and pudgy, Goya's has the proportions of an adult, adding to his overall anonymity.

Rubens allows the surrounding cosmos with its visible virtues to temper the violence. By the very decision to paint it, he acknowledges that however violent the world can be, a larger vision of virtue still presides over absolute evil. Goya's image is sheer trauma, for the subject, for the artist, and for the viewer. It is savagery with no sight of innocence or tragedy. It is pure horror without remainder.

Goya's level of honesty and vulnerability appeals to modern sensibilities. But he also confronts us with a new challenge. Many of the grotesques that preceded him were done in service of the church, and thus the implicit "optimism" of the paintings reflected the relative optimism of the painter. Thus, we can theologically account for the grotesque aesthetic more easily when a painting is created as praise or offering to the church (especially if commissioned as an altar piece). Even Picasso's work gives itself to reflection on transcendence, as his obscure or reduced images procure such a palpable effect that one really encounters Picasso in the "beyond" of his paintings. Goya kept *Saturn* along with the other "Black Paintings" for himself, and painted them on the walls of his home near the end of his life, which is a telling contrast to the ecclesial setting of many historic grotesques. In what way then does Goya's work disclose the holy, not in spite of paintings like *Saturn*, but precisely through them?

While *Saturn* is graphic, and a rich resource for discussion of the holy, Goya still has more problematic images. To the extent that *Saturn* is mythic, the painting resonates with traces of the demonic, the otherworldly, and the imagination, which all in some way signal transcendence. The image is obviously unreal. But earlier, in October of 1808, Goya was sent to Saragossa, the city in which he was raised, to paint the success of Spanish soldiers over the Napoleonic invasion. Instead, Goya witnessed the remains of a French massacre, but he still rendered it and the subsequent horrors with a series of etchings called "The Disasters of War" ("*Los Desastres de la Guerra*"). These 80 plates contain a variety of images that are ironic, satirical, and morbid. An image like *A Heroic Feat! With Dead Men! (Grande hazana! Con muertos!*), Plate 39, poses a greater challenge because it is at least equally as disturbing as *Saturn* but with "real" subject matter. In this etching, three Spanish bodies variously mutilated or castrated are strung over the remaining branches of a half-dead tree. The men are entirely exposed, and one feels that Goya has held nothing back. The etching is more tactile than *Saturn*, and what is more, due to the nature of this tragically historic war act, as a public deterrent to others, Plate 39 stirs one to consider other such instances of horror. If *Saturn* was something of a gateway to the ethereal or demonic, than this image is a gateway to the real, and the real is grotesque. Even here, Goya has not reached absolute nihility, because the Spanish bodies are classically proportioned and quite beautiful, which dignifies the victims and thus exposes a remnant of belief in the good.

Goya's work offers us images from which the singularity of horror emanates. But however truly brutal his etchings are, however raw, honest, and genuinely traumatized, they still evince a beautifying impulse. And by "beautifying," I am talking about more than the obviously artistic features such as the classically proportioned bodies of the Spaniards. By the very act of rendering an image, the artist re-deems the horrific event with beauty, even if the artist has no intention to salvage anything beautiful about the event. The artist may want to accomplish nothing more than to capture the naked truth of an unredeemable violence, but in so doing, he or she recasts the event through overtly aesthetic means.

Such an artist desires to capture the horror properly, and is thus thrown into all the aesthetic questions that make art possible: what palette, angle, or technique gives the appropriate effect? How best can I depict the horror I saw? In light of this aesthetic matrix, we must acknowledge also that even the way we retell, or narrate, the event to others is as "artistic" as a painting. What details, tone, and plot development best capture the event, in light of what one believes about the event, or what they believe the event to be? We need to adjust our focus only slightly to see that the artistry of perception, the aesthetic judgement through which the narrative re-lives the event in a new created medium (namely the story), happens also in the phenomenological appearance of the event itself, the firsthand encounter. The event is perceptible only by a gaze that aesthetically measures and construes the original event, and thus at once helps to "create" that event.⁵⁶ There is no horror, out there as it were, that is not one's horror.⁵⁷

While Goya's work evinces a beautifying impulse, that impulse still serves a morose end. He achieves remarkable honesty in his paintings precisely by giving horror the primary word, whether that was through the gritty portrayals of wartime atrocities, or through the astral dread of the monstrous. Is Goya then irretrievably gloomy? Insofar as he achieves horror without remainder, does he advocate for hopelessness, nihilism, and meaninglessness in the face of such violence? No matter how hopeless Goya, or anyone, feels, horror is only possible as reverence. Therefore, however genuinely horrified, one continues to believe, see, and encounter the holy.

Holiness saves horror. Goya's "Disasters of War" etchings would be even more heinous if they weren't horrifying. Goya's overwhelming gloom may appear to flaunt a meaningless existence, but that is a lie. Goya's work is powerful only because it has a deep feeling for meaning. Otherwise, why

---

56. John Milbank speaks of construal: "Hamann persistently claims, in 'Aesthetica in Nuce' and elsewhere, that we only see things when they speak to us, or that we cannot have sight if we are deaf. What exactly can this mean? . . . What he seems to mean is that we never grasp a thing in isolation, but only as articulated with something else, and yet that in such articulation there is a necessary 'talking together,' or reading of the conjunction over and above what merely appears: for example a tree does not appear to me as one tree, rather I construe this. Yet if such a reading or construing is taken as non-arbitrary this means that what is invisible in the tree 'speaks' to me as one tree. . . . It is for this reason that Hamann always links the 'depth' in things with the depth in the human subject which images the creative power of God. . . . Day may speak to day, and night to night, but I know this only if I creatively express it, and make the sign 'day' a non-identically repeatable expression" (Milbank, "Theological Critique of Philosophy," 27). When Milbank says that the tree's objectivity alone is not responsible for its appearance, he is recognizing the marvel that within a material world shapes, forms, and natures emerge, which cannot be reduced to the material. Jean-Luc Marion makes the same point: "Without the work of the invisible, what we perceive as visible actually would offer only a rhapsodic spectacle and confusion of colored spots" (Marion, *Crossing*, 12). Moreover, "the invisible of the gaze is stretched out, arranged and displaying the chaos of the visible as harmonious phenomena" (Marion, *Crossing*, 5). For the differences between Milbank and Marion on this point, see Milbank, "Beauty and the Soul," 26. This is all another way of indicating the simultaneously active and passive aspects of consciousness with regard to "objects." For example, the red of a rose is not in the rose itself in any objective sense, independent from the perception of sight, which construes redness. So if asked, in what way is the rose "really" red, we must say that it is indeed actually red, but only so as a interconnected reality between subject and object. See further Hart, *Experience of God*, 179.

57. This is the same logic as Michel Henry's, there is no suffering that is not one's suffering. See Henry, "Phenomenology of Life," 249.

should anyone consider such moments of violence to be remarkable? In a truly meaningless, nihilistic world, why take a second glance at these mutilated bodies? Why should the horrors of war be any different than a fallen leaf on the ground, or a gardener trimming hedges? If these events are considered nihilistically, then surely one gains nothing from rendering and displaying them, for what effect could one hope for in such a scene? The violence would be no more surprising or disturbing then the trampled blade of grass.

But Goya's work does have a powerful effect. It is loud. It screams with the "scream of nature" ("*Der Schrei der Natur*," the original title of Munch's famous painting "The Scream"). Such a scream is not on account of nothing, but the magnitude of what has been violated. More precisely, horror arises from the violation of sanctity. We can make an exact correlation: more horror equals more sanctity. This explains why among the possible heinous acts, the sexual abuse of children is of the most repulsive kind. It incorporates (among other things) the innocence and purity of children, the intimacy of sex, which belongs to the sacrament of marriage, and the guardianship of adults over children. Horror is thus predicated upon sanctity, and increases to the degree that sanctity increases. Horror proclaims, identifies, and thereby *reveres* the holy. Therefore, what harrows also hallows.[58]

THE GROTESQUE WILL SAVE THE WORLD

In Fyodor Dostoevsky's novel *The Idiot* we read those now famous words, "beauty will save the world."[59] If merely attributed to the fictitious Christ-figure, the idiotic Prince Myshkin, in Dostoevsky's novel, the saying became all the more tangible when it came from the pen of Rome's Christ-figure,

---

58. Flannery O'Connor, that learned observer of the grotesque, said that she employed distortion in order to disclose the sanctity of a thing: "When I write a novel in which the central action is a baptism, I am very well aware that for a majority of my readers, baptism is a meaningless rite, and so in my novel I have to see that this baptism carries enough awe and mystery to jar the reader into some kind of emotional recognition of its significance. To this end I have to bend the whole novel—its language, its structure, its action. I have to make the reader feel, in his bones if nowhere else, that something is going on here that counts. Distortion in this case is an instrument; exaggeration has a purpose, and the whole structure of the story or novel has been made what it is because of belief. This is not the kind of distortion that destroys; it is the kind that reveals, or should reveal" (O'Connor, "Novelist and Believer," 162).

59. Dostoevsky, *Idiot*, 383.

namely Pope John Paul II. In his *Letter to Artists*, John Paul II speaks to the timeliness of wonder: "People of today and tomorrow need this enthusiasm if they are to meet and master the crucial challenges which stand before us"; and thanks to this enthusiasm, humanity will be able to navigate through life's many trials by setting itself upon the right path, and thus "In this sense it has been said with profound insight that 'beauty will save the world.'"[60]

If I say that the grotesque will save the world I make no attempt to counter Dostoevsky or John Paul II, but detail, restrict, or focus their contention. The grotesque is an aesthetic genre or mood and thus an aspect of beauty. For the grotesque is a perennial motif in all aesthetic mediums, as grotesques prove to be deeply mesmerizing and attractive. It is especially pertinent because it captures the point at which beauty vanishes. In an obvious sense, grotesques often show mutilated and disproportionate figures, which is a visible rupture of classically beautiful standards. However, grotesques please the eye not in spite of their disproportion, obscurity, and dread, but because of them. The combined elements of attraction and terror that together offer a more total beauty paradoxically appears in a way "beyond beauty." In light of the eclipse of the holy (or the white light of holiness), grotesques capture that moment, that stasis, when beauty returns upon the inscrutable white light of holiness. The visible *anti*-aesthetic speaks to the *ante*-aesthetic, namely the holy. Such encounters allow spectators to traverse beauty's return, its apotheosis. Therefore, the grotesque is an especially timely, though enduring, medium of beauty and holiness.

What exactly do I mean by grotesque? Historically, one finds a variety of definitions, classifications, and standards, but I mean "grotesque" in the broadest, and yet deepest terms.[61] The grotesque is what aesthetically renders the singularity that simultaneously generates attraction and fear. The "singularity" involved here is synonymous with the "holy." In other words, the grotesque aesthetically depicts luminous darkness (ὑπέρφωτον

---

60. John Paul II, "Letter to Artists," 16.

61. Wolfgang Kayser sees the grotesque beginning with the late fifteenth-century discovery of Roman work and traces it to the present. Kayser, *Grotesque*, 13–29. Mikhail Bakhtin takes a rather ahistorical view of the grotesque as exemplified in the carnivals and festivals of the medieval era. Bakhtin, *Rabelais and His World*. Others such as Ewa Kuryluk and Geoffrey Harpham see the grotesque as formally bound to historic forms, which cannot be repeated accurately in the general malaise of contemporary culture. Kuryluk, *Salome and Judas*; Harpham, *Grotesque*. See also Yates, "Introduction to the Grotesque," 1–40.

γνόφον).⁶² To the degree the pseudo-grotesque fails to be "luminous" or compelling, it becomes inane, pretentious, or boring. To the degree it fails to be "dark," is becomes trite, oppressive, and apathetic.

The grotesque is timely not only because it is formally mystical and holy, but because our time is begging for it, seeking it, and creating it. Grotesqueries saturate our culture, and can be seen as the unspecified cry of Israel to the beyond (Exod 3:7-8; cf. 2:23-24). Moreover, Christianity has the greatest capacity to render the grotesque. On the one hand, Christianity positively accounts for grotesque-induced terror by refusing to see it as a limited quality of demonic darkness, opposed to angelic light. This duality would limit and thus belittle both divine light and the scope of the darkness one encounters in ominous dread. This fear would only reach as far as the counter-border of light and no further. Rather, Christianity sees the divine light itself not only as "fearful too," but as *the* originary terror in which and to which all subsequent instances of terror stand. On the other hand, while Christianity can maximize the darkness of the grotesque more than any other worldview, it can also best save the inherent liberating power of the grotesque because it overcomes all ontological violence. A philosophy resigned to violence, whether in the guise of fate, determinism, or nihilism, will inevitably mute the grotesque by limiting ahead of time the extent of its power. The real poignancy of grotesques is that whatever violence is depicted on the surface, a "higher," more inscrutable, more frightening, more

---

62. Dionysius, *Mystical Theology*, 997B. On this *analogical* connection between Dionysian light and the grotesque: Otto von Simson asks the rhetorical question, how can God be manifest in human creations (namely through the gargoyles and features of the gothic cathedral)? He says, "The Pseudo-Areopagite answered this question by pointing to the frailty of our intellect, which is incapable of perceiving God face to face. Therefore, God interposes images between Him and us. Holy Writ as well as nature are such 'screens'; they present us with images of God, designed to be imperfect, distorted, even contradictory. This imperfection and mutual contradiction, apparent even to our minds, is to kindle in us the desire to ascend from a world of mere shadows and images to the contemplation of the Divine Light itself. Thus it is, paradoxically enough, by evading us that God becomes gradually manifest; He conceals Himself before us in order to be revealed" (Simson, *Gothic Cathedral*, 53). Moreover, Simson emphasizes that the connection is predicated upon analogical metaphysics: "At the basis of all medieval thought is the concept of *analogy*. All things have been created according to the law of analogy, in virtue of which they are, in various degrees, manifestations of God, images, vestiges, or shadows of the Creator. The degree to which a thing 'resembles' God, to which God is present in it, determines its place in the hierarchy of beings" (Simson, *Gothic Cathedral*, 54). In his important study *On the Grotesque: Strategies of Contradiction in Art and Literature*, Geoffrey Harpham uses Simson's passage on Dionysius to explicate the grotesque. Harpham, *Grotesque*, 109-10.

powerful One forever remains "beyond" and sovereign. The real power here is that while the grotesque can make its attempt to incite violence and evil, it delivers its greatest threat as it bespeaks that divine Other who is wholly unaffected by and still more frightening than any particular moment of evil.

The apocalyptic drama in the book of Revelation displays this dynamic, namely that the grotesque is dreadful to the degree it conjures a still-more-frightening Other. The forces of darkness are led by the Red Dragon, that ancient serpent called the devil or Satan (Rev 12:9). He has seven heads with ten horns. With him are two beasts. The greater of the two emerged from the sea, and also had seven heads with ten horns, but also had the appearance of a leopard with feet like a bear and a mouth like a lion (13:1–2). Upon his head were blasphemous names. The lesser of the two rose out of the earth and had two horns like a lamb, and he spoke like a dragon (13:11–13). These creatures are symbols of power and fear. But those who make war against the Lamb will be conquered, "for he is Lord *of* lords and King *of* kings" (17:14).[63] Even here, the supremacy of the Lamb over the Dragon and his beasts is comically absurd. The lamb is typically a symbol of meekness, but here the Lamb stands on Mount Zion with his followers who have the Father's name written on their heads (14:1–2).

God sends forth seven "holy angels" with seven plagues to destroy the beast and all its worshippers (14:10). Before the destruction, God sent forth one of his angels to proclaim an "eternal gospel" to every nation and tribe, language and people, "*Fear God* and give him glory, for the hour of his judgment has come; and worship him who made heaven and earth, the sea and the springs of water" (14:7).[64] Those who withstood the beast and did not succumb to him in fear sang the song of the Lamb, in which we hear, "Lord, who will not fear and glorify your name? For you alone are holy" (15:4). When the first three angels poured their bowls upon the earth, the sea, and the rivers, which brought terrible sores to the people and turned all the water into blood, the angel in charge of the waters said, "Just are you, O Holy One, who is and who was" (16:5). When all the plagues had finished, multitudes rejoiced in heaven, and the twenty-four elders and the four living creatures worshipped God saying, "Praise our God, all you his servants, and all who fear him, small and great" (19:5).

---

63. Emphasis mine.
64. Emphasis mine.

These four living creatures are presented as the greatest of all creatures. Each is clothed in eyes and takes to flight by six wings. The first is like a lion, the second like an ox, the third has the face of a man, and the fourth is like an eagle (4:6–8). Forever they utter these words: "'Holy, Holy, Holy, is the Lord God Almighty,' who was, and is, and is to come" (4:8). They are mutated, grotesque figures, part animal, part human, part angel, with unsightly, even beastly features. Yet what is most remarkable about them is that these monstrous creatures, who would otherwise be among the most frightening things we could envision, are themselves filled with fright. In Isaiah's vision, which depicts similar creatures, the Seraphim fly with two wings, which one can imagine are Jurassic-like, while with another two they hide their faces, cowering, and with the remaining two, they cover their feet (Isa 6:1–3).

From an initial assessment, one would imagine that the Red Dragon and his beast are the most dreadful, and thus the most grotesque of Revelation's characters. But this is only to believe the demonic lie, which claims the dread of the holy for itself. The lesser beast reveres the greater, and the greater beast reveres the Dragon. Though the Dragon refuses to fear God, he is nevertheless conquered by him. Therefore, in the end, the Red Dragon's might only testifies to the superior might of the One who conquered him. The angels are terrifying because of their power, and though we know little of their appearance, they exercise this power exactly as worship and service to God. Above them are the four grotesque living creatures who magnify our reverence of God, because though they are terrifying, they are still terrified of another. The Lamb, the perfect Son of the Father, absolutely hallows the Father and has supreme power and authority. If the four living creatures were dreadful because they were "obviously" monstrous and powerful beings, the Son is even more dreadful because he wields more power than any other being but does so as the nonthreatening, vulnerable, and grazing animal that is the common lamb. Therefore, the power that we know he has is incomprehensible and unexpected. He is so entirely "beyond" created beings that nothing is in any way truly competitive with him. His supremacy is of another order, whereby he stands unrivaled though nonthreatening. He is, therefore, a dazzling, haunting, and truly ominous symbol of fear and power. But still, this grotesquery is predicated upon his manifestation of the Holy Father. He is most harrowing because he is pure hallowing.

Nevertheless, one might object that the church is no place for the grotesque. For the church, one might say, ought to be welcoming, not a horror house or some exhibition. Agreed, but however hospitable the church is, we have to keep that singularity which lures attraction and fear. Granted, a grotesque in a church will affect those who enter. One might wander in and shudder at the first glance of it. The one who brings a newcomer may feel the need to prepare his or her guest as they approach it. Children may need to be cautioned as they pass by it. Those who are in the throes of deep agony may need to avert their gaze from the grotesque. All this inconvenience may be the very reason why some feel we should abandon all grotesques. But let us imagine the impossible thing that we had the holiness of God in a glass jar and placed it upon a shelf in the church for all to see. Those who passed it would be shocked. Children would need to be cautioned and newcomers prepared. The same kind of dynamics are at play with the imaginary jar and the grotesque. If the holiness of God was bottled up, the very sight of it would be deeply disruptive to the otherwise natural order of our lives. An awe-inducing grotesque commands a certain kind of consecration that displays a structural affinity with the holy itself.

But is fear really a fitting response to God who has not given us a "spirit of fear" but of love (2 Tim 1:7)? Indeed, God has given a spirit of love, but before doing away with fear altogether, we should ask, what kind of person is without fear? A purely fearless person sees every impending threat to his or her health and safety as inconsequential. For reasons not yet specified, this person has given up on themselves and abandoned the task of survival. The implications extend beyond the confines of individual security. This person is altogether indifferent to the suffering of others. They cannot even acknowledge suffering as such because they have no connection to the dread of suffering. Nothing can phase this fearless person, and yet he or she will be alienated by the world, a world that is incomprehensible because of the economy of fear upon which it depends. In a fallen and violent world, the fearless person cannot receive life as a gift, as he or she is entirely unmotivated to protect it and thus receive it.

Because this person is fearless, the fretting of others can only appear silly. The more one is alienated from others the more one's "amusement" towards suffering becomes sinister, as he or she is disconnected from their deepest concerns and motivations that invariably guide their every decision. Also, fearlessness usually has the luxury of power, which liberates one from fear-inducing violence. Thus the fearless person exercises a certain tyranny, and is liable to find pleasure in torture. Without an acute, immanent knowledge of fear and thus the fear of those who suffer, one cannot distinguish between play, joking, and suffering.[65]

But does life so entirely submit to fear as to depend upon it and thus violence also? In the absolute sense, no. For the basic creaturely fears that we all have are met by God, who though being incomparably frightening and powerful loved us before we loved him. God's fortuitous love comforts us, namely as God's Love who is the Spirit, the Comforter. By so loving us, God raises our fears towards himself and they become awe, wonder, and delight, though never a delight that is wholly untroubled, but the weighty delight that is as shocked as it is grateful. Therefore, God's love is hauntingly beautiful, humbling in majesty, and incomprehensibly true. In other words,

---

65. In his fascinating work *God Is Watching You: How the Fear of God Makes Us Human*, Dominic Johnson provides anthropological and sociological evidence for why the fear of the Lord is integral to human nature, and subsequently human flourishing. He argues that "belief in supernatural reward and punishment is no quirk of western or Christian culture. It is a *ubiquitous phenomenon of human nature* that spans cultures across the globe and every historical period, from indigenous tribal societies, to ancient civilizations, to modern world religions—and includes atheists too. Heaven and hell may be the best-known versions of supernatural reward and punishment, but they are mirrored by a panoply of others that are thought to occur in this life—notably negative outcomes such as misfortune, disease, and death—as well as in the hereafter. And while we in the West tend to think of a single, omnipotent God as our judge, in other cultures rewards and punishments may come from a pantheon of gods, angels, demons, shamans, witches, ancestors, ghosts, jinns, spirits, animals, sorcerers, and voodoo. In other cases there is no specific agent at all, but supernatural consequences still come as the result of karmic forces of nature and the universe. The variation is remarkable, but there is a clear underlying pattern: our behavior is strongly influenced by the anticipated supernatural consequences of our actions. They make us question our selfish desires, deter self-interested actions, and perform remarkable acts of generosity and altruism—even when alone and even when temptation comes knocking at our door" (Johnson, *God Is Watching*, 7). Moreover, Johnson argues that while there are indeed "many scientists who argue that religion is an accidental byproduct of human cognitive mechanisms that evolved for other reasons, there are many other scientists who argue that religion is the polar opposite of an evolutionary accident—rather, that it is an evolutionary *adaptation*. New work in anthropology, psychology, and evolutionary biology suggests that not only do religious beliefs and practices bring important advantages in today's world (such as promoting cooperation and collective action), but that they were actually *favored by* Darwinian natural selection because they improved the survival and reproductive success of believers in our ancestral past. This offers a scientific alternative to the Dawkins model of God-as-accident. It also offers a striking twist on the old science and religion debate: religion is not an alternative to evolution, it is a *product of* evolution" (Johnson, *God Is Watching*, 11). For a more holistic account of religion and evolutionary theory from the Christian metaphysical perspective see Cunningham, *Pious Idea*.

God's love is holy, and it fulfills the basic creaturely impulses of fear by the glory of reverence.

Besides being passably Christian, why should the church consider implementing grotesqueries? By creating and engaging grotesques, we create innumerable opportunities to correct excesses and vices that plague the church. We also reach a new depth of profundity and insight that is otherwise inaccessible.

First, grotesques are acts of solidarity and compassion. This can be seen straightforwardly in images and music that speak directly to injustices and evil, and so empathize with the suffering of the world.[66] Whatever the chosen medium, one has the ability to say with a grotesque, "I feel what you feel, I see what you see, I hurt how you hurt." The insecurities that can accompany a newcomer to church can be addressed in love before any formal meeting. Will I be accepted, or judged? Are my sins too many, too heinous? Can they handle a drug addict, a prostitute? Is the church more than a bandage for sentimental folk; can it address the horrors I've seen, I've committed? We can speak Christ's "Yes and Amen" without uttering a word (cf. 2 Cor 1:20). Also, by taking up the challenge to create grotesques, we will be made more sensitive to the pain of others, and therefore be all the more ready to love. Moreover, these kinds of grotesques can also critique and condemn the latent apathy in many churches. One may be unwilling to compassionately put themselves in others' shoes, as it were, nor go out into the world to see its hurt, but a confrontation with a powerful, and yet still appropriate, grotesque will be an immanent word of admonition.

Second, grotesques save us from nihilism. One may find this idea counterintuitive because the grotesque is often a symbol of nihilism itself. Here we might think of the contemporary master of the genre, Francis Bacon. But to retrieve the point about the sanctity *of* horror, the sanctity in-and-beyond horror, the act of painting is a way of bringing meaning about in a meaningless world. However resigned to nihilism one may be, he or she defies such nihilism by the creative process. Painting is thus an unwillingness to surrender all truth, goodness, and beauty to nothing, even if this crusade for meaning has the false humility of one who says, "this life is all there is so we might as well do something with it." Nihilism is not the logical, coherent theory that best accounts for human experience, but is

---

66. See my article "On the Humanity of *Mad Max*," in which I seek to demonstrate how *Mad Max*, a thoroughly grotesque action film, exudes a deeply compassionate sensibility. See Roberts, "*Mad Max*."

instead a lament. Therefore, grotesques can subtly defend life by its "pleasing" and persuasive articulation of the lament that is nihilism.

In addition to this overt nihilism, grotesques critique modernist rationality (and its post-modern offspring), that ethos of belief that seeks to "get" the truth once and for all, whether this is the positivism based upon scientific method, theological foundationalism, or the various kin of dialectics. Ultimately, the grotesque has the power to undercut false confidence. Its effect is not tied to any single philosophy or ideology, but always stands beyond one's grasp and finds a way of disrupting the status quo with an inconvenient truth.

Third, grotesques critique every form of puritanism, self-righteousness, and elitism. In this way, Christ's parables anticipate the grotesque satire of Goya's etchings, "The Disasters of War" and the "*Caprichos.*" In the latter, Goya uses the image of a donkey to undercut the elitism of his time. Plate 37, "Perhaps the Pupil Knows Better?," depicts a student donkey instructing the teacher, who is also a donkey, on the basics of the alphabet. In Plate 38, "Bravissimo!," a monkey serenades a donkey with a guitar, and in Plate 40, "Of What Ill Will He Die?," a donkey physician attends to a patient on his death bed. But Christ's grotesque exceeds Goya's. For Christ, the absurdity comes positively from the truth itself—as with the offensive and ignoble love of the prodigal's father—and is the paradoxical "darkness" of the light. Goya's absurdity goes no farther than a negative critique. Thus, Goya's image implicitly suggests that we ought to move away from the absurd, where Christ's suggests that we must move into it. The grotesque has the capacity to cut across every dividing line: across races, countries, tribes, and classes; it is blind to wealth and poverty, purity and guilt, honor and shame. For these reasons, the grotesque is in sync with gospel itself.

If the grotesque critiques this kind of puritanism, it does not obliterate purity as such. True purity is deeply grotesque. The world is so violent that to see someone or something untainted by it is as mysterious as any other phenomenon. In light of true purity, we ask, "From where does its power and delicacy come?" Purity in its proper form is thus ominous. It stands over against the economies of violence and declares the supremacy of another order. But it also threatens like all grotesques, for those sullied by the world know that if this purity were to reign, they would be wholly consumed (at least all they know of themselves).

Fourth, grotesques mediate transcendence. Our discussion of Picasso and Goya has already indicated the phenomenological profile of transcendence that accompanies the grotesque. But this transcendent moment reaches farther than the confines of art galleries and represents God in the collective imagination of a culture. We may belong to a secular age, but people are as indulgent in alternative modes of transcendence as ever. The examples are endless. Consider the unprecedented commercial success and cultural dominance of mega-franchises such as *Harry Potter*, *The Lord of the Rings* and *The Hobbit*, *Star Wars*, *Star Trek*, and what has now become superhero fanaticism. We also see the grotesque prominently in video games, which have become a multi-billion dollar industry. We see the new levels of devotion at fan expos and conventions at which devotees arrive in full costume (cassock?) and may be able to speak Klingon or Elvish.

This imaginative, transcendent alternative to religious consciousness is more than a chance to escape life, it is a chance to *finally* experience life. These fantasies are not a rival to religion and Christianity, but the "religious" cultus of a people victimized by a secular age. They are cultural "high places" at which one can feel something of the ominous holy. Behind the lure of these franchises is a stunning, beautiful, and profound disclosure of the holiness of God through the darkness of grotesques. *The Lord of the Rings* (and *The Hobbit*) not only have an exquisite variety of mesmerizing grotesque creatures (e.g., orcs and Uruk-hai), but the integrity of the story itself is predicated upon the ghost of Sauron, whose great eye burns within the walls of Mordor.[67] Frodo and Sam set out to destroy the ring of power under the impending threat of Sauron's bodily return. In other words, Sauron haunts Middle-earth. *Harry Potter* has its own dazzling grotesques, but again, its overall persuasiveness is tied to the looming threat of "He-Who-Must-Not-Be-Named," Voldemort, who is ethereally absent/present. This is exactly the play of the holy itself, which was discussed in chapter 1 and 2 regarding the holy as the name that cannot be named and its present/absent dynamic. Video games can be equally as grotesque and dark.

One might ask whether or not grotesques are inappropriate for children to see. Granted, children are uniquely vulnerable, and we must consider that when introducing grotesques. But we delude ourselves and harm our children if we think that they need to be shielded from or kept oblivious to the darkness in life. Moreover, children and youth are compelled by the grotesque. Old Disney films are deeply ominous (e.g., *Fantasia*, *Snow White and the Seven Dwarfs*, *Pinocchio*). While these films mostly reserve such dread for the baddies, we have seen a movement from seeing hidden beauty

---

67. See Milbank, *Chesterton and Tolkien*.

in the grotesque "other" (*Beauty and the Beast*), to making grotesques central to the storyline or even as protagonists (e.g., *Shrek, Hotel Transylvania, Nightmare Before Christmas, Despicable Me, Monsters Inc., Megamind*). The grotesque has proved to appeal to children's sensibilities and educate them by gaining compassion for the "other." A powerful symbol of the grotesque's universal appeal is Kim Adams's sculpture *Breugel-Bosch Bus*. The sculpture is a 1960 Volkswagen that has been transformed into a diorama. Adams re-interprets two classic grotesques, *Tower of Babel* by Pieter Bruegel (1525–1569) and *The Garden of Earthly Delights* by Hieronomous Bosch (1450–1516), by creating a scene made entirely of toys. By studying the grotesque in contemporary American film and literature, Schuy Weishaar describes the workings of the grotesque in remarkable continuity with our thesis: "The grotesque is the prism at the center of this process, constantly fragmenting and obfuscating, but in such a way that it adds variety, intensity, and color to the visions we perceive," and "Just as the prism refracts all light that tries to penetrate it, the grotesque effects a kind of leveling of those worlds that writers/artists 'shine' through it."[68] This "initiates the

---

68. Weishaar, *Masters*, 4. In *Masters of the Grotesque*, which deals extensively with *Nightmare Before Christmas* creator Tim Burton, Schuy Weishaar ties a number of our themes together: "the comic and tragic drama of life persists simultaneously as we fruitlessly exert ourselves in our attempts to bring resolutions, to make them. They are parallel but particular blanknesses that can devastate and horrify as much as they astound or delight because they invite contradiction, opposition, conflict, combination, fragmentation, synthesis, and scission . . . the grotesque names this level of our conflict-ridden interchange . . . with reality aesthetically expressed. As with Ishmael's uncanny moment of recognition in the dark, his realization about the ineffability of whiteness, or Pip's mad sea-born sagacity, our categories, the contents of these categories, the meanings and associations with which they are invested, and the crippling effects their confusion entails for us—these are the junctures whereat the grotesque can emerge as the (meta-physical) aesthetic context within which such confusion arises, can be recognized, and/or expressed. It works according to a principle of macerated mimesis in its isolation, application, inversion, division, unification, etc. of any of the competing poles of the paradoxes between which human being finds itself drawn: light and dark, high and low, inside and outside, body and essence, contentment and anxiety, creation and destruction, life and death, good and evil, pleasure and pain, transcendence and obfuscation, the divine and the demonic, movement and stasis, self and other, official and carnival, imaginativeness and bleak materialism, reason and madness, mythic and modern, and the list goes on. Whether the grotesque finds expression as a literary mode, an artistic style, an aesthetic dimension, a pattern of thought (archetype, etc.), a metaphysical reality, a social ideology, or something else, it is utterly bound up with the human. Perhaps this is why its fruits seem forbidden but necessary. Perhaps this is why it can elicit desire and disgust, laughter and revulsion—or, simply put, love and hate and everything that comes with them—all at once. The grotesque is caught up with the breadth, depth, and

critic/theorist of the grotesque on a spiraling journey both into and out from the seats of contradition and/or paradox."[69]

Fifth and finally, the grotesque restores humor, which for many people is not associated with the church. As discussed above, grotesques share the absurd with comedies. Thus, comedy regularly employs the grotesque to invoke the absurd for the end of humor. Inversely, grotesques regularly employ comedic elements, which we see spectacularly in Goya's etchings (e.g., in Plate 42 of the *Capricho* series, Goya depicts two donkeys riding on the backs of two poor men, which is an indictment against the nobility, who are thought to have profited while metaphorically riding on the backs of the hard working poor). Therefore, humor ought to be a vital aspect of the church's charisma. We can look back to the uniqueness of Israel's Scriptures that are charmingly self-deprecating of Israel's own national identity and of its individual heroes. Christianity's grammar is comedically humbling all the way along, and one can argue that if we lose this *sense* of humour, we may lose it all. Though the church ought to be a humorous people, that does not mean it should be frivolous and trite.

On the contrary, humor is divine, for it is that profoundly rendered understanding of the depth and importance always at stake with an equal awareness of our fragility, vulnerability, and general inability. Consider the likes of Winston Churchill or Abraham Lincoln, whose political achievements were so intimately tied to their sense of humor, both because it brought opposing and hostile parties together, but also for the way in which it kept these men sane in insane times.[70] This kind of humor is the resolve of courage without self-aggrandizement. Therefore, humor may be one of our greatest teachers in times of darkness and sorrow. By "sanctioning" humorous grotesques, we guide the church towards incorporating reverent humor

---

confusion of what it means to be human" (Weishaar, *Masters*, 193). For Weishaar's argument that Dr. Seuss may be more subversively grotesque than Bruegel, Bosch, and Bacon, see Weishaar, *Masters*, 2–4.

69. Weishaar, *Masters*, 4.

70. In *The Humorous Mr. Lincoln*, Keith W. Jennison wrote: "Mr. Lincoln's use of humor changed. During the wilderness years he told jokes and stories without trying to prove anything at all; he told them simply because it was natural for him to do so. After he became a lawyer he found that his wit and his acute sense of the ridiculous were effective courtroom tools. As a politician he handed the weapon of satire as a stiletto or a broadax as the occasion demanded. During the first few months of his Presidency he used humor many times as a roundabout way of saying 'no.' As his responsibility grew and became almost unendurable he took to telling jokes again, trying to lessen the tensions in himself and those around him" (Jennison, *Humorous Mr. Lincoln*, 1).

into its life, which will at once relieve pressing anxieties and inspire acts of courage. One can see how ancient Spartan warriors were humorous to the extent they were fearless.[71] Because the singularity of humor can simultaneously maximize humility and courage, which appear oxymoronic while paradoxically harmonious.

Christ himself is inconceivable apart from the absurd. He is a human person who hungers and thirsts, though claims to have created food and drink. He is the author of life put to death. He serves us though he is our master. He humbles the exalted and exalts the humble. Thus, theology itself must be comedic and grotesque, not simply to "represent" the subject matter but to participate in it. For the very idea that we can speak learnedly about God is at once humorous and grotesque because of how "beyond" he is; and yet, he is the beyond "in" our midst, which makes the creation of comedic grotesques desirable over absolute silence.

CONCLUSION

Bulgakov recognized the dark spiritual power of Picasso's paintings, but wholly resisted them as demonic temptations. But the church must consider the wider question: with whom does this power ultimately lie? The demonic omits a distinct spiritual quality that we can name with Otto as numinous fear, which is an originary feature of holiness. So what are the consequences of opposing demonic dread and divine dread? Either we absolutize the difference between light and darkness in ontological dualism, or we suggest that evil is an actual reality created by God. Both disrupt sound Christian convictions. Rather, the demonic is the idolatrous distortion of numinous fear, but nevertheless always a participation in the holiness of God. Thus, we can see a qualitative affinity between the demonic, or grotesque, and the holy.

By comparing Kayser's account of the grotesque with the holy, we also discovered a structural affinity. Kayser says the grotesque depicts a pregnant depth "in and behind" the image, which makes all contemplation and language regarding the "It" of the grotesque inherently posterior. Also, as a play of the absurd in an estranged world, the grotesque ruptures, fractures, and crosses all our finite categories and shows how tenuous our concepts and names are. In order to maintain estrangement, the grotesque must occupy a "suspended middle" between what is alien and what is familiar. All

---

71. See Feickert, "Fighting in the Shade," 119–36.

of these features accord with the dynamics of the white light of holiness. Moreover, the grotesque is mystical on a formal level, as the mystic sensibility is that which apprehends the aesthetic measure of paradox that unveils the holy. Therefore, the grotesque participates in the eternal gaze of the Son upon the Invisible Father.

Moreover, this chapter argued that not only does holiness "fit" with the problematic of horror, but that holiness alone saves horror. Goya's etchings are an example of horror without remainder, and we saw that these gloomy images are not powerful because they parade a meaningless existence, but rather that they are powerful because of the magnitude of what has been violated. For why should these etchings, or any heinous act for that matter, be in any way offensive, horrifying, or even inconvenient if they do not violate some perceived sanctity? Thus we see a direct equivalence: more horror equals more sanctity. Horror identifies, proclaims, and thus reveres the holy. What harrows also hallows.

With this renewed connection between the divine and the grotesque in mind, I suggested that in Dostoevsky's "beauty will save the world," that beauty be replaced by the grotesque. For metaphysically, the grotesque captures that moment, that stasis, when beauty returns upon the inscrutable white light of holiness. The grotesque's *anti*-aesthetic speaks to the ontological *ante*-aesthetic, namely the holy. Such encounters allow spectators to traverse beauty's return to the holy. The grotesque is then what aesthetically renders the singularity that simultaneously generates attraction and fear, this "singularity" being synonymous with the holy.

Moreover, culture craves and seeks transcendence in the grotesque, and Christianity has the greatest capacity to render it. Additionally, I offered five concrete reasons why the grotesque will connect the world and the church, elevating both: it is an act of solidarity and compassion, it saves us from nihilism, it condemns a certain puritanism, it mediates transcendence, and it restores humor. In the end, I believe the grotesque will save the world, partially for the theoretical reasons I suggest, but really because all such reasons are predicated upon this basic truth, the grotesque has saved the world. For in weakness and fear we proclaim the mystery of God, Christ and him crucified, who is that morbid if still radiant light of the world (1 Cor 2:2).

5

The Secret

"For my part I am convinced that no creature, not even an angel, is permitted to comprehend this secret of divine love, so holy and so august."[1]

—Bernard of Clairvaux, *Song of Songs*.

"The faith that you have, keep between yourself and God."

—Rom 14:22

INTRODUCTION

As mentioned above, if the holy is a transcendental, then the nature of holiness becomes relevant to everything in existence. The previous chapter considered a single, glaring, issue in relation to this thesis, namely how can we say that everything is holy in light of the many atrocities we see in the world. This chapter will begin to demonstrate the breadth of the holy's reach by connecting it to "the Gift," an already established social dynamic that has been shown to comprehend the entirety of inter-personal life. This

---

1. Bernard of Clairvaux, *Song of Songs*, 8.2.

chapter will argue that the gift is predicated upon "the Secret," and just as the gift is the dynamic of the good, the secret is the dynamic of the holy. The gift is a symbol of excess that keeps the secret holy and keeps the holy secret. First, this chapter will seek to show how the sociality of the gift discloses secrecy as its precondition. Second, it will argue that because secrecy is the dynamic of the holy, keeping secret is a preeminent Christian virtue and an integral aspect of love. Finally, in light of the dynamics of secrecy, it will argue that the mask is an inherent and quintessential aspect of consciousness, insofar as the mask reveals by concealing.

SECRECY AND THE GIFT

As a philosophical theme, the gift has captured the imagination of various disciplines and has proved to be a fundamental aspect of human social relationships.[2] The gift is involved in our most concrete concerns, such as "What will I give my wife for our anniversary?" But it also extends to the very reaches of God himself. Is all that *is* an accident of material causes, or a "creation" formed into something like a gift to be received? The gift alters the way one thinks about society and economics. Are we bound together only through contracts, without which we would have no inherent need for or connection with others? Or are we more fundamentally bound through mutual gift-giving?[3]

If the gift is so central to humanity, then what is the nature of gift-giving? What makes it different from contract? Can one give a "pure" gift that seeks no reward in return? This brings up the question of whether or not the only morally good act is that which expects nothing in return. For

---

2. See for example, Milbank, *Politics of Virtue*; López, *Unity of Being*; Barclay, *Paul and the Gift*; Mauss, *Gift*; Marion, *In Excess*; *Being Given*; Komter, *Gift*.

3. Marcel Mauss's seminal study—entitled *The Gift*—argues that reciprocal gift-giving is more original to society than practices of trade and contract. Moreover, any such form of social bond infiltrates the whole of society, and thus has profound moral ramifications. He says, "As we shall note that this morality and organization," namely that of the gift, "still function [sic] in our own societies, in unchanging fashion and, so to speak, hidden, below the surface, and as we believe that in this we have found one of the human foundations on which our societies are built, we shall be able to deduce a few moral conclusions concerning certain problems posed by the crisis in our own law and economic organization. There we shall call a halt. This page of social history, of theoretical sociology, of conclusions in the field of morality, and of political and economic practice only leads us after all to pose once more, in different forms, questions that are old but ever-new" (Mauss, *Gift*, 4).

some, any trace of self-interest in the original gift is seen as defilement. Is this purely one-way gift desirable or even possible?

Additionally, the nature of the gift concerns the most basic reality, the ground of the Absolute, or the original "stuff" out of which all *is*. For example, Jean-Luc Marion argues that the tendency to separate God from his act of giving is misguided. For Marion, God is not a giver, strictly speaking, but Givenness *par excellence*, which is "beyond being."[4] God is pure givenness or the Gift. Marion's philosophical method is phenomenological because everything *is* only in its givenness. He rejects any metaphysical speculation about divine "being." On the contrary, theologians within the Christian metaphysical tradition consider being (*esse*) according to a triune mode of reciprocity. David Bentley Hart says, "In the Trinity the gift is entire, and entirely 'exposed': the Father gives himself to the Son, and again to the Spirit, and the Son offers everything up to the Father in the Spirit, and the Spirit returns all to the Father through the Son, eternally," and "creation is always already implicated in this giving of the gift because it is—in being inaugurated by the Father, effected by the Son, and perfected by the Spirit—already a gift shared among the persons of the Trinity, in transit, a word spoken by God in his Word and articulated in endless sequences of the Spirit and offered back to the Father."[5]

The gift is anchored in the divine nature. It is the social dynamic of the transcendental Divine Name "Good." Just as the Good is the transcendent "cause" of movement and the choreographer of existence, the gift is like the social manifestation of this movement in the form of giving and receiving. The Good "gives" creation by self-outpouring kenosis and "receives" it (*exitus–reditus*) by luring all things through desire. The gift then is the inter-personal face of the Good. On the spectrum of the triad being-life-intelligence (*esse–vivere–intelligere*), the Good is on the side of being while

---

4. Marion says that givenness is unrelated to whether or not something can be regarded as an "unconstituted given" in epistemological philosophy of consciousness; rather, it is to proceed from the conviction that "everything that shows itself must first give itself... [which] implies that one is questioning givenness as *a mode of phenomenality*, as the *how* or *manner* (*Wie*) of the phenomenon" (Marion, *Reason of the Gift*, 19). See also Marion, "Metaphysics and Phenomenology," 295; *Being Given*, 86.

5. Hart, *Infinite*, 268. Thus, "Love of, the gift to, and delight in the other is one infinite dynamism of giving and receiving, in which desire at once beholds and donates the other."

the gift is that of life and intelligence. Thus, John Milbank calls the gift a "social transcendental."[6]

However prevalent the gift is, it has a certain understated element that is determinative for the gift as such, namely *secrecy*. At a practical level, a gift must be concealed before it is given. Parents hide their children's Christmas presents, even if the children are likely to find the gifts. For if they do find the gifts, the parents will likely choose an even better hiding place the next year, because secrecy "builds" the weight of the gift. In other words, secrecy "gives" the gift. Not only are presents themselves hidden, but the entire gift-giving process is born out of secrecy. One contemplates the kind of gift that should be given away from the recipient, and when a decision has been reached, then he or she must act in secrecy to go acquire or prepare the gift.

But givers act from a still more profound sense of secrecy than whether or not the gift has been pre-exposed. For a great gift gives the feeling that *this* person is the only one who could have given *this* gift. Having received this kind of true gift, we can imagine someone saying, "You know me so well," "Coming from you, this means so much," or "Just what I always wanted!" A true gift requires "insider" knowledge, which cannot be bought, only mutually created. One cannot force themselves into a bond of secrecy. For a true gift is welcomed. It speaks to the bond already in place, but in so creatively expressing that bond through giving a good gift, it also further deepens and enriches the secret between the giver and the recipient.

Like the giver who must be "secretive," the recipient must also maintain the gift in secret. No matter how small a gesture of gratitude one gives, the recipient is always placed in a position to respond to the gift, and thus we can see that a bad gift is a form of violence, which might disappoint, offend, or obligate. When a gift elicits nothing in the recipient but an obligatory response of gratitude, the atmosphere is more like a contractual relationship than one of true gift-giving. I give you something, and you are obliged to respond accordingly. In such a contractual relationship, the recipient has no invested personal interest that their expressed form of gratitude might be received back as a good counter-gift. The recipient then makes no ecstatic reach beyond contractual duty. The giver and the recipient are not "in

---

6. Milbank, *Future of Love*, 360–61. "Christendom, therefore, the sphere of the *ecclesia* as necessarily both personal and material, is the fulfillment of gift-exchange as the social transcendental which is also a metaphysical and theological transcendental: indeed nothing less than the Holy Spirit as gift, or the bond of reciprocal loving union between Father and Son" (Milbank, *Future of Love*, 361).

one another" as thoroughly social beings, but "touch" only indirectly in the neutral territory of the contract. Thus, even subtle forms of contract, seen as apathetic gift-exchange, limit the reaches of human sociality.

In addition to apathy, a recipient can destroy the gift through untempered joy. If the recipient feels compelled to return the gift in full, not out of disinterested duty but overwhelming appreciation, then he or she will undermine the fortuity and grace of the gift by "measuring" its precise worth in the hope of returning an exactly equivalent gift. This kind of measured exchange views the gift more like a commodity, and thus returns to the structure of contract. This untempered counter-giving can be as simple as when someone will not allow a friend to pay for dinner, or when finally conceding, he or she *demands* they go out again to return the favour. Additionally, even if no such concrete demands about returning the favour are made, one can in theory still undermine the gift by trying to *fully* express its meaning, namely by exhausting its every hint of beauty and surprise. Such a recipient has an insatiable need to make it known just how meaningful the gift is, which is seen as a form of counter-gift in gratitude. But if the gift's meaning was ever finally exhausted, which is actually impossible, then the recipient would have reached the boundary-line between gratitude as a counter-gift and indifference, thus delimiting the gift itself. By so drawing a boundary around the gift's meaning, one can do nothing else but contractually exchange the newly commodified non-gift. While the limits of the gift can never truly be found, the recipient still undermines it by *hoping* to reach its limits through a gratitude so comprehensive that nothing about the gift's meaning remains unexpressed.

While the gift is recognizable, it is still inexhaustible. For even a simple gift is irretrievably woven into the entire fabric of human sociality, which itself is an analogical non-identical repetition of a plenitudinous infinity of gifts in the Trinity. In this way, a gift cannot be thought of as any single act or object, but an ineffable touching of souls. Therefore, the giver and the recipient of a gift must maintain the intimacy of secrecy with one another through a measured and virtuous adherence to the logic of the secret. Moreover, the dynamics of giving and receiving discussed thus far have already disclosed the gift's most definitive formal quality, namely that the gift is a symbol of excess that mediates the secret. In gift-giving, the original gift of the giver and the counter-gift of the recipient are true to the extent that they declare an "unspeakable" joy that can only be hinted at through the mediation of symbols (even a symbol as simple as a smile). Thus, the gift itself keeps secret.

If the gift is the dynamism of the good, we can see that both have their essence only as a "praise" to what is beyond, though this beyond still paradoxically contains them. Both have their essence "in-and-beyond" their existence. In doxology, the gift emerges from and returns upon the secret, and the good returns upon the divine essence. Moreover, these two doxological relationships actually overlap. Because the good itself is a symbol of excess from the divine essence, the secret keeping essence of the gift goes back through the good to the divine essence. Therefore, we can say that as the gift is the dynamic of the good, the secret is the dynamic of the divine essence, which we have named Holy.

While Jacque Derrida does not see the gift as a reciprocal bond between persons but rather a unilateral self-sacrifice unto death, he still perceives the inherent connection between the gift and the secret. In his book, *The Gift of Death*, Derrida argues that "The gift is the secret itself, if the secret *itself* can be told. Secrecy is the last word of the gift which is the last word of the secret."[7] Derrida sees the secret as standing in the place of the "essence without essence," which we can see as the *hyper*-essence of Dionysius.[8] He says that a gift that could be recognized "in the light of day, a gift destined for recognition, would immediately annul itself."[9] Therefore, the most decisive paradox is a recognition of "the *gift that is not a present*, the gift of something that remains inaccessible, unrepresentable, and as a consequence secret."[10] Derrida also connects the secret with the *mysterium tremendum* of a Wholly Other to which we respond with fear and trembling.

The *mysterium tremendum* is a "frightful mystery, a secret to make you tremble."[11] Derrida reflects on Paul's phrase "work out your own salva-

---

7. Derrida, *Gift of Death*, 29–30.
8. Derrida, *Gift of Death*, 29.
9. Derrida, *Gift of Death*, 29.
10. Derrida, *Gift of Death*, 29.
11. Derrida, *Gift of Death*, 54. Moreover, "As different as dread, fear, anxiety, terror, panic, or anguish remain from one another, they have already begun in the trembling, and what has provoked them continues, or threatens to continue, to make us tremble. Most often we neither know what is coming upon us nor see its origin; it therefore remains a secret. We are afraid of the fear, we anguish over the anguish, and we tremble. We tremble in that strange repetition that ties an irrefutable past (a shock has been felt, a traumatism has already affected us) to a future that cannot be anticipated; anticipated but unpredictable; *apprehended*, but, and this is why there is a future, apprehended precisely *as* unforeseeable, unpredictable; approached *as* unapproachable."

tion with fear and trembling" (Phil 2:12) and says that the disciples are asked to work in the darkness of knowing all along that it is God who decides. The Other "has no reason to give to us and nothing to settle in our favor, no reason to share his reasons with us."[12] We fear and tremble because we are in the hands of God, under his gaze, though we do not see him or know his will. Derrida says we cannot know his reasons for wanting this or that, our life or death, our salvation or perdition. Thus "we fear and tremble before the inaccessible secret of a God who decides for us although we remain responsible, that is, free to decide, to work, to assume our life and our death."[13] In the Philippians passage, Paul commands the disciples to work towards their salvation in the absence (*apousia*) of their master, not his presence (*parousia*).[14] Therefore, Derrida says we are given over to "absolute solitude."[15] Precisely at the moment God is to be obeyed, he is "absent, hidden and silent, separate, secret."[16] God does not have to explain his motives "if he has any."[17] Otherwise, he would not be God, and we would not be dealing with "the Other as God or with God as *wholly other*."[18] If God explained himself all the time to us, he would be without secrecy. For these reasons, Derrida finally says that one does not speak "with God or to God."[19]

This is where Jesus' good tidings enlightens the "absolute solitude" of life in God's absence. We have been shown God's perfect will in Jesus, who knows and sees all that the Father does (John 5:19–20). Jesus reveals these things to us because we are friends of God, and therefore invited in on the secret (John 15:15). We are grateful to Derrida for connecting the secret and the gift with the *mysterium tremendum*. We also see the melancholy of his secret. For Derrida, the secret, like the gift, has an impossible vocation in which it annihilates itself in living out itself. As John Caputo describes, "The secret is divulged as soon as it is kept; it is divulged by being kept; the

---

12. Derrida, *Gift of Death*, 56.
13. Derrida, *Gift of Death*, 56.
14. Derrida, *Gift of Death*, 56–57.
15. Derrida, *Gift of Death*, 57. He says, we must obey "without either seeing or knowing, without hearing the law or the reasons for the law. Without knowing from whence the thing comes and what awaits us, we are given over to absolute silence. No one can speak with us and no one can speak for us; we must take it upon ourselves, each of us must take it upon himself."
16. Derrida, *Gift of Death*, 57.
17. Derrida, *Gift of Death*, 57.
18. Derrida, *Gift of Death*, 57.
19. Derrida, *Gift of Death*, 57.

promise to keep the secret is broken as soon as it [is] made, is broken in being made.... As soon as I say 'I have a secret,' the secret of the secret has been divulged."[20] By contrast, the Christian *kerygma* is of a lush, hospitable, secret. It is a place of abiding and *rest*, and is thus holy. In Christ, the moments of absence and presence are united by an overarching story of faith, hope, and love in which joy is the enduring *telos* of all longing.

FAITH AS SECRET KEEPING

As Jesus told us, if we want to see God, we must go where he is. The Father is "in secret" (ἐν τῷ κρυπτῷ) and called the one who "sees in secret" (ὁ βλέπων ἐν τῷ κρυπτῷ) (Matt 6:6). This is not the cultic secrecy of Gnosticism, which builds divisions where Christ tore down walls. Gnostic secrecy, along with every exclusivist variation of the secret, seeks to distinguish itself in rivalry with the other. However, Christianity does not keep secret *from* others, but *for* others. It keeps the secret *of* the other, that which belongs to the other and that which the other is.

Jesus' secrets are hospitable, empathetic, and generous. They are also intimate, somatic, and friendly. Many of Jesus' miracles were kept hidden, because in order to be understood they require one to approach through the narrow path of secret keeping. Since they are acts of love, and secret keeping is an aspect *of* love, then his signs and miracles can only be properly understood and received in the secrecy of love. By seeking to publicize Jesus' miracles, the crowd would betray them, destroy their meaning, and thus expose the secret.

When Christ's secret keeping does exclude others, it is in proportion to the callousness of those who "deem themselves" unworthy of eternal life (Acts 13:46). In contrast to Gnostic secrecy, the secret of Christ is so fully revealed that it is "hard" to see. The secret is stated so clearly that many find

---

20. Caputo, *Prayers and Tears*, 33. Caputo says of the secret in Derrida, "There is no escape from the surface of the text, and hence no way to put to rest our interpretive controversies. If our heart are restless until they rest in the secret, then, in this Jewish Augustinianism, they will never rest. Indeed, that is just what is *productive* about the secret and why it impassions. There is no privileged access to a *hyperousios*, beyond the name of God, to some deep truth that arrests the play of traces in the text. There is nothing beneath the surface of the text—*scriptura et traditio*—or the trace that is left in a text that is tormented and disturbed by the desire to efface itself before the wholly other. That secretless secret is a matter of permanent provocation, and it is necessary to talk about it" (Caputo, *Prayers and Tears*, 34).

it offensive, suspect, or simply irrelevant. Thus the hiding and disclosing of the secret are intimately tied. Jesus says, "Is a lamp brought in to be put under the bushel basket, or under the bed, and not on the lampstand? For there is nothing hidden, except to be disclosed; nor is anything secret, except to come to light. Let anyone with ears to hear listen!" (Mark 4:21–23).

Even though Jesus chose to tell ambiguous parables and only explain their meaning to his disciples, he is aesthetically revealing the *secrecy* of the secret. By speaking *so that* the Pharisees would not understand, he was in another sense speaking clearly about their spiritual blindness. Through his parables, Jesus was able to bring to the surface the deep disorientation of their hearts. The secret of the parables revealed the truth of their blindness. If they saw themselves as "blind" to the truth of Jesus' life, then they could approach Jesus in humility, and thus "see" (cf. John 9:41). Paradoxically, therefore, Jesus further reveals his secret by keeping it, which then itself becomes a more profound form of keeping secret. More secrecy means more revelation, and vice versa.

The secret then can only be perceived, contemplated, and deepened through a certain mode of apprehension that is the highest degree of truth, namely faith. For faith is that trusting, committed, growing intimacy which "*is*" through secret keeping. God has been revealed "from faith to faith" (Rom 1:17). Thus Schleiermacher spoke accurately when he said, "Religion, however, as I wish to show it, which is to say, in its own original, characteristic form, is not accustomed to appear openly, but is only seen in secret by those who love it."[21]

But all of these moments of secret keeping in Jesus' life point toward a climax. What Jesus taught about the "open secret"—the secret that is so revealed that it is hard to see—takes full form in the enigma of the cross. The Passion is at once the result of the world's wickedness and Christ's faithfulness. This makes the cross a kind of *hyper*-parable that precisely

---

21. Schleiermacher, *On Religion*, 26–27. Schleiermacher describes this hidden aspect: "It is true that religion is essentially contemplative. You would never call anyone pious who went about in impervious stupidity, whose sense is not open for the life of the world. But this contemplation is not turned, as your knowledge of nature is, to the existence of a finite thing, combined with and opposed to another finite thing. . . . The contemplation of the pious is the immediate consciousness of the universal existence of all finite things, in and through the Infinite, and of all temporal things in and through the Eternal. Religion is to seek this and find it in all that lives and moves. . . . Without being knowledge, it recognizes knowledge and science. In itself it is an affection, a revelation of the Infinite in the finite, God being seen in it and it in God" (Schleiermacher, *On Religion*, 36).

by *concealing* the truth of the injustice in it becomes an infinitely greater *disclosure* of that truth.

Judas departed from the intimacy of the Lord's Supper to hand Jesus over, or "betray" his secrecy. In connection with the previous discussion of how the betrayal of the gift creates a commodity, Judas exchanges Jesus for money. Knowing his arrest was imminent, Jesus went to the Garden of Gethsemane with his disciples, and despite telling them to stay vigilant in prayer, they fell asleep—failing to maintain the secret. When the guards moved to arrest him, one of Jesus' disciples drew his sword and sliced the ear of a guard. Jesus rebuked him and said, "Put your sword back into its place; for all who take the sword will perish by the sword. Do you think that I cannot appeal to my Father, and he will at once send me more than twelve legions of angels?" (Matt 26:52–53). Thus even here, Jesus "keeps secret" the legions at his fingers, like he also did when tempted by Satan (Matt 4:1–11). Rather than resist, and in a sense publicize the secrecy of his life, Jesus touches the man's ear, heals him, and goes calmly.

Throughout Jesus' arrest, his captors mocked his inconspicuous manner. Some spat in his face, slapped him, and said, "Prophesy to us, you Messiah! Who is it that struck you?" (v.68). Such insults belittled his reputation of being a prophet, and countered his secret status by playing with the secrecy of those who struck him. The high priest stripped him naked and thus betrayed the decency of his human form (Matt 26:65). Afterwards, Peter was approached by a servant girl, and when she asked him if he knew Jesus, he denied it (or betrayed the trust built in secrecy with Christ) (vs. 69–70).

Later, when Pilate asked Jesus if he was king of the Jews, he spoke ambiguously and thus most truthfully, for the truth of his claim to kingship can only been seen in the secrecy of faith, which one must approach in humility. In response, Jesus says, "You say so" (27:11). Instead of heeding Jesus' reputation as king, the guards paraded him around with a crown of thorns and a scarlet robe, and said, "'Hail, King of the Jews!' They spat on him, and took the reed and struck him on the head" (27:27–30).

Once nailed to the cross, the crowds began to scoff at him, which the book of Proverbs puts in the context of secrecy, "Whoever goes about slandering reveals secrets, but he who is trustworthy in spirit keeps a thing covered" (Prov 11:13, ESV). In contrast to the obnoxious guards and spiteful crowds, Jesus kept the Secret. In Isaiah we read of him, "He was oppressed, and he was afflicted, yet he did not open his mouth; like a lamb that is led to the slaughter, and like a sheep that before its shearers is silent, so he did not open his mouth" (Isa 53:7).

THE MASK AND ITS RITUALS

If the *incognito* of Christ's bloodied face conceals the secret of his divinity, then we ought to think of it as a mask. Like Christ's parables, the mask reveals by concealing. We can see this in the Apostle Paul's language of "putting on" Christ. Paul insists that he has permanently taken upon himself Christ's mask. In Galatians he says, "I have been crucified with Christ; and it is no longer I who live, but it is Christ who lives in me. And the life I now live in the flesh I live by faith in the Son of God" (Gal 2:19–20). He also encourages fellow disciples to "put on [ἐνδύσασθε] the Lord Jesus Christ, and make no provision for the flesh" (Rom 13:14). He also uses this verb, "put on," to describe donning the armour of God (Eph 6:11). By so putting Christ on, "I" no longer live, but Christ lives *in* me. This is for Paul a new human being. This newness is also the basis of all his interactions with others, and the possibility of his great authority *in* great humility. For he says, "we regard no one from a human point of view; even though we once knew Christ from a human point of view, we know him no longer in that way. So if anyone is in Christ, there is a new creation" (2 Cor 5:16–17).

Though Paul insists that he no longer lives (or his "I"), this is not a total annihilation of the I. For Paul is still the one speaking of this death. Rather than a total destruction of the self, Paul speaks of a new found freedom, "the life I now live in the flesh I live by faith in the Son." He is *more* truly himself in the secrecy of faith kept through the mask. He has a healthy indifference about whether he lives or dies, acquires wealth or lives in poverty. The life of flesh has itself received the distance proper to reverence. The flesh is no longer treated as the main priority to a life fixated on survival. Paul has freely "died" and has distanced himself from the life of the flesh, but paradoxically, this distancing only further fulfills the flesh and the self by allowing each to be shown more prominently in their own natures through their reverence of the secret.

The features of a mask are often more pronounced or exaggerated than a human face. By wearing it, one takes on the mood of the mask, and thus it has a certain deifying quality. Because the mask is still "other," it gives one greater freedom to live into and through the mask. Thus, in his acting manual *Behind the Mask*, Bari Rofle says, "Masks, though, can offer everyone a certain self-knowledge; through a false face one can find a true face," and "A mask is a medium of truth, for even when it is meant to lie, its very use to hide or cover reveals the subterfuge."[22] Rolfe says that "Playwright John Arden discovered that the actor in a mask cannot behave as though he were not wearing it."[23]

While we often talk about insincerity towards others as "wearing a mask," the truth is that insincerity comes from *not* wearing a mask. By donning a mask, one is *announcing* something and thus drawing attention in a certain way. A mask is as much about revealing as hiding, and it allows one to more fully express themselves than ever without it. Thus by living "behind" the mask of Christ, we no longer fixate on what is superficial or inadequate, but live freely *as if* we were Christ—or more accurately, *as* Christ—and regard others in the same way. The mask of Christ creates a "loose association" between us and our particularities, which gives way to a more total unconditional love that covers a multitude of sins. Derrida was aiming for this kind of response to the other, but needed a richer notion of self-mediation in the mask: for he says, everyone really is "this unique person whose secret remains hidden behind the social mask."[24]

---

22. Rofle, Behind the Mask, 2. Rofle describes the mask in terms of mediating an anterior paradox that is simultaneously attractive and frightening, present and absent: "The theatre's twin masks of comedy and tragedy originated as the representations of Dionysius, father of drama, god of wine, and patron deity of Greek drama festivals. The link of comedy and tragedy in one god is typical of the paradoxes and dualities that surround Dionysius and the mask, both symbols of drama. For one, there is his own double mask. Then, unlike other deities, he was a god who came down from Olympus and moved among mortal men. Also, the mask is a man-made object, yet it inspires fear and exaltation—as though it was beyond mortal touch. It is presence and absence. It is death and life. The mask is a complete object in itself, but it lacks a reverse side; thus it invites a living participant to wear and thereby complete it" (Rofle, Behind the Mask, 7). Moreover, "Because the mask confers freedom it is safe; it is an object to hide behind physically, and a characterization to hide behind emotionally. But the mask hides *and* reveals. When the face is hidden the wearer feels entirely hidden . . . so the body is left free to respond expressively, unself-consciously" (Rofle, Behind the Mask, 11).

23. Rofle, Behind the Mask, 15. "Mary Wigman found that she could not move contrary to what the mask 'decreed,' that she could not impose movement upon the mask but had to listen to its requirements" (Rofle, Behind the Mask, 15). Moveover, Eugene O'Neill commented on a performance of his Great God Brown that "after using the masks for a time, the actors reacted to the demand made by the masks that their bodies became alive and expressive. He observed that, once mastered, its lessons were retained by the body and the mind even when masks were not worn" (Rofle, Behind the Mask, 15–16).

24. Derrida, Gift of Death, 36. He says, "Inauthentic dissimulation, that of the masked role, bores to the extent that it claims to unveil, show, expose, exhibit, and excite

Sanctum Sanctorum

Rather than a physical prop, the mask is more like a dynamic throughline that goes all the way down from the flesh to the soul. The mask is a part of spiritual creatures, or an aspect of the self. William Desmond has recognized the significance of the mask. He says that we both "are as we appear and are not as we appear, that is, we are masks."[25] Thus humanity reveals a unique capacity of "*self-othering*."[26] Desmond says that with the double mediation of the "metaxological sense of being," the mask also brings out into the open what would otherwise be lost in "labyrinthine inwardness."[27] The "shy, gauche person becomes a flamboyant actor."[28] Moreover, Desmond says that normal self-consciousness may "paralyse efforts at self-revelation, or even merely being oneself."[29] While only a thin paper barrier, the mask "miraculously lifts the psychic veil that repressed presence."[30]

---

curiosity. By unveiling everything it hides that whose essence resides in its remaining hidden, namely, the authentic mystery of the person. Authentic mystery must *remain* mysterious, and we should approach it only by letting it be what it is in truth—veiled, withdrawn, dissimulated. Authentic dissimulation is inauthentically dissimulated by the violence of unveiling" (Derrida, *Gift of Death*, 37).

25. Desmond, *Philosophy and Its Others*, 78. "Being aesthetic is here related to the emergence of 'being true.' The latter is complex, since the self being true to its own intermediate being discovers itself, not only in relation to others, but discovers itself as the power to present itself as other than itself."

26. Desmond, *Philosophy and Its Others*, 78. He says, "With the mask, we come across a distinction between 'seeming' and 'being' that allows us to deceive and dissimulate. We mask ourselves in our appearances, such that our identity becomes opaque and enigmatic, even twisted. We reveal self obliquely, and sometimes have to be unmasked, so elusive can be our ambiguous inwardness. We inwardly hide our own ambiguous otherness in response to the ambiguity of the otherness surrounding us."

27. Desmond, *Philosophy and Its Others*, 78.

28. Desmond, *Philosophy and Its Others*, 78. "A person dons a mask and is suddenly transformed."

29. Desmond, *Philosophy and Its Others*, 78.

30. Desmond, *Philosophy and Its Others*, 78. "All rigid roles are suspended; being becomes fluid again and, as in childhood, open to magical transformation. . . . Of course, it is the actor who knows most intimately the power of the mask. A mask creates a new identity, catapults the actor into the different world of an other self. It originates a new self, makes impersonation possible, the injection of living energy into a merely imaginary role. It actualizes an imaginary possibility; the appearance invent a reality. It makes possible the multiplication of identities, showing forth the open potency of the unfinished self. In fact, the first actors wore actual masks; the mask was the persona; the actor was agent of the mask, servant of the persona. Now an actor, shedding the physical mask (though never entirely, as the use of make-up shows), must make himself into an invisible, imaginary mask. His service to the persona becomes interiorized—inward imaginative identification with the role of the other" (Desmond, *Philosophy and Its Others*, 78–79).

Because this pluralizing of identity can "*open* the self to even the most radical *otherness*," Desmond connects the power of the mask to the "religious mystery, the holy in its terrifying and overwhelming enigma."[31] Even in the sedated atmosphere of a museum, ritual dance masks seem to emanate a forceable demonic presence; how much more "primordial" must this have been in the mask's original setting?[32] When donning the mask of the ritual animal, the dancer "*becomes* the animal power"; when one dons the god's mask, the dancer "*is* the god dancing."[33] Moreover, the mask "releases the dancer from quotidian consciousness," and makes him or her a vessel of savage power.[34] Desmond says that in the religious mask archaic humanity dances its identity "with the energy of the whole. The mask becomes the presencing of unmastered otherness."[35]

The mask is not simply an object of ritual, but is a ritualistic dynamic, and insofar as conscious beings are en-masked beings, they are ritualistic by nature. We learn from the mask a number of guidelines for ritual itself. We learn that the "face" of God in the mask must be the superficially "obvious" center of focus. The character in the performance is the mask itself, which also drives the story. The actor plays the mask, and the audience sees and responds to the mask. But however rendered, the mask does not deny the actor, but makes possible for the actor what without the mask would be impossible. The actor is given greater, more profound, resources in the mask than what is already at his or her disposal. The mask gives a gift to the actor that actually further recognizes and celebrates the actor. We ought to cultivate aesthetic habits and inform our contemplation so that the mask of Christ is superficially "seen" throughout our performances. We thus also require donning rituals to realize the dynamism of the mask.

In *Beyond Good and Evil*, Nietzsche says, "Everything profound loves masks; the most profound things go so far as to hate images and likenesses."[36] As with the secrecy of love discussed above, Nietzsche says that some events are "so delicate that it is best to cover them up with some coarseness

---

31. Desmond, *Philosophy and Its Others*, 79.
32. Desmond, *Philosophy and Its Others*, 79.
33. Desmond, *Philosophy and Its Others*, 79.
34. Desmond, *Philosophy and Its Others*, 79.
35. Desmond, *Philosophy and Its Others*, 79.
36. Nietzsche, *Beyond Good and Evil*, §40. "Wouldn't just the *opposite* be a proper disguise for the shame of a god? A questionable question: it would be odd if some mystic hadn't already risked something similar himself."

and make them unrecognizable."[37] Such an event might be an act of love or extravagant generosity "in whose aftermath nothing is more advisable than to take a stick and give the eye-witnesses a good beating."[38] Nietzsche argues that every person has shame, and some do well to conceal it in profound secrecy. One so hidden instinctively uses speech to generate silence and concealment, and tirelessly evades communication. Thus he "wants and encourages a mask of himself to wander around, in his place, through the hearts and heads of his friends."[39] If this is not what he wants, "he will eventually realize that a mask of him has been there all the same—and that this is for the best."[40] In the end, "Every profound spirit needs a mask: what's more, a mask is constantly growing around every profound spirit."[41]

If Christ is the image of God, and we take his whole life to be "image," we might think of his face as the mask of the faceless Father, the Wholly Inscrutable One disclosed in hiddenness and revealed in his Son as the

---

37. Nietzsche, *Beyond Good and Evil*, §40.

38. Nietzsche, *Beyond Good and Evil*, §40. "Many people are excellent at obscuring and abusing their own memory, so they can take revenge on at least this one accessory—shame is highly resourceful. It is not the worst things that we are the most ashamed of. Malicious cunning is not the only thing behind a mask—there is so much goodness in cunning. I could imagine that a man with something precious and vulnerable to hide would roll through life, rough and round like an old, green, heavy-hooped wine cask; the subtlety of his sham will want it this way. A man with something profound in his shame encounters even his fate and delicate decisions along paths that few people have ever found, paths whose existence must be concealed from his closest and most trusted friends. His mortal danger is hidden from their eyes, and so is his regained sense of confidence in life."

39. Nietzsche, *Beyond Good and Evil*, §40.

40. Nietzsche, *Beyond Good and Evil*, §40.

41. Nietzsche, *Beyond Good and Evil*, §40. This growing mask is "thanks to the consistently false (which is to say shallow) interpretation of every word, every step, every sign of life he displays." William Desmond adds, "The masquerade is not just for hardhearted seducers. It also is the daily play of deceit and betrayal that wears the mask of reliable decency. There are indecent things in the inner heart of decency that decency cannot confess to itself. It has worn the mask so long that the memory of its other face has grown vague. To remove the mask would be like having its face flayed. I want to say the masquerade is *constitutive* of our ethical situation. The grief of being ethical arises out of the hiddenness of good and evil, in their very showing of themselves. If the showing is double, it is as much secrecy as it is manifestation. Such equivocal showing conditions the possibility of deceit, and lies and distortion and cunning and conspiracy and other treacheries. It also conditions the possibility of man's innerness, which as innerness never completely shows itself, even as it shows itself" (Desmond, *Ethics and the Between*, 278).

Unbegotten "in repose."[42] Thus our "play" in the mask is not merely an anthropological ploy in response to shame alone. Rather the sociality of the mask participates in the Triune God whose faceless face we see in concealment. Also, we must respond to others in love and secrecy and thus fortify others' masks, even if they lack the subtlety and peace to remain "behind" the mask. We extend a love that covers sins and keeps secret when we *revere* the hiddenness of others, but this is a hiddenness *mediated* by and in continuity with every revelation of the self. In his collection of sermons called *Reverence for Life*, Albert Schweitzer recognized this reverential aspect involved in loving others.[43] He says that love for others eclipses purely "ethical" duty. For if our love is to reflect our love for God, than we must extend the "reverent love" we have for God to everyone.[44] He says, "God is infinite life. Thus the most elementary ethical principle, when understood by the heart, means that out of reverence for the unfathomable, infinite, and living Reality we call God, we must never consider ourselves strangers toward any human being."[45]

CONCLUSION

Having considered the social ubiquity of the gift, this chapter discussed a certain understated element of the gift, namely secrecy. The very practicality of arranging and giving a gift requires secrecy. But more profoundly

---

42. Marius Victorinus sees that the Father as the Preexistent is repose, while the Son is the Existent and begotten: ""[God] produces therefore the existent, and does so by an ineffable begetting; he produces existence, the *nous* and life, not as one who is these things but as above all things. If, therefore, God is not the nonexistent, he is, however, what is above that which exists, which is truly *on* (existent), the potentiality of the *on* (existent) itself, potentially which, when the begetting act is awakened in it, will beget in an ineffable motion to the fully perfect *On* (existent), an *On* (existent) proceeding in its totality from the totality of potentiality; it follows that God is the total *Proon* (preexistent), and Jesus is the total *On* (existent), but the absolutely existent and already totally perfect in existence, in life, in knowledge" (Victorinus, *Letter of Victorinus to Candidus*, 62).

43. Schweitzer, *Reverence*.

44. Schweitzer, *Reverence*, 113.

45. Schweitzer, *Reverence*, 113. "Wherever you see life—that is yourself! What is this recognition, this knowledge within the reach of the most scientific and the most childlike? It is reverence for life, reverence for the unfathomable mystery we confront in our universe, an existence different in its outward appearance and yet inwardly of the same character as our own, terribly similar, awesomely related. . . . Reverence for the infinity of life means removal of the alienation, restoration of empathy, compassion, sympathy" (Schweitzer, *Reverence*, 115).

still, the gift is always given "from the inside" of a mutually shared realm of secrecy. Thus the giver and the recipient can only give true gifts insofar as those gifts are symbols of the excess of the secret that is shared and enriched between them. The gift then *mediates* the depth of the secret.

As the gift is part of the Trinitarian life of God, and analogously the nature of God's being in virtue of the Good, so the secret is part of the life and nature of God. For the gift mediates the secret, which is ultimately the social dynamic of the Holy. In this way, we can see how far-reaching the holy is by seeing its relation to the gift as its ultimate ground. We see this virtue of secret keeping exemplified in Jesus, the founder and perfecter of our faith. For as *the* Gift, Christ also preeminently keeps the Father's secret which is himself. Finally, this chapter also discussed the mask as a mediating "other" that makes the self more itself precisely by concealing the self, and by so concealing it becomes our psychic-somatic means of "keeping secret."

Bibliography

Aertsen, A. J. "Good as Transcendental and the Transcendence of the Good." In *Being and Goodness: The Concept of the Good in Metaphysics and Philosophical Theology*, edited by Scott MacDonald, 56–73. Ithaca: Cornell University Press, 1991.
———. *Medieval Philosophy and the Transcendentals: The Case of Thomas Aquinas*. Leiden: Brill, 1996.
———. *Medieval Philosophy as Transcendental Thought: From Philip the Chancellor (ca. 1225) to Francisco Suárez*. Leiden: Brill, 2012.
Allen, R. E. *Plato's Euthyphro and the Earlier Theory of Forms*. Vol. 1. Routledge Library Editions. London: Routledge, 2013.
Ambrose. *On the Christian Faith*. In *Ambrose: Select Works and Letters*, edited by Philip Schaff and Henry Wace, 199–314. Translated by De Romestin. Vol. 10 of *Nicene and Post-Nicene Fathers, Second Series*. Peabody, MA: Hendrickson, 2012.
———. *On the Holy Spirit*. In *Ambrose: Select Works and Letters*, edited by Philip Schaff and Henry Wace, 91–158. Translated by De Romestin. Vol. 10 of *Nicene and Post-Nicene Fathers, Second Series*. Peabody, MA: Hendrickson, 2012.
Aquinas, Thomas. *De Veritate*. Translated by Robert W. Mulligan. Chicago: Regnery, 1952.
———. *Summa Theologiae*. Translated by Fathers of the English Dominican Province. Lander, WY: Aquinas Institute, 2012.
Aristotle. *Metaphysics*. In *Aristotle in 23 Volumes*. Vols. 17–18. Translated by Hugh Tredennick. Cambridge, MA: Harvard University Press, 1989.
Augustine. *The Confessions*. In *The Confessions and Letters of Augustin, with a Sketch of His Life and Work*, edited by Philip Schaff, 45–208. Vol. 1 of *Nicene and Post-Nicene Fathers, First Series*. Peabody, MA: Hendrickson, 2012.
———. *Homilies on the Gospel of John*. In *Augustin: Homilies on the Gospel of John, Homilies on the First Epistle of John, Soliloquies*, edited by Philip Schaff, 7–452. Vol. 7 of *Nicene and Post-Nicene Fathers, First Series*. Peabody, MA: Hendrickson, 2012.
———. *On the Holy Trinity*. In *Augustine: On the Holy Trinity, Doctrinal Treatises, Moral Treatises*, edited by Philip Schaff, 1–228. Vol. 3 of *Nicene and Post-Nicene Father, First Series*. Peabody, MA: Hendrickson, 2012.
Ayres, Lewis. *Augustine and the Trinity*. Cambridge: Cambridge University Press, 2010.
Balthasar, Hans Urs von. *Cosmic Liturgy: The Universe According to Maximus the Confessor*. Translated by Brian E. Daley. Communio. San Fransisco: Ignatius, 2003.
———. *The Glory of the Lord: The Realm of Metaphysics in the Modern Age*. Vol. 5 of *A Theological Aesthetics*. San Fransisco: Ignatius, 1990.
———. *Theology of Henri de Lubac*. Communio. San Francisco: Ignatius, 1976.

Bibliography

Barclay, John M. G. *Paul and the Gift*. Grand Rapids: Eerdmans, 2017.

Basil of Caesarea. *On the Holy Spirit*. In *Basil: Letters and Select Works*, edited by Philip Schaff and Henry Wace, 1–50. Translated by Blomfield Jackson. Vol. 8 of *Nicene and Post-Nicene Fathers, Second Series*. Peabody, MA: Hendrickson, 2012.

Bell, David N. "Esse, Vivere, Intelligere: The Noetic Triad and the Image of God." *RTAM* 52 (1985) 5–43.

Berkhof, Louis. *Systematic Theology*. New Combined Edition. Grand Rapids: Eerdmans, 1996.

Bernard of Clairvaux. *Commentary on the Song of Songs*. https://archive.org/stream/StBernardsCommentaryOnTheSongOfSongs/StBernardOnTheSongOfSongsall#page/no/mode/2up.

Blans, Bert. "Cloud of Unknowing: An Orientation in Negative Theology from Dionysius the Areopagite, Eckhart, and John of the Cross to Modernity." In *Flight of the Gods: Philosophical Perspectives on Negative Theology*, edited by Ilse Bulhof and Laurens ten Kate, 58–77. New York: Fordham University Press, 2000.

Boersma, Gerald P. *Augustine's Early Theology of Image: A Study in the Development of Pro-Nicene Theology*. Oxford Studies in Historical Theology. Oxford: Oxford University Press, 2016.

Borgmeyer, David. "Modernism, Orthodoxy, and Russian Identity: Pablo Picasso and Sergei Bulgakov." In *Cultural Identity and Civil Society in Russia and Eastern Europe: Essays in Memory of Charles E. Timberlake*, edited by Andrew Kier Wise et al., 152–71. Newcastle: Cambridge Scholars, 2012.

Bradshaw, David. *Aristotle East and West: Metaphysics and the Division of Christendom*. Cambridge: University of Cambridge Press, 2004.

———. "In Defence of the Essence/Energies Distinction: A Reply to Critics." In *Divine Essence and Divine Energies: Ecumenical Reflections on the Presence of God in Eastern Orthodoxy*, edited by Constantinos Athanasopoulos and Christoph Schneider, 256–73. Cambridge: James Clarke, 2013.

Bulgakov, Sergius. "The Corpse of Beauty." In *A Bulgakov Anthology*, edited by Nicolas Zernov and James Pain, 67–77. London: SPCK, 1976.

———. *Icons and the Name of God*. Translated by Boris Jakim. Grand Rapids: Eerdmans, 2012.

Bychkov, Oleg V. "'Metaphysics as Aesthetics': Aquinas's Metaphysics in Present-day Theological Aesthetics." *Modern Theology* 31 (2015) 147–78.

Chao, Shun-Laing. *Rethinking the Concept of the Grotesque: Crashaw, Baudelaire, Magritte*. Legenda Studies in Comparative Literature. Oxford: Legenda, 2010.

Clark, Mary T. "The Neoplatonism of Marius Victorinus the Christian." In *Neoplatonism and Early Christian Thought*, edited by H. J. Blumenthal, 153–59. London: Variorum, 1981.

Clement of Alexandria. *Stromata*. In *Fathers of the Second Century: Hermas, Tatian, Athenagoras, Theophilus, and Clement of Alexandria (Entire)*, edited by Alexander Roberts and James Donaldson, 409–520. Vol. 2 of *Ante-Nicene Fathers*. Peabody, MA: Hendrickson, 2012.

Coakley, Sarah. *God, Sexuality, and the Self: An Essay "On the Trinity."* Cambridge: Cambridge University Press, 2013.

Congar, Yves. *After Nine Hundred Years: The Background of the Schism Between the Eastern and Western Churches*. New York: Fordham University Press, 1998.

Bibliography

Cooper, Stephen Andrew. "The Life and Times of Marius Victorinus." In *Marius Victorinus's Commentary on Galatians*, 16–40. Translated by Stephen Andrew Cooper. Oxford Early Christian Studies. Oxford: Oxford University Press, 2005.

Coulter, Dale M. *Per Visibilia ad Invisibilia: Theological Method in Richard of St. Victor (d. 1173)*. Bibliotheca Victorina. Turnhout, Belguim: Brepols, 2006.

Cunningham, Conor. *Darwin's Pious Idea*. Interventions. Grand Rapids: Eerdmans, 2010.

———. "Suspending the Natural Attitude: Transcendence and Immanence from Thomas Aquinas to Michel Henry." In *Transcendence and Phenomenology*, edited by Conor Cunningham and Peter M. Chandler, 241–59. Translated by Nick Hanlon. Veritas. London: SCM, 2008.

De Chardin, Pierre Teilhard. *Divine Milieu: An Essay on the Interior Life*. New York: Harper, 1960.

Derrida, Jacque. *Of Grammatology*. Translated by Judith Butler. Fortieth Anniversary Edition. Baltimore: Johns Hopkins University Press, 2016.

Descartes, René. *Meditations*. In *The Method, Meditations, and Philosophy of Descartes*, edited and translated by John Veitch, 206–82. Washington: Dunne, 1901.

Desmond, William. *Being and the Between*. New York: State University of New York Press, 1995.

———. *Ethics and the Between*. New York: State University of New York Press, 2001.

———. *God and the Between*. Illuminations. Oxford: Blackwell, 2008.

———. *Is There a Sabbath for Thought?* Perspectives in Continental Philosophy. New York: Fordham University Press, 2005.

Dionysius the Areopagite. *Divine Names*. In *The Works of Dionysius the Areopagite*, edited by John Parker, 2–86. Translated by John Parker. London: Aeterna, 2014.

———. *Ecclesiastical Hierarchy*. In *The Works of Dionysius the Areopagite*, edited by John Parker, 193–249. Translated by John Parker. London: Aeterna, 2014.

———. *Mystical Theology*. In *The Works of Dionysius the Areopagite*, edited by John Parker, 87–95. Translated by John Parker. London: Aeterna, 2014.

Dostoevsky, Fyodor. *The Idiot*. Translated by Constance Garnett. New York: MacMillan, 1913.

Eckhart, Meister. "Sermon 9." In *Meister Eckhart: Teacher and Preacher*, edited by Bernard McGinn, 255–60. The Classics of Western Spirituality. New Jersey: Paulist, 1986.

Eco, Umberto. *The Aesthetics of Thomas Aquinas*. Translated by Hugh Bredin. Cambridge, MA: Harvard University Press, 1988.

Edwards, Justin D., and Rune Graulund. *Grotesque*. The New Critical Idiom. New York: Routledge, 2013.

Edwards, Mark J. "Being, Life and Mind: A Brief Inquiry." *Syllecta Classica* 8 (1997) 191–206.

———. "Marius Victorinus and the Homoousion." *Studia Patristica* 46 (2010) 105–18.

———. "Porphyry and the Intelligible Triad." *The Journal of Hellenic Studies* 110 (1990) 14–25.

Elders, Leo J. *The Metaphysics of Being of St. Thomas Aquinas in Historical Perspective*. Leiden: Brill, 1993.

Feickert, Sabrina. "'Fighting in the Shade': Comic Representations of Sparta and Coming to Terms with Fearsome Otherness." In *Humour and Laughter in History: Transcultural Perspectives*, edited by Elisabeth Cheauré and Regine Nohejl, 119–36. Transcript. New York: Columbia University Press, 2014.

Bibliography

Finlay, Robert. "Weaving the Rainbow: Visions of Color in World History." *Journal of World History* 18 (2007) 383–431.

Flogaus, Reinhard. "Palamas and Barlamm Revisited: A Reassessment of East and West in the Hesychast Controversy of the Fourteenth-Century Byzantium." *St. Vladimir's Theological Quarterly* 42 (1998) 1–32.

Fritz, Peter Joseph. "Black Holes and Revelations: Michel Henry and Jean-Luc Marion on the Aesthetics of the Invisible." *Modern Theology* 25 (2009) 415–40.

Gambero, Luigi. *Mary and the Fathers of the Church: The Blessed Virgin Mary in Patristic Thought*. Translated by Thomas Buffer. San Francisco: Ignatius, 1999.

Golitzin, Alexander. "Dionysius the Areopagite in the Works of Saint Gregory Palamas." *St. Vladimir's Theological Quarterly* 46 (2002) 189–90.

———. *Mystagogy: A Monastic Reading of Dionysius Areopagita*, edited by Bogdan G. Bucur. Cistercian Studies Series. Minneapolis: Liturgical, 2013.

Goroncy, Jason. *Hallowed Be Thy Name: Sanctification of All in the Soteriology of P. T. Forsyth*. T. & T. Clark Studies in Systematic Theology. London: T. & T. Clark, 2013.

Gregory of Nazianzus. *The Fifth Theological Oration*. In *Cyril of Jerusalem, Gregory of Nazianzen*, edited by Philip Schaff and Henry Wace, 318–27. Vol. 7 of *Nicene and Post-Nicene Fathers, Second Series*. Peabody, MA: Hendrickson, 2012.

———. "On the Arrival of the Egyptians." In *Cyril of Jerusalem, Gregory of Nazianzen*, edited by Philip Schaff and Henry Wace, 334–38. Vol. 7 of *Nicene and Post-Nicene Fathers, Second Series*. Peabody, MA: Hendrickson, 2012.

———. *Oration on Holy Baptism*. In *Cyril of Jerusalem, Gregory of Nazianzen*, edited by Philip Schaff and Henry Wace, 360–77. Vol. 7 of *Nicene and Post-Nicene Fathers, Second Series*. Peabody, MA: Hendrickson, 2012.

———. *The Second Theological Oration*. In *Cyril of Jerusalem, Gregory of Nazianzen*, edited by Philip Schaff and Henry Wace, 288–300. Vol. 7 of *Nicene and Post-Nicene Fathers, Second Series*. Peabody, MA: Hendrickson, 2012.

Gregory of Nyssa. *Answer to Eunomius's Second Book*. In *Gregory of Nyssa: Dogmatic Treatises, Etc*, edited by Philip Schaff and Henry Wace, 250–314. Translated by M. Day. Vol. 5 of *Nicene and Post-Nicene Fathers, Second Series*. Peabody, MA: Hendrickson, 2012.

———. *On the Holy Spirit*. In *Gregory of Nyssa: Dogmatic Treatises, etc.*, edited by Philip Schaff and Henry Wace, 315–25. Vol. 5 of *Nicene and Post-Nicene Fathers, Second Series*. Peabody, MA: Hendrickson, 2012.

———. *On the Holy Trinity*. In *Gregory of Nyssa: Dogmatic Treatises, etc.*, edited by Philip Schaff, 326–30. Translated by H. A. Wilson. Vol. 5 of *Nicene and Post-Nicene Fathers, Second Series*. Peabody, MA: Hendrickson, 2012.

———. *On "Not Three Gods."* In *Gregory of Nyssa: Dogmatic Treatises, etc.*, edited by Philip Schaff, 331–36. Translated by H. A. Wilson. Vol. 5 of *Nicene and Post-Nicene Fathers, Second Series*. Peabody, MA: Hendrickson, 2012.

———. *On Virginity*. In *Gregory of Nyssa: Dogmatic Treatises, etc.*, edited by Philip Schaff and Henry Wace, 343–71. Vol. 5 of *Nicene and Post-Nicene Fathers, Second Series*. Peabody, MA: Hendrickson, 2012.

Hadot, Pierre. "Etre, vie, pensee chez Plotin, et avant Plotin." *Les Sources de Plotin* 5 (1960) 107–57.

———. "L'Image de la trinité dans l'âme chez Victorinus et chez Saint Augustin." *Studia Patristica* 81 (1962) 409–42.

———. *Porphyre et Victorinus*. 2 Vols. Paris: Études augustiniennes, 1968.

Hankey, W. J. *God in Himself: Aquinas's Doctrine of God as Expounded in the Summa Theologiae.* 2nd ed. Oxford: Oxford University Press, 2000.

Harpham, Geoffrey Galt. *On the Grotesque: Strategies of Contradiction in Art and Literature.* New Jersey: Princeton University Press, 1982.

Harrington, "Introduction." In *A Thirteenth-Century Textbook of Mystical Theology at the University of Paris: The Mystical Theology of Dionysius the Areopagite in Eriugena's Latin Translation with the Scholia translated by Anastasius the Librarian and Excerpts from Eriugena's* Periphyseon, edited by L. Michael Harrington, 1-3. Dallas Medieval Texts and Translations 4. Paris: Peeters, 2004.

Hart, David Bentley. *The Beauty of the Infinite: The Aesthetics of Christian Truth.* Grand Rapids: Eerdmans, 2003.

———. *The Experience of God: Being, Consciousness, Bliss.* New Haven: Yale University Press, 2013.

———. "Hidden and the Manifest: Metaphysics after Nicaea." In *Orthodox Readings of Augustine*, edited by George E. Demacopoulos and Aristotle Papanikolaou, 191-226. New York: St. Vladimir's Seminary Press, 2008.

Hartley, J. E. "Holy and Holiness, Clean and Unclean." In *Dictionary of The Old Testament: Pentateuch*, edited by T. Desmond Alexander and David W. Baker, 420-31. Downers Grove, IL: InterVarsity, 2003.

Hayward, Robert. "The Sanctification of Time in the Second Temple Period: Case Studies in the Septuagint." In *Holiness Past and Present*, edited by Stephen C. Barton, 168-92. London: T. & T. Clark, 2003.

Hazelton, Roger. "The Grotesque, Theologically Considered." In *The Grotesque in Art and Literature: Theological Reflections*, edited by James Luther Adams and Wilson Yates, 75-82. Grand Rapids: Eerdmans, 1997.

Hegel, George Wilhelm Friedrich Hegel. *The Philosophy of History.* Translated by J. Sibree. New York: Dover, 1956.

Heidegger, Martin. *Martin Heidegger: Basic Writings from Being and Time (1927) to The Task of Thinking (1964)*, edited by David Farrell Krell. Modern Thought. New York: HarperPerennial, 2008.

Hemmerle, Klaus. "Holy I. 2-4, II." In *Encyclopedia of Theology: A Concise Sacramentum Mundi*, edited by Karl Rahner, 639-41. Mumbai, India: St. Pauls, 2004.

Henry, Michel. *Barbarism.* Translated by Scott Davidson. London: Bloomsbury, 2012.

———. *I Am the Truth: Toward a Philosophy of Christianity.* Translated by Susan Emanuel. Cultural Memory in the Present. Stanford: Stanford University Press, 2003.

———. *Material Phenomenology.* Translated by Scott Davidson. Perspectives in Continental Philosophy. New York: Fordham University Press, 2008.

———. "Phenomenology of Life." In *Transcendence and Phenomenology*, edited by Peter M. Candler Jr. and Conor Cunningham, 241-59. Translated by Nick Hanlon. Veritas. London: SCM, 2008.

Heraclitus. *Diels.* Translated by John Burnet, 1912. http://philoctetes.free.fr/heraclitus.htm.

Heschel, Abraham Joshua. *God in Search of Man: A Philosophy of Judaism.* New York: Harper, 1966.

Hesiod. *Theogony.* In *The Homeric Hymns and Homerica*, 78-153. Translated by Hugh G. Evelyn-White. Cambridge, MA: Harvard University Press, 1914.

Hodge, Charles. *Systematic Theology.* Vol. 1. Grand Rapids: Eerdmans, 1981.

Bibliography

Howe, John. *The Blessedness of the Righteous Opened, and Further Recommended from the Consideration of the Vanity of This Mortal Life: In Two Treatises, on Psalm XVII. 15 and Psalm LXXXIX. 47*. New York: Haven, 1835.

Husserl, Edmund. *The Crisis of European Sciences and Transcendental Phenomenology: An Introduction to Phenomenological Philosophy*. Translated by David Carr. Evanston, IL: Northwestern University Press, 1970.

Janicaud, Dominique. "The Theological Turn of French Phenomenology." In *Phenomenology and the "Theological Turn": The French Debate*, 16–106. Translated by Bernard G. Prusak. New York: Fordham University Press, 2000.

Jennison, Keith Warren. *The Humorous Mr. Lincoln: A Profile in Wit, Courage, and Compassion*. Expanded Edition. New York: Countryman, 1988.

John Chrysostom. "Homilies on the Gospel of St. John." In *Chrysostom: Homilies on the Gospel of Saint John and the Epistle to the Hebrews*, edited by Philip Schaff, 1–334. Vol. 14 of *Nicene and Post-Nicene Fathers, First Series*. Peabody, MA: Hendrickson, 2012.

John of the Cross. *The Dark Night*. In *John of the Cross: Selections from The Dark Night and Other Writings*, edited by Emilie Griffin, 1–17. Translated by Kieran Kavanaugh. New York: HarperSanFrancisco, 2004.

John of Damascus. *Exposition of the Orthodox Faith*. In *Hilary of Poitiers, John of Damascus*, edited by Philip Schaff and Henry Wace, 1–99. Translated by S. D. F. Salmond. Vol. 9 of *Nicene and Post-Nicene Fathers, Second Series*. Peabody, MA: Hendrickson, 2012.

John Paul II. "Letter to Artists." April 23, 1999. https://w2.vatican.va/content/john-paul-ii/en/letters/1999/documents/hf_jp-ii_let_23041999_artists.html.

Johnson, Dominic. *God Is Watching: How the Fear of God Makes Us Human*. Oxford: Oxford University Press, 2016.

Johnson, Keith L. *Karl Barth and the Analogia Entis*. London: T. & T. Clark, 2010.

Jones, Tamsin. "Dionysius in Hans Urs von Balthasar and Jean-Luc Marion." *Modern Theology*. 24 (2008) 745–54.

Jordan, Mark D. "The Evidence of the Transcendentals and the Place of Beauty in Thomas Aquinas." *International Philosophical Quarterly* 29 (1989) 393–407.

———. "The Grammar of *Esse*: Re-reading Thomas on the Transcendentals." *The Thomist* 44 (1980) 1–26.

Judson, Lindsay. "Carried Away in the *Euthyphro*." In *Definition in Greek Philosophy*, edited by David Charles, 31–61. Oxford: Oxford University Press, 2010.

Kant, Emmanuel. *Critique of Pure Reason*, edited by Paul Guyer and Allen W. Wood. The Cambridge Edition of the Works of Immanuel Kant. Cambridge: Cambridge University Press, 1998.

Kayser, Wolfgang. *The Grotesque in Art and Literature*. Translated by Ulrich Weisstein. New York: McGraw-Hill, 1966.

Kelly, J. N. D. *Early Christian Doctrines*. Revised Edition. New York: HarperCollins,1978.

Knepper, Timothy D. *Negating Negation*. Eugene, OR: Wipf and Stock, 2013.

Komter, Aafke E., ed. *The Gift: An Interdisciplinary Perspective*. Amsterdam: Amsterdam University Press, 1996.

Kovacs, Judith, and Christopher Rowland. *Revelation: The Apocalypse of Jesus Christ*. Oxford: Blackwell, 2004.

Kuryluk, Ewa. *Salome And Judas In The Cave Of Sex: The Grotesque Origins, Iconograpy, Techniques*. Evanston, IL: Northwestern University Press, 1987.

LaCugna, Catherine Mowry. *God For Us: The Trinity and the Christian Life*. San Francisco: HarperSanFrancisco, 1993.
Lewis, C. S. *Mere Christianity*. In *The Complete C.S. Lewis Signature Classics*, 1–178. New York: HarperOne, 2007.
López, Antonio. *Gift and the Unity of Being*. Eugene: Cascade, 2013.
Lossky, Vladimir. *In the Image and Likeness of God*. New York: St. Vladimir's Seminary Press, 1976.
———. *The Vision of God*. New York: St. Vladimir's Seminary Press, 1983.
Loudovikos, Nikolaos. "Striving for Participation: Palamite Analogy as Dialogical Synenergy and Thomist Analogy as Emanational Similitude." In *Divine Essence and Divine Energies: Ecumenical Reflections on the Presence of God in Eastern Orthodoxy*, edited by Constantinos Athanasopoulos and Christoph Schneider, 122–48. Cambridge: James Clarke, 2013.
Majercik, Ruth. *The Chaldean Oracles: Text, Translation, and Commentary*. Studies in Greek and Roman Religion. Leiden: Brill, 1989.
Marion, Jean-Luc. *Being Given: Toward a Phenomenology of Givenness*. Translated by Jeffrey Kosky. Stanford: Stanford University Press, 2002.
———. *The Crossing of the Invisible*. Translated by James K. A. Smith. Cultural Memory in the Present. Stanford: Stanford University Press, 2004.
———. *God Without Being: Hors-Texte*. Translated by Thomas A. Carlson. Chicago: University of Chicago Press, 1995.
———. *Idol and Distance: Five Studies*. Translated by Thomas A. Carlson. New York: Fordham University Press, 2001.
———. *In Excess: Studies of Saturated Phenomena*. Translated by Robyn Horner and Vincent Berraud. New York: Fordham University Press, 2004.
———. "Metaphysics and Phenomenology: A Relief for Theology." In *Religion: Beyond a Concept*, edited by Hent de Vries, 283–98. Translated by Thomas A. Carlson and Christina M. Gschwandtner. 3rd ed. New York: Fordham University Press, 2008.
Maritain, Jacques. *Art and Scholasticism: With Other Essays*. Whitefish, MT: Kessinger, 2003.
Marius Victorinus. *Marius Victorinus: Theological Treatises on the Trinity*, 89–304. Translated by Mary T. Clark. The Fathers of the Church. Washington, DC: Catholic University of America Press, 1981.
Mauss, Marcel. *The Gift: The Form and Reason for Exchange in Archaic Societies*. London: Routledge, 1990.
Maximus the Confessor. *Maximus Confessor: Selected Writings*, edited by George Berthold. The Classics of Western Spirituality. New Jersey: Paulist, 1985.
McGinn, Bernard. *The Presence of God: A History of Western Christian Mysticism*. 4 Vols. New York: Crossroads, 1991.
McInerny, Ralph. *Aquinas and Analogy*. Washington, DC: Catholic University of America Press, 1996.
Melville, Herman. *Moby Dick or the White Whale*. http://www.planetpublish.com/wp-content/uploads/2011/11/Moby_Dick_NT.pdf.
Merleau-Ponty, Maurice. *The Visible and the Invisible*. Edited Claude Lefort. Translated by Alphonso Lingis. Northwestern University Studies in Phenomenology and Existential Philosophy. Evanston, IL: Northwestern University Press, 1968.
Merton, Thomas. *No Man Is an Island*. Garden City: Image, 1967.

Bibliography

Meyendorff, John. *St. Gregory Palamas and Orthodox Spirituality*. New York: St. Vladimir's Seminary Press, 2002.

Milbank, Alison. *Chesterton and Tolkien as Theologians: The Fantasy of the Real*. New York: T. & T. Clark, 2009.

Milbank, John. "Beauty and the Soul." In *Theological Perspectives on God and Beauty*, by John Milbank, 1–34. London: T. & T. Clark, 2003.

———. "Christianity and Platonism in East and West." In *Divine Essence and Divine Energies: Ecumenical Reflections on the Presence of God in Eastern Orthodoxy*, edited by Constantinos Athanasopoulos and Christoph Schneider, 158–209. Cambridge: James Clarke, 2013.

———. "Commentary: Ecumenical Orthodoxy—A Response to Nicholas Loudovikos." In *Encounter Between Eastern Orthodoxy and Radical Orthodoxy: Transfiguring the World through the Word*, edited by Adrian Pabst and Christoph Schneider, 156–64. Farnham, UK: Ashgate, 2009.

———. "Knowledge: The Theological Critique of Philosophy in Hamann and Jacobi." In *Radical Orthodoxy: A New Theology*, edited by John Milbank, et al., 21–37. London: Routledge, 1999.

———. "Sophiology and Theurgy: The New Theological Horizon." In *Encounter Between Eastern Orthodoxy and Radical Orthodoxy: Transfiguring the World through the Word*, edited by Adrian Pabst and Christoph Schneider, 45–85. Farnham: Ashgate, 2009.

———. *Theology and Social Theory: Beyond Secular Reason*. Oxford: Blackwell, 1993.

———. *The Word Made Strange: Theology, Language, Culture*. Oxford: Blackwell, 1997.

Milbank, John, and Adrian Pabst. *The Politics of Virtue: Post-Liberalism and the Human Future*. New York: Rowman & Littlefield, 2016.

Mills, Robert. "Jesus as Monster." In *The Monstrous Middle Ages*, edited by Bettina Bildhauer and Roberts Mills, 28–54. Toronto: University of Toronto Press, 2003.

Moberly, R. W. L. "Isaiah's Vision of God." In *Holiness Past and Present*, edited by Stephen C. Barton, 122–40. London: T. & T. Clark, 2003.

O'Connor, Flannery. "Novelist and Believer." 1963. http://www.nyu.edu/classes/gmoran/FLO'C.pdf.

O'Meara, Thomas F. *Erich Przywara: His Theology and His World*. Notre Dame: University of Notre Dame Press, 2002.

Origen. *Commentary on The Gospel of Matthew*. In *The Gospel of Peter, The Diatessaron of Tatian, The Apocalypse of Peter, The Vision of Paul, The Apocalypse of the Virgin and Sedrach, The Testament of Abraham, The Acts of Xanthippe and Polyxena, The Narrative of Zosimus, The Apology of Aristides, The Epistle of Clement (Complete Text), Origen's Commentary on John, Books 1–10 and Commentary on Matthew, Books 1, 2, and 10–14*, edited by Allan Menzies, 411–93. Vol. 9 of *Ante-Nicene Fathers*. Peabody, MA: Hendrickson, 2012.

O'Rourke, Fran. *Pseudo-Dionysius and the Metaphysics of Aquinas*. Notre Dame: University of Notre Dame Press, 2005.

O'Sullivan, Michael. *Michel Henry: Incarnation, Barbarism, and Belief*. Oxford: Peter Lang, 2006.

Otto, Rudolf. *The Idea of the Holy: An Inquiry Into the Non-Rational Factor in the Idea of the Divine and Its Relation to the Rational*. Translated by John Wilfred Harvey. London: Oxford University Press, 1923.

Owens, Joseph. *An Elementary Christian Metaphysics*. Milwaukee: Center for Thomistic Studies, 1985.
Pabst, Adrian. *Metaphysics: The Creation of Hierarchy*. Interventions. Grand Rapids: Eerdmans, 2012.
Palamas, Gregory. *Gregory Palamas: The Triads*, edited by John Meyendorff. Translated by Nicholas Gendle. New York: Paulist, 1982.
Pannenberg, Wolfhart. *Systematic Theology*. Translated by Geoffrey W. Bromiley. Vol. 1. Grand Rapids: Eerdmans, 2010.
Parmenides. *Diels*. http://philoctetes.free.fr/parmenides.pdf.
Pascal, Blaise. *Pensées*. Edited by Roger Ariew. Indianapolis: Hackett, 2005.
Paul VI. "Lumen Gentium." November, 21, 1964. http://www.vatican.va/archive/hist_councils/ii_vatican_council/documents/vat-ii_const_19641121_lumen-gentium_en.html.
Perl, Eric D. "Pseudo-Dionysius." In *A Companion to Philosophy in the Middle Ages*, edited by Jorge J. E. Gracia and Timothy B. Noone, 540–49. Blackwell Companions to Philosophy. Oxford: Blackwell, 2002.
———. *Theophany: The Neoplatonic Philosophy of Dionysius the Areopagite*. SUNY Series in Ancient Greek Philosophy. New York: State University of New York Press, 2007.
Pickstock, Catherine. *After Writing: On the Liturgical Consummation of Philosophy*. Challenges in Contemporary Theology. Oxford: Blackwell, 1998.
Pink, Arthur W. *The Attributes of God*. Grand Rapids: Baker, 1975.
Plato, *Euthyphro*. In *Plato in Twelve Volumes*, edited by W.R.M. Lamb, 3–85. Translated by Harold North Fowler. Vol. 1. Cambridge, MA: Harvard University Press, 1966.
———. *Phaedo*. In *Plato in Twelve Volumes*, edited by W.R.M. Lamb, 57–118. Translated by Harold North Fowler. Vol. 1. Cambridge, MA: Harvard University Press, 1966.
———. *Philebus*. In *Platonis Opera*, edited by John Burnet, 11–67. Oxford: Oxford University Press, 1903.
———. *Republic*. In *Plato in Twelve Volumes*. Translated by Paul Shorey. Vols. 5–6. Cambridge, MA: Harvard University Press, 1969.
———. *Symposium*. In *Plato in Twelve Volumes*. Translated by Harold North Fowler. Vol. 9. Cambridge, MA: Harvard University Press, 1925.
Plotinus. *Enneads*. Translated by Stephen Mackenna and B. S. Page. http://www.documentacatholicaomnia.eu/03d/0204-0270,_Plotinus,_The_Six_Enneads,_EN.pdf.
Pöltner, Günter. *Schönheit Eine Untersuchung Zum Ursprung des Denkens Bei Thomas V. Aquin*. Freiburg: Herder, 1978.
Proclus. *The Elements of Theology*. Translated by E. R.Dodds. 2nd ed. Oxford: Clarendon, 1963.
Przywara, Erich. *Analogia Entis: Metaphysics: Original Structure and Universal Rhythm*. Translated by John R. Betz and David Bentley Hart. Ressourcement. Grand Rapids: Eerdmans, 2013.
Raphael, Melissa. *Otto and the Concept of Holiness*. Oxford: Clarendon, 1997.
Rebidoux, Michelle. "Given Life: The Phenomenology of Michel Henry." *ARC* 35 (2007) 159–87.
Rhodes, Michael Craig. *Mystery in Philosophy: An Invocation of Pseudo-Dionysius*. Lanham, MD: Lexington, 2012.

Bibliography

Richard of St. Victor. *The Mystical Ark.* In *Richard of St. Victor: The Book of the Patriarchs, The Mystical Ark, Book Three of the Trinity*, 149–370. Translated by Grover A. Zinn. Classics of Western Spirituality. New Jersey: Paulist, 1979.

Ricoeur, Paul. *Interpretation Theory: Discourse and the Surplus of Meaning.* Fort Worth, TX: Texas Christian University Press, 1976.

Roberts, Justin Mandela. "On the Humanity of *Mad Max.*" *The Other Journal* 25 (2016). http://theotherjournal.com/2016/02/25/on-the-humanity-of-mad-max/.

———. *Sacred Rhetoric: Dietrich Bonhoeffer and the Participatory Tradition.* Eugene, OR: Wipf and Stock, 2015.

Rorem, Paul. *Biblical and Liturgical Symbols within the Pseudo-Dionysian Synthesis.* Toronto: Pontifical Institute of Mediaeval Studies, 1984.

Sammon, Brendan Thomas. *The God Who Is Beauty: Beauty as a Divine Name in Thomas Aquinas and Dionysius the Areopagite.* Princeton Theological Monograph Series. Eugene, OR: Pickwick, 2013.

Santayna, George. *The Sense of Beauty: Being the Outline of Aesthetic Theory.* New York: Dover, 1955.

Schäfer, Christian. *Philosophy of Dionysius: An Introduction to the Structures and the Content of the Treatise on the Divine Names.* Philosophia Antiqua. Leiden: Brill, 2006.

Schindler, David L. "Catholicity and the State of Contemporary Theology: The Need for an Onto-Logic of Holiness." *Communio* 14 (1987) 426–50.

———. *Hans Urs von Balthasar and the Dramatic Structure of Truth: A Philosophical Investigation.* Perspectives in Continental Philosophy. New York: Fordham University Press, 2004.

———. "Trinity, Creation, and the Order of Intelligence in the Modern Academy." *Communio* 28 (2001) 406–28.

Schmemann, Alexander. *For Life of the World: Sacraments and Orthodoxy.* New York: St. Vladimir's Seminary Press, 1973.

Sevier, Christopher Scott. *Aquinas on Beauty.* London: Lexington, 2015.

Šijaković, Bogoljub. *The Presence of Transcendence: Essays on Facing the Other through Holiness, History, and Text.* Los Angeles: Sebastian, 2013. Kindle edition.

Simson, Otto von. *The Gothic Cathedral: Origins of Gothic Architecture and the Medieval Concept of Order.* Expanded Edition. Bollingen Series. New Jersey: Princeton University Press, 1988.

Sinkewicz, Robert E. "The Doctrine of the Knowledge of God in the Early Writings of Barlaam the Calabrian." *Mediaeval Studies* 44 (1982) 181–242.

Sloane, Patricia. *Visual Nature of Color.* New York: Design, 1989.

Splett, Jörg. "Holy I. Phenomenology and Philosophy." In *Encyclopedia of Theology: A Concise Sacramentum Mundi*, edited by Karl Rahner, 639–41. Mumbai, India: St. Paul's, 2004.

Stăniloae, Dumitru. *The Experience of God: Revelation and Knowledge of the Triune God.* Vol. 1. Orthodox Dogmatic Theology. London: T. & T. Clark, 2000.

Stechow, Wolfgang. "Hieronymus Bosch: The Grotesque and We." In *The Grotesque in Art and Literature: Theological Reflections*, edited by James Luther Adams and Wilson Yates, 113–24. Grand Rapids: Eerdmans, 1997.

Strickland, Deborah. "The Holy and the Unholy: Analogies for the Numinous in Later Medieval Art." In *Images of Medieval Sanctity: Essays in Honour of Gary Dickson*, edited by Deborah Strickland, 101–20. Visualizing the Middle Ages. Leiden: Brill, 2007.

Symeon the New Theologian. *The Discourses*. Translated by George Maloney. The Classics of Western Spirituality. New Jersey: Paulist, 1980.
Thompson, Leonard L. *The Book of Revelation: Apocalypse and Empire*. Oxford: Oxford University Press, 1997.
Underhill, Evelyn, ed. *Cloud of Unknowing*. 2nd ed. London: Watkins, 1922.
Vasilijević, Maxim. *History, Truth, Holiness: Studies in Theological Ontology and Epistemology*, edited by Daniel Mackay. Contemporary Christian Thought Series. Alhambra, CA: Sebastian, 2011. Kindle edition.
Vlastos, Gregory. *Platonic Studies*. 2nd ed. Princeton: Princeton University Press, 1981.
Von Hildebrand, Dietrich. *The Art of Living*. Steubenville: Hildebrand, 2017.
Ware, Kallistos. "Praying with the Body: The Hesychast Method and Non-Christian Parallels." *Sobornost Incorporating Eastern Churches Review* 14 (1992) 6–35.
Wear, Sarah Klitenic, and John Dillon. *Dionysius the Areopagite and the Neoplatonist Tradition: Despoiling the Hellenes*. Farnham, UK: Ashgate, 2007.
Webster, John. *Holiness*. Grand Rapids: Eerdmans, 2003.
Weinandy, Thomas. *The Father's Spirit of Sonship: Reconceiving the Trinity*. London: T. & T. Clark, 1995.
———. "Trinitarian Christology: The Eternal Son." In *The Oxford Handbook of the Trinity*, edited by Gilles Emery and Matthew Levering, 387–400. Oxford: Oxford University Press, 2011.
Weishaar, Schuy R. *Masters of the Grotesque: The Cinema of Tim Burton, Terry Gilliam, the Coen Brothers, and David Lynch*. Jefferson, NC: McFarland, 2012.
Wenham, Gordon. *Genesis 1–15*. Word Biblical Commentary. Grand Rapids: Zondervan, 1987.
Wesley, John. *Explanatory Notes upon the New Testament*. New York: Lane and Scott, 1850.
White, Thomas Joseph, ed. *The Analogy of Being: Invention of the Antichrist or Wisdom of God?* Grand Rapids: Eerdmans, 2011.
Williams, A. N. *The Ground of Union: Deification in Aquinas and Palamas*. Oxford: Oxford University Press, 1999.
Williams, James. "Gilles Deleuze and Michel Henry: Critical Contrasts in the Deduction of Life as Transcendental." *Sophia* 47 (2008) 265–79.
Willis, E. David. *Notes on the Holiness of God*. Grand Rapids: Eerdmans, 2002.
Yannaras, Christos. "Orthodoxy and the West." Translated by Fr Theodore Stylianopoulos. *Eastern Churches Review* 3 (1971) 286–300.
Yates, Wilson. "An Introduction to the Grotesque: Theoretical and Theological Considerations." In *The Grotesque in Art and Literature: Theological Reflections*, edited by James Luther Adams and Wilson Yates, 1–68. Grand Rapids: Eerdmans, 1997.
Young, Edward J. *The Book of Isaiah*. Vol. 1. Grand Rapids: Eerdmans, 1965.
Zordan, Davide. "Seeing the Invisible, Feeling the Visible: Michel Henry on Aesthetics and Abstraction." *CrossCurrents* 63 (2013) 77–91.

Index of Names and Subjects

Art, 43–44, 126–30
    Christ as, 74–77
Augustine, 7, 11, 12, 51n122, 59,
    60n12, 62n20, 80, 83n133, 112n60

Basil of Caesarea, 14, 29, 92n5, 94,
    97–99
Beauty
    and darkness, 116–17, 131, 136
    and holiness,15–16
    issue of being a transcendental, 8–10
Being
    and the Holy, 37, 40–41, 46
    in repose, 58–65
Bernard of Clairvaux, 91, 112
Bosch, Hieronomous, 140, 141n68
Bruegel, Pieter, 141n68,
Bulgakov, Sergei, 50, 116–17, 118–19,
    125, 142

Derrida, Jacque, 27n27, 149–51,
    155–56
Desmond, William, 46–47, 71, 104–6,
    156–58
Dionysius the Areopagite, 7–9, 20–38,
    42–46, 48–50, 54, 56, 59, 62–63,
    80, 82n130, 84, 85n141, 88n145,
    119, 123, 132n62, 149, 155n22
Disney, 139–40
Divine Names, 11, 21–28, 33, 111
    onomastic theurgy, 26–27
Dostoevsky, Fyodor, 130–31, 143

Eckhart, Meister, 38n65, 42

Eclipse of the Holy, 41–56, 61–62, 75,
    119, 123, 131

Forsyth, P. T., 17

Gift, 25, 87–89, 104, 135 144–51
    and God, 145
Good, 22–33, 102–3
Goya, Francisco, 126–30, 138, 141, 143
Gregory of Nazianzus, 34n51, 36,
    54n137, 56
Gregory of Nyssa, 11–12, 15–16, 30,
    36–37, 42, 45, 78, 83, 96, 98
Gregory Palamas, 36, 48, 50–51, 54
Grotesque, 42–44, 123–26 , 131–42

Harry Potter, 139
Hart, David Bentley, 27n25, 31n43,
    34n53, 45, 50–51, 93n6, 100n26,
    103, 146
Henry, Michel, 33n50, 37–39, 58,
    66–74, 76n96, 129n57
Holy
    Christ as the form of, 74–80
    preeminent over the Good, 22–26,
    28–31
    problem of definition, 1–5
    views of, 13–18
    white light of, 21, 42–43
Holy Spirit
    and distance, 100–103
    as Consecrator 95–97
    as Sanctuary, 98–99, 114
    rationale for its hypostasis, 91–95
Horror, 115, 118, 122, 126–30, 137

Index of Names and Subjects

Humor, 141–42
Husserl, Edmund, 66–67, 71
Hyperbole and Oxymoron, 37n63, 44–45, 47, 56, 63, 76, 88n145, 142

John of Damascus, 15, 54
John Paul II, Pope, 76, 131

Kayser, Wolfgang, 120–24, 131, 142

Light, 33, 36, 54–56
  color refraction, 36, 41–42, 56, 119
  divine rays, 22–23
Lord of the Rings, 139

Marion, Jean-Luc, 24, 27n27, 42, 49–50, 58, 67n55, 72n82, 75–78, 81–82, 122, 129n56, 145n2, 146
Mary, 25, 87–90
Merleau-Ponty, Maurice, 67n55, 106–7
Merton, Thomas, 18
Milbank, John, 44–45, 50, 56, 75–76, 78, 91, 93–94, 107, 113, 129, 139, 145n2, 147
Moby Dick, 42–43
Mysterium Tremendum, 44, 58, 79, 89, 149–50

Nietzsche, Friedrich, 157–59

One, 35–36, 42
Otto, Rudolf, 5–7, 17–18, 25, 30n42, 31n46, 42–44, 47, 57–58, 72–73, 78–79, 93, 117–18, 123, 132n62, 142

Paradox, 24, 27, 42 45, 49, 83–84, 86, 88–89, 97–98, 107, 124–25, 131, 138, 140n68, 141–43, 149, 152, 155n22
Phenomenology, 24n15, 33n50, 37n65, 66–71, 74, 146n4

and touch 106–8
Picasso, Pablo, 116–17, 119, 127, 138, 142
Plato, 3–5, 7, 13–14, 34
Przywara, Erich, 27, 34, 37–39, 56, 60, 71–74, 80, 124

Reverence, 38, 46–47, 78–80, 104–6
Rubens, Peter Paul, 126–27

Sanctum Sanctorum (Holy of holies), 16, 19, 31, 37, 39, 47, 50, 56, 80, 96, 114, 124
Schindler, David L., 17, 40–41
Schleiermacher, Friedrich, 152
Schmemann, Alexander, 17
Schweitzer, Albert, 159
Secret, 144–60
  and Jesus, 151–54
  and the Mask, 154–59
Šijaković, Bogoljub, 17
Stăniloae, Dumitru, 16
Superessential Essence, 22, 27–29, 42, 46
  super-luminous darkness, 44, 54, 83–84, 119
Symeon the New Theologian, 36

Transcendentals
  and distance, 103
  definition and criteria, 10–13
  hallowing the Holy, 33–39
Truth, 100–102

Vasilijević, Maxim, 17
Victorinus, Marius, 33n50, 42, 58–65, 69–70, 73–76, 81, 83, 89–90, 92, 94–98, 102–3, 112–14, 123, 159

Webster, John, 2–3
Wesley, John, 18

www.ingramcontent.com/pod-product-compliance
Lightning Source LLC
Chambersburg PA
CBHW052058230426
43662CB00036B/1693